Women Saints in World Religions

McGill Studies in the History of Religions,
A Series Devoted to International Scholarship
Katherine K. Young, editor

Women Saints in World Religions

edited by
Arvind Sharma

State University of New York Press

Published by
State University of New York Press, Albany

Printed in the United States of America

For information, address State University of New York Press
90 State Street, Suite 700, Albany, New York 12207

Production by Dana Foote
Marketing by Patrick Durocher

Library of Congress Cataloging-in-Publication Data

Women saints in world religions / edited by Arvind Sharma.
p. cm. — (McGill studies in the history of religions)
Includes bibliographical references and index.
ISBN 0–7914–4619–0 (alk. paper) — ISBN 0–7914–4620–4 (pbk. : alk. paper)
1. Women saints. I. Sharma, Arvind. II. Series.

BL488.W65 2000
200′.92′2—dc21
[B]
00–044060

10 9 8 7 6 5 4 3 2 1

For
My Daughter
Bhakti

Men achieve sainthood:
women are saints?

—Anonymous

Contents

PREFACE

The comparative study of religion goes back to the middle of the last century, whereas studies of women in religion to the middle of this century. This book brings together these two approaches to the study of religion.

The theme chosen for orienting the discussion is the category of women saints. In the literature of world religions one reads more about a woman's curious and even dubious ability to corrupt a saint than to become one. And some have ruefully, if equally dubiously, wished that she make saints of them, if they cannot make a sinner of her! In more generous accounts of women in saintly literature, this is precisely what some women accomplished—made saints out of men—either by intent or accident.

But producing a saint is not the same as being one. This book sets out to correct this parasitic perception of women in relation to sainthood. It presents new material, in translation from original sources previously unavailable in English, around the life of a figure considered "saintly" within the traditions of Judaism, Christianity, Islam, Hinduism, Buddhism, and Taoism. The implication of this material for the concept of sainthood within the tradition is also examined, as well as the implication for "women saints" as a cross-cultural category. In doing so the book hopes to not only deepen our understanding of the concept of sainthood (as applied to women), but also to bring to light original material pertaining to women, as the table on the following page illustrates. It has been said that the merit of originality consists not in its novelty but rather sincerity. We hope that the readers will find the book original in both the senses, even if it is ostensibly translational at the conceptual and also a more literal level.

To the various contributors who made this volume possible—Katherine K. Young, Judith Baskin, Marie Anne Mayeski, Jane Crawford, Valerie Hoffman, Rajeshwari Pandharipande, Miriam Levering, and Suzanne Cahill—one can only offer one's heartfelt thanks, for bringing off a project even more successfully than one had initially dared to hope. If we are a part of all whom we meet, then how much more those we collaborate with, a part of us.

Religious Tradition	Woman Saint	Date	Original Language of Text	Author
Judaism	Dolce of Worms	Twelfth Century	Hebrew	Her husband, Rabbi Eleazer
Christianity	Saint Radegund	c. 525–587	Latin	Nun Baudonivia
Islam	Sayyida Nafīsa	762–824	Arabic	Aḥmad al-Shihāwī Sa'd Sharaf al-Dīn
Hinduism	Janābāī	c. 1263–1350	Marathi	Janābāī herself
Buddhism	Miao-tsung	Twelfth Century	Chinese	Ssu-ming T'an-hsiu (compiler)
Taoism	Pien Tung-hsüan	Ninth Century	Chinese	Master Tu Kuang-T'ing

I
Introduction

Katherine K. Young

Much has been written recently about the lives of saints, usually in Christianity but occasionally in other world religions as well. This scholarly activity has both inspired and responded to the new interest in vernacular literatures and popular religions. When the topic is female saints, it has also been stimulated by the desire of women to know more about powerful, female religious figures in the past and the desire of feminists to find role models for women in the present. This book tries to fill some important gaps by introducing some neglected female saints: each author presents translations of excerpts from their works (or from other sources about their lives) that had not yet been translated and discusses the general concept of sainthood (or its functional equivalent in non-Christian religions).[1] This volume also presents the first comparative analysis of female sainthood. But first, a word about these particular saints and the religions they represent.[2]

Judaism

Judith Baskin discusses the Dolce of Worms, a twelfth-century exemplar of Ashkenazi piety in Germany. The study is based on Baskin's translation of a biography written by the Dolce's scholarly husband Rabbi Eleazar of Worms, well-known as a pietist and mystic. The daughter of one rabbi and the wife of another, the Dolce belonged to a circle of Jews in Germany (the Hasidei Ashkenaz) known not only for the fervor of their pietism but also for their esoteric, mystical works. The Dolce took care of her family. She was also a major banker and moneylender, activities undertaken to allow her husband, her son, and her husband's students to spend their time studying the Torah. And more than that, she made parchment for scrolls, thread and wicks for ritual items, and food for the students. Her altruistic activities included those for the women of the community. She helped adorn brides; taught other women about religion (drawing on extensive education from her husband); recited prayers in Hebrew; and sang hymns sweetly. She visited the sick, bathed the dead, and made their shrouds. Tragedy hit this family when two men entered the home and used their swords to strike everyone. Wounded, the Dolce fled. She cried out for help. When the attackers followed her, her husband managed to lock the door behind them. This saved his own life and that of his son (his two daughters and his wife, however, died from the attack). In the rabbi's lament, he repeatedly describes his good wife as a "saint" (*hasidah*) and a righteous woman (*tzadeket*).

Christianity

Marie Ann Mayeski and Jane Crawford have translated the story of Saint Radegund, a sixth-century Merovingian queen of France, as told by the nun Baudonivia and preserved in the *Scriptorum Rerum Merovingicarum.* As a child, Radegund was caught in an internecine struggle that virtually obliterated her family (the Thuringians). Rescued from the battlefield by Clothar, king of the Franks, Radegund was raised to become one of his many wives. After her husband killed her last brother, she left Clothar and moved to one of the villages that belonged to her dowry. When Clothar wanted her back, she fled to Poitiers and managed, through the intervention of a bishop, to have him endow a convent there for her and others. Radegund is said not only to have been a remarkable exemplar of virtues, but also to have had supernatural abilities: protecting the convent from demons by making the sign of the cross every night; banishing noisy birds by uttering blessings; healing the sick; and expunging demons from possessed women. In addition to religious powers, she continued to exercise political ones, drawing on her family's name for its connections with ecclesiastical and secular authorities. Of her passing, we are told that she chose a significant day on the Christian calendar; after dying, she was taken by angels to heaven. Meanwhile, the bishop arrived and saw an angel where her body, with its still-radiant face, was lying. While her corpse was being transported to Saint Mary's basilica, a blind man was cured. After her entombment, the basilica became famous as a site of miracles.

Islam

Valerie Hoffman describes the life of Sayyida Nafīsa bint al-Ḥasan (762–824), a member of the Prophet Muḥammad's family (more specifically, the great-granddaughter of the Prophet's grandson al-Ḥasan). Hoffman's contribution is to translate excerpts from the *Al-Sayyida Nafīsa, Daughter of Sīdī Ḥasan al-Anwar,* by contemporary Egyptian preacher and prayer leader Aḥmad al-Shihāwī Sa'd Sharaf al-Dīn. Sayyida was so well-educated that legal scholars came to consult her. She was known for her beauty and piety (rigorous in fasts, prayers, and pilgrimages), even though some accounts say that she was shy, modest, and weak. Biographical sources mention a pivotal spiritual experience while visiting the tomb of Abraham. Hoffman describes how she asked "God to immerse her heart in the blessings and fragrances of the Friend, and to cause her to be complete with his divine effusions and graces. . . ." Dozing at the tomb, "she saw the Friend of God in her sleep welcoming her and greeting her, speaking to her spirit, counselling her, and telling her of her high standing with God." When the Prophet's family was persecuted by Sunni Caliphs, Sayyida moved with her husband and children to Egypt. She became very popular there. Not only did ordinary people bring their problems to her, so did scholars and government officials. According to biographies, she gained a reputation for miracles. She united in herself the special status of belonging to the Prophet's family, and that of a close relationship with God, signified by her ability to perform miracles. Despite her saintliness, Sayyida's personal life was one of tribulations. Her husband abandoned her. Then came the deaths of her father, her daughter, and finally her son. Her own death was extraordinary. Even though she was struck by a severe illness, she did not stop her fasting during Ramadan. When her doctor commanded her to resume eating, she got rid of him (not caring whether she lived or died). Then, she had a curtain removed to reveal the grave in which she wanted to be buried. She told those assembled that she had recited the entire Qur'ān there 1,000 times, performed *rak'as* (prayer cycles) 100,000 times, and uttered God's name 200,000 times. After saying that she would break her fast only in heaven, she began to recite the Qur'ān, and then just the name of God, until "her pure spirit and her blameless soul returned to their maker, rising to the heavenly council."

Hinduism

Rajeshwari Pandharipande's chapter marks the debut in English of the story of Maharashtrian saint Janābāī (circa 1263–1350). For this project, she translates from Janābāī's own poems (*abhanga*) found in the *Śrī Nāmadeva Gāthā* (collected works of her guru Nāmadev) and various hagiographic sources in Marathi. Pandharipande shows how Janābāī, daughter of a low-caste tailor, became a maid servant (*dāsī*) in an upper-caste household after being orphaned. A son of this family, and her junior, would later become a famous saint known as Nāmadev. At first, Janābāī was his maid. Eventually, she began to think of herself as his disciple (a relationship that had already existed, according to her, through several births) even though she continued to perform chores for him and his family. Finally, in her own eyes, she surpassed Nāmadev. In fact, she claimed to be the supreme deity himself: Lord Viṭṭhal. This realization was caused by an experience of the "divine flood of self-knowledge," observes Pandharipande, that overcame Janābāī and blinded her, even though she tried to resist it: "What I eat is divine, what I drink is divine, my bed is also divine. The divine is here, and it is there. There is nothing empty of divine. Jani says—Vithabai [the Lord] has filled everything from the inside out." All worldly distinctions have disappeared and the servant is now one (*advaita*) with the supreme Lord, or, in her own words, "*santa* is God and God is *santa*" (saint). She, too, had an unusual death; the hagiography states that she entered a final meditative trance and "died" at the same moment as did her teacher, Nāmadev.

Buddhism

Miriam Levering writes about the female Ch'an (Zen) masters in China from the tenth to the thirteenth century, "the first period when women in Ch'an were publicly visible and had their sacred biographies composed and recorded." She translates excerpts from the sacred biography of the nun and Ch'an teacher Miao-tsung (twelfth century) along with material from other genealogical histories. Miao-tsung was the granddaughter of a prime minister during the southern Sung period. Although she had an early spiritual experience and wanted to pursue a religious path, she was pressured into marriage by her parents. Because of her spiritual proclivities, marriage was not to her liking, and so she began to seek the guidance of Ch'an masters. This well-educated woman was more than the equal of any monk; she was a master of verbal debate, and the epitome of sanctity with her quick wit and dialectical mind (which was recognized by other masters according to traditional accounts). These things indicated that she had reached a high level of attainment on the *bodhisattva* path, and therefore, that of sainthood. She donned the robe of a monastic and went into concealment, practicing an ascetic life. Later, she became the abbess of a convent; wrote sermons and poetry; taught and preached. Her writings were widely disseminated. After sanctification, her body and relics came to be venerated. (Prior to this time, the bodies of exemplary Buddhist founders of lineages or masters were preserved and displayed as "flesh bodies." These were considered eternal sources of power, because they did not decay; this was due to an unusual technique of mummification.[3] This became common for female saints in the Sung period, which suggests the increasing status of Ch'an nuns).

Taoism

Suzanne Cahill writes about Pien Tung-hsüan, a Taoist saint of the T'ang Dynasty (618–907). The essay is based on her translation of a biography in the "Records of the Assembled Transcendents of the Fortified Walled City," which is part of the *Cheng t'ung Tao tsang* by Taoist master Tu Kuang-t'ing (850–933). Tung-hsüan, like most other saints, showed early signs of spirituality: feeding wild animals and birds during winter, for instance, and saving the lives of tiny creatures. Although she refused to marry, her parents pressured her to follow the norm. Before anything transpired, though, her parents died. During the long mourning period, she fasted almost to the point of death. Then she decided to join a monastery and become a master. Like others in this convent, who supported themselves by spinning yarn and weaving silk, Tung-hsüan worked industriously. Fasting for years, according to her biography, she gave the "five grains" (a euphemism for food) to animals, even rats. In addition, she stored these "five grains" and gave them to people during famines. The only things Tung-hsüan consumed were elixir drugs, such as cinnabar. Then she met an old man, also on the spiritual path, who had to help a fellow seeker. He gave her some special pills and promised that, within fifteen days of taking them, she would ascend to heaven. She flew immediately to the top of a nearby building. On the day of her ascent to heaven, crowds collected, music spontaneously filled the air, as did a strange fragrance.

The Problem of Naming and Classifying

All anthologies presuppose selection. That presupposes definition. And that, in turn, presupposes some degree of arbitrariness in the formation of categories. The term "saint" is an obviously Western term with a Christian heritage. Early Christian martyrs who submitted to persecution and death rather than renounce their faith were called *hagioi* (holy men) or *hagiai* (holy women).[4]

The term *hagioi/hagiai* then developed a different connotation in Christianity: someone who has extraordinary religious qualities—

charismatic gifts or powers—and has conquered death in some extraordinary way before entering heaven. Because martyrs are supposed to be emulated, many saints have willed their own deaths. Their tombs contain the resulting power and have become the venues of posthumous miracles, where God conveys his own power by enabling his followers to exemplify virtues and dispense his power by miraculously transferring it to others in order to solve problems such as illness, danger, or sin. Transference has been facilitated at specific places (especially the tombs of saints) or times (annual public ceremonies held to commemorate their lives).[5]

Some historians of religions today—when scholars are especially sensitive to "cultural diversity," thanks to the intellectual fashion of postmodernism—have worried about using the Christian term "saint" as a cross-cultural category. Robert Cohn, for instance, comments that historians of religions "have liberated the category of sainthood from its narrower Christian associations and have employed the term in a more general way to refer to the state of special holiness that many religions attribute to certain people. . . . The problem for the historian of religions is whether the term *sainthood* so broadly applied retains any meaning. Can a category that grows out of one religion be properly and usefully extended cross-culturally?"[6]

Gerardus van der Leeuw understands saints as figures through whom divine power is revealed. As conduits, their very bodies are important. The key signs of this corporeal power are their miracles during life and their bodies (as relics) after death. For him, in fact, saints are preeminently the power of the tomb or relic; their roles during life (and there are many different ones) are incidental to their power after death. These features distinguish saints from other figures such as prophets, preachers, and teachers.[7]

Joachim Wach compares saints across religions. He, too, thinks that they are different from other types of religious figures: founders, prophets, mystics, or teachers. They are more passive, he suggests, than prophets, less authoritative than founders, and more charismatic than teachers. Saints, according to Wach, are people who achieve fame primarily because of their religious experiences, which often occur early in life. Because of their experiences and the resulting charisma, they become guides for others (but usually in a personal rather than in an institutional manner). Sometimes, of course, categories overlap.[8]

Other scholars include prophets, mystics, teachers, and so forth among the saints. Despite his initial concern about the difficulties of cross-cultural comparisons, Cohn points to a very wide range of types. He lists the following as representative saints in various religions: the Jewish *hasid* or *tsaddiq,* the Muslim *waliy,* the Zoroastrian *fravashi,* the Hindu *ṛṣi* or *guru,* the Buddhist *arahant* or *bodhisattva,* the Taoist *sheng-jen,* and the Shinto *kami.* Despite the variety, he concludes that three basic paths lead to their fame: 1) the moral (involving discipline, asceticism, chastity, and control, martyrdom being the latter's most extreme form); 2) the intellectual (contemplation of the self, world, and ultimate reality); and 3) the emotional (unqualified love that heals or redeems others). Cohn is especially interested in how religions define spiritual perfection. With that in mind, he argues that sainthood can be understood as imitable (a model for behavior) or inimitable and venerable (a power to be tapped for intercession with a yet higher power for direct help, especially in the form of miracles). He emphasizes death-defying acts.

John Stratton Hawley, following Cohn's basic definitions, writes that inimitability consists of extraordinary signs, powers, miracles, or transgressions of conventional morality. Saints who have these are remembered especially by their relics.[9] And Charles Keyes defines saints as those charismatics who have had contact or union with chaos and have domesticated it to manifest the ineffably sacred or to communicate with it. This is indicated by signs of charisma representing the domestication of chaos by death-conquering acts (resurrection, martyrdom, symbolic death), curative acts, unitive acts of any duration (vision quests, initiation rites, spiritual disciplines), and miracles.[10]

It is striking that only one of these authors discusses any differences between male and female saints—and very briefly, at that. At the end of his article, Cohn notes that female saints are less common than male ones, because the path is less accessible to them in Judaism, Hinduism, and Confucianism. And where the path does exist, it is more rigidly or supernaturally defined. Moreover, the paths for women place greater emphasis than those for men on penitance (especially to purge female sexuality, as in the higher stages of the Mahayana *bodhisattva* path), nurturing, and helping others.

In this book, Baskin argues that there is a Jewish analogue to the Christian concept of sainthood for men and women: the ethical person characterized by three closely related virtues: *kedushah* (sanctity through Torah), *tzedakah* (righteousness), and *hasidut* (piety that goes beyond the demands of Torah). People with these virtues obey God, emulate him, follow the commandments of the law (*halakhah*), and maintain purity for his sake. Because Judaism recognizes the categorical limitations of human nature (which distinguish human beings from God), these virtues must remain ideals.[11] Even so, some people come closer than others to perfection. Those who have deep experiences of holiness (mysticism)—the goal of which is communion with God who extends his grace to complete the efforts made by people—are said to have acquired *hasidut,* which has been translated into English as "saintliness." Their lives are considered exemplary. Most men and women who have been remembered earned their reputations by fulfilling the normative ideal (established by the Torah's commandments) and acting altruistically (that is, beyond the selflessness required by duty). And those who have died rather than deny their faith, the martyrs, are the most exemplary of all. Women in this category are represented by the postbiblical story of Hannah who watched her seven sons die (they would not bow down to idols, thereby refusing to become apostates) and then followed them in martyrdom. She was the prototype of the Dolce of Worms, who heroically sought help when her house was attacked, thereby saving her husband and son, though she herself died in the process. (Her husband describes her as a "saint" rather than a martyr for the faith. In my opinion, it is not inconceivable, however, that he could have considered her a martyr, not only because of Jewish precedents but also because Judaism in Germany during the twelfth and thirteenth centuries was under the influence of Christianity, which had established a close connection between martyrdom and sainthood.)

Apart from these prevailing virtues and the occasional martyrdom by which Jews of both sexes have earned reputations for saintliness, a closer look at authoritative texts reveal examples of Jewish saints more akin to the Christian model. Rabbinic (postbiblical) Judaism had described extraordinary people with extraordinary powers. In the Babylonian Talmud, for example, people of outstanding piety perform miracles.[12] In some sources (elaborated in folklore and mystical works), the good deeds of righteous ancestors can be transferred to others. And in the mystical tradition (especially Hasidism),[13] the ultimate goal of piety is communion with God.[14]

Baskin points to a second source for concepts of sainthood: the fact that women's religion takes place mainly in the private realm of the home and often in exclusively female circles such as women's prayer groups.[15] Women usually pray spontaneously for themselves and their families, and in vernacular languages.[16] In this context, they often have invoked the merits of the biblical mothers (Sarah, Rebecca, Leah, and Rachel)—just as men remember the merits of the biblical fathers (Abraham, Isaac, and Jacob).[17] Although women have not traditionally studied

Torah in terrestrial academies, which is obligatory for men, they have maintained the hope (in one prayer) of doing so in the celestial academy. There, they hope to study under the guidance of an extraordinary biblical woman. That poses no problem for orthodoxy, in theory, because the celestial academy is a feature of life in the World to Come. In fact, though, it presents a potential problem. Women could use this idea to legitimate their own renegade piety in their own separate domain.

Next, take the example of intercession. Baskin points out the example of prayers in which women ask deceased female relatives to intercede for the petitioner. One example would be the seventeenth-century text, *Shloyse sheʿorim* by Sarah bas Tovim: "May God have mercy upon me and upon all Israel. May I not long be forced to be a wanderer, by the merit of our Mothers, Sarah, Rebecca, Rachel, and Leah, and my own dear mother Leah pray to God, blessed be He, for me, that my being a wanderer may be an atonement for me for my sins." (Traditional Jews have two problems with the notion of intercession, whether by women or men: 1) it suggests that some people are more than human, which would contradict the strict demarcation between God and creature; 2) the popularity of intercession in Christianity might have worried and troubled the rabbis in a context of extreme Christian hostility. Therefore, belief in the intercession of Jews living in Christian countries carried the danger of inspiring a renegade tradition.[18] With the invention of the printing press, women's prayers were collected and disseminated. This, according to Baskin, created the potential for widely disseminating a "Little Tradition" of female Judaism.

Yet another source for concepts of sainthood would be popular Islam, which might well have influenced Sephardic Jews (most of whom, after the fifteenth century, lived in Islamic countries). Drawing on Susan Sered's research, Baskin observes that, in the Middle East, martyred Jewish ancestors (male and female) have been recognized as saints. In the popular imagination, moreover, they have been considered 1) part human, part divine; 2) able to cross the boundary separating these two realms; 3) able to intercede on the behalf of women (and men) who want help for their families; and 4) approachable through dreams, prayers, candle lighting, visits to cemeteries, and pilgrimages to tombs.[19]

Baskin observes that the sexual segregation which has characterized Judaism (though modern denominations have desegregated) might have influenced the number of women publicly recognized for saintliness. Some men have had the opportunity to choose a life of study, which could lead to extraordinary piety in the public world, or of mysticism.[20] Some Hasidic men have also practiced prolonged sexual abstinence,[21] despite the antiascetic bias of Judaism, and this was also said to qualify them for mysticism. All these have contributed, thinks Baskin, to the recognition of *extraordinary* behavior and to its public recognition as sainthood.

But Torah learning (and even prolonged abstinence in some cases), which has contributed to public acclaim for piety and mysticism, has been strictly forbidden to women because this would undermine duties to their husbands and families. (The kabbalistic tradition, for instance, has produced no female leaders that we know of). Baskin explains this in connection with sexual segregation. Women's religion belongs in the domestic realm, men's in the public one. Women such as the Dolce of Worms have had some public functions in relation to other women, of course: helping arrange their marriages and dowries, say, or instructing them in prayers and domestic rituals. In addition, they have visited the sick and performed other acts of charity. But they have been especially esteemed for supporting the Torah study of their husbands and sons. This support has been based on their dowries as well as their own financial skills, initiative in business, and (in the past) moneylending. For these activities, they have become literate in the vernacular languages and skilled in bookkeeping. Their work has provided the essentials of life, relieving the men from responsibilities that would prevent them from studying Torah. Women have produced parts of the *tefilin*—sometimes known as "phylacteries," these are small boxes containing parchment inscriptions, which are worn on the forehead and arm during weekday liturgies—made candles for synagogues or schools, and so on. In addition, their work has made it possible to hire other teachers and to buy parchment, books, or oil. They have cared for the (male) students of their husbands by mending their clothes, feeding them, and repairing their books. Baskin thinks that few "extraordinary women" are *remembered* by the Ashkenazi Jewish tradition because of the self-effacing nature of these *supportive* activities and lack of opportunities for Torah study.[22]

Hoffman discusses the Islamic notion of sainthood in terms of *walaya* (or its variant *wilaya*), from the word *walī* (plural *awliyā*) meaning a "friend of God." According to a sixteenth-century Egyptian biographical dictionary of Sufis, a *walī* is: "one who has been brought near to Him, granted special favour enabling him to be diligent in worship, purify his soul of its base passions, and receive mystical illumination."[23] The roots of this concept are found in the Quranic reference to *awliyā* as people who believe and are pious (10:63–64). This definition is often embroidered onto the cloths covering saints' tombs. It is also elaborated in a *ḥadīth* (an authority second only to the Qur'ān) that eulogizes servants who fulfill religious obligations and perform altruistic deeds; these are the most beloved of God and recipients of his favor. For Sufi adepts, this culminates in a state of nearness to Him in which they are free from error, indifferent to the physical world, and channels of divine "grace, blessings, and guidance to humanity." The concept of *awliyā* is characteristic of the Sufi tradition, but it has influenced popular forms of Islam as well. In the latter, it signifies those who have especially close relationships with God. In addition, therefore, it signifies those who have contact with the *baraka:* spiritual power that entered the world with Muḥammad and can be transmitted, in turn, to others. The friends of God are usually those who perform miracles, dispense blessings, and act as intercessors.

Descriptions of Sufi saints often include reversal motifs. The Sufi philosopher and mystic, Ibn ʿArabī (1165–1240), who had himself had a female teacher, radically reversed customary gender restrictions in his description of the Sufi path. Hoffman describes how the Sufi should become as if female, viewing himself in continuous coition as a female in the passive role, becoming pregnant, and giving birth. After this, he may keep company with women and love them without harm.

Closer yet to God, and in a third category, are those belonging to the family of the Prophet, the *ahl al-bayt* (literally, the people of the house) and descendants of the Prophet (*sharīf;* plural *ashrāf*). These include Muḥammad, his daughter Fāṭima, his cousin and son-in-law ʿAlī ibn Abī Ṭalīb, and the sons of Fāṭima and ʿAlī (Ḥasan and Ḥusayn) as well as their descendants. They are the "ultimate exemplars of holiness and purity." These "people of the house" provided links by family (blood or marriage) and virtue between the Prophet and the common people. They did so within the Prophet's lifetime, and they do so in perpetuity through his descendants. The Shiʿis claim the descent of their *imāms* from the family of the Prophet.

Pandharipande notes that the conventional meaning of *santa* (the Hindu word for "saint" in Hindi and other North Indian languages) comes to include the virtues of "compassion, love, and selflessness." Virtues can be signs of either divinity (in the form of incarnations, *avatāra*) or human perfection (people who are liberated on earth and in this life, *jīvanmuktas*). Both *avatāras* and *jīvanmuktas* are recognized as saints. In addition, the category of *saint* can include those who are endowed with divine qualities. Pandharipande considers a variety of figures over the long history of Hinduism: *ṛṣis* who had the *apauruṣeya,* or suprahuman vision of ultimate truths; priests whose own divine powers ensured the efficacy of the sacrifice; heroes as divine incarnations who saved the world; learned philosophers and teachers (*ācāryas*), who taught paths leading toward enlightenment; teachers and guides (*gurus*); and devotees (*bhaktas*). If a broad definition of sainthood is warranted, I would add to this list the following: the great souled ones (*mahātmas*), a term now of universal fame, thanks to Mahatma Gandhi; *yogis,* beings with special powers as a result of their ascetic regimens (*siddhas*); and heroes (*vīras*). After surveying the typologies provided by various historians of religions.

Miriam Levering prefers those of Wach and Keyes. She finds them most helpful for understanding the Ch'an Buddhist concept of sainthood,[24] because they note fluid boundaries between the concepts of teacher and saint. (Remember that her topic is a female "teacher-saint.") Levering observes that students published the *words* of their male and female teachers as a direct manifestation of the Dharma-body of the Buddha, which could instigate enlightenment in others." In other words, teaching was the medium for direct contact with the Buddha. (This implies, I would add, that the teacher is a channel for the transformative power of the Buddha.)

The Taoist notion of sainthood, according to Suzanne Cahill, is captured in the term "transcendent." Taoist adepts are called "transcendents," because they follow a path specifically designed to take them beyond the ordinary moral world. They vow not to marry; refine the body through special fasts, adopting dietary regimens including the consumption of alchemical substances such as cinnabar; feed wild birds and animals; and physically ascend to heaven.

I will return to the problem of definitions and discuss distinctions between male and female saints at the conclusion of this introduction. But first, several dimensions of female sainthood warrant discussion.

Sainthood, Asceticism, and Monasticism

It has been said many times before, and must be said again, that officially separate space provides women with more opportunities for religious experiences and for cultivating leadership roles. In Christianity, the convent provides this. In voluntary monastic communities, women experience love and mutual support, service to others, constant prayer, reading from scripture, preaching sermons, almsgiving, and ascetic practices. Christianity took a major step away from Judaism in providing an alternative role for women. Care was taken, of course, to prevent it from undermining the role of women in reproduction and family life. This was done by sanctifying marriage[25] and by making convent life ascetic (which would be too demanding for most people). Mayeski and Crawford ask whether the Christian convent represents nothing more than "safety and closure, which have always been held out to women as the ideals of female destiny"? But they conclude that the story of Radegund exemplifies a struggle to control life within the limits of social and political realities.

Like Christianity, Buddhism has established convents (though the female order has died out in some countries), thereby providing women not only with an alternative to marriage but also with a separate space in which they can pursue enlightenment and develop leadership skills. At the same time, Buddhism has recognized an official lay orientation for householders. Moreover, it has maintained a symbiotic relation with other religions, such as Hinduism and Confucianism, that support families in no uncertain terms. Levering introduces the subject of female Ch'an saints by observing their choice of celibacy and asceticism over marriage and their practice of Buddhism, culminating in sudden "awakening" or enlightenment. The latter has been interpreted as a sign of their sacred knowledge and their charisma. But an even more important sign, points out Levering, is their capacity to preach, teach, and spar intellectually with the monks. As with Miao-tsung, this illustrates their high attainment along the bodhisattva path and their worthiness for veneration after death.

Taoism, too, has provided alternatives for women. Few of the female Taoist transcendents marry; they remain celibate and childless. In his "Records of the Assembled Transcendents of the Fortified Walled City," Tu Kunag-t'ing describes the Taoist path. It begins with a spontaneous expression of faith, good works, and spiritual practices (chastity, fasting, mediation, visualization, the study and teaching of scripture). It culminates in physical youthfulness, divine knowledge, communication with the deities, magical powers, and ascension to heaven. The really great saints visibly ascend to heaven, an event witnessed by others; the lesser ones appear to die but actually leave their bodies and go to paradise. Because there were more accounts of male than of female transcendents, Tu wrote a separate book on the latter. It was modeled on the biographical genre used by the Confucians and Buddhists. His description of the path for women, and his references to their titles, indicates important differences between male and female adepts. Women face some specific problems, for instance, even before beginning their spiritual journeys. They are expected to marry. Some avoid marriage (in fact, this is a sign of their ability to leave ordinary society and their necessary discipline for the arduous path). Most others enter the monastic order only after their children have grown up or after they have become widows. (Tu is quick to point out that the Taoist Order does not threaten the family system. The families of those who join benefit, because the virtue of these women helps save their relatives; this makes it a superior form of filial piety. It also helps support the emperor and the mandate of heaven, thereby making it a superior form of loyalty to the state.) Sexual or gender differences are factors even within the path. Cahill observes that these differences need not be interpreted in terms of inequality; they can be interpreted in terms of complementary—along the lines of *yang* and *yin* (male and female) in Taoist cosmology. Both men and women follow their separate paths according to their own virtues and skills. Ultimately, both attain immortality and positions in the heavenly bureaucracy.

Hoffman points out that those Muslim women who have broken out of material restrictions have been primarily Sufis. The asceticism of this path provided an opportunity to circumvent marriage, dependence on and obedience to men, and the responsibilities of motherhood, although some Sufis were married. (The same applies to many men who join monastic orders or semi-institutional ascetic groups to avoid marriage. Many women belonging to Sufi orders have been widows. Others has been divorced; joining Sufi orders has been a convenient way to maintain their chaste reputations, while waiting for the opportunity to remarry. It is true that the lists of Sufi saints found in the biographical dictionaries consist mainly of men. And of the women, most are nameless (being listed as the wives of male Sufis). Nonetheless, some male leaders have established just for women—Sufi teachers, retreat houses (*ribāṭs*), or sections of retreat houses. A few have acknowledged that women can attain the supreme spiritual rank (*quṭb*) or become teachers. Two famous examples are the *shaykha* Zaynab Fāṭima bint al-ʿAbbās (died 1394) and Ḥāgga Zakiyya ʿAbd al-Muṭṭalib Badawī (1899–1982). Sayyida, the Muslim saint discussed in this volume, also practiced ascetic regimens, especially during the month of Ramadan. In Egypt, the great Sufis of the day visited her home. Some of them even received *from her* the principles of asceticism. Given her life of fasting, it is befitting that she died during a fast. Her biography has Sufi images.

Memory and Sainthood

Sainthood is intimately related to genre. Hagiography, a term derived from the Greek word *hagios* (martyr; saint), though popular, originated as a literary genre. According to Paul Connerton, written accounts are often about elite, spiritual men whose lives progress as they accumulate influence or power. Oral accounts, by contrast, are more cyclical than linear.[26] It is worth asking from the outset, therefore, whether the lives of the female saints under consideration here have been transformed by a literary genre created for elite men. Does this distort the lives of upper-class (often literate) women? Does it distort the lives of lower-class (often illiterate) women even more?

In the field of religious studies, we consider biography factual and hagiography not factual, because it traffics in the supernatural.[27] Those who study religions that have traditions of "historical" writing (although these might be more like hagiographies than the modern concept of *history* would allow) prefer the category *biography*. The Chinese tradition, for instance, includes a genre of history, so scholars prefer to translate the term *zhuan-ji* as "biography." Sinologists have recognized the limitations of the term "biography" for this genre, however, recognizing that early tales were about the "marvellous" and that some originated in the tales of shamanistic Taoist women. Nevertheless, among the first "biographies" were the *Lieh-nü chuan* (*Biographies of Women*) written between 80 and 9 B.C.E. by Liu Hsiang[28] and the somewhat later *History of the Latter Han* by Fan Yeh (died 445 C.E.). The Chinese biography begins with general geneological data—the person's name, historical era, lineage (offices of male ancestors), class, birth registry, career, and place. Kathryn Ann Tsai shows how the genre of historical writing in China has as its raison d'être not just reportage, but moral guidance, inspiration, and remembrance for both men and women. Biographies of Confucian women are often shorter than those about men, because they are based on vignettes that illustrate Confucian virtues (righteousness, say, or human-heartedness) and vices. These are used for the didactic purpose of instilling feminine norms. The most prominent feminine virtues cited are associated with marital duties and roles in the patrilineal family: producing sons, and performing acts of filial devotion. Women are praised, moreover, or blamed because of their effects on fathers, husbands, or sons—the three types of man to whom they should be obedient throughout their life. Women are praised, moreover, for choosing death not only in cases of conflict between duties but also to preserve their reputations or those of their families (this is martyrdom for Confucianism). In other words, they promote Confucian morals in both life and death (as do men).

Once this genre was established, it was adopted and transformed by other religions in China.[29] Consider the case of Taoism. In Taoist biographies, the general genealogical details are followed by details of the saint's childhood: special talents, signs of saintly behavior such as spontaneous and "natural" reverence, faith, or selection by the deity. Although the Taoist canon had preserved stories of the lives of many male "transcendents," it had preserved few of women. This was corrected by Tu Kuang-t'ing in his "Records of the Assembled Transcendents of the Fortified Walled City," which presents twenty-eight accounts of female Taoist "transcendents" from the late T'ang dynasty.

Next consider the case of Buddhism. In the preface to his *Pi-ch'iu-ni chuan* (*Lives of the Nuns*),[30] the Buddhist Pao-ch'ang mentions his method of collection: "The achievement of their aspirations is not yet collected into books and writings, and I have frequently deplored this. It is a long time since I first began extensively to gather epitaph eulogies, widely searching in notes and collections. Sometimes I interviewed those who had heard a lot about it; sometimes I inquired from old people. Explaining and ordering [the material] from beginning to end, I wrote down their biographies. . . . I worked to preserve the essential facts hoping that those who seek liberation will exert the wish to emulate [the nuns'] virtue."[31] Because this author collected information between the fourth and the sixth centuries, he was sometimes far removed from the subject; his details can be questioned. Nevertheless, his treatment is interesting. He classifies nuns as follows: virtuous and wise; chaste and obedient; intellectual and capable of reasoning; ascetic; contemplative; faithful and steadfast; and teachers of great influence. He is most impressed by the ascetics, who perform self-willed death in honor of the Buddha; the steadfast, who escape marriage by daring means; the contemplatives, who become like wood or stone in their trances; and the teachers, who have hundreds of disciples. In his discussion of the lives of the nuns, Pao-ch'ang highlights the Buddhist aspects of their lives (keeping the precepts, say, or teaching the law). But sometimes, he draws on Confucian virtues such as filial piety and obedience as well. That is because he wants Buddhism to uphold tradition as well. According to Tsai, Pao-ch'ang collected everything available to serve his didactic and laudatory goal, which made the genre more akin to hagiography than biography.[32] And yet, these "biographies" do reveal some details that could well be factual: The saints' high degree of literacy, for example, or the marital problems that prompted them to take refuge in the order. Tsai observes that biographies from the Ch'i and Liang dynasties, with their sober tone, might be closer to historical circumstances than other biographies.[33] Each Buddhist lineage had its own source, as did the Ch'an source used by Levering in this book.

Islam, too, has a tradition of "historical" reporting. Scholars of Islam have been more inclined to use the term "biography," even though the accounts of Sufi saints and others, with their channels of divine power, make them seem supernatural in the modern or common imagination—and therefore closer to the genre of hagiography. Hoffman notes that Sufi biographies are usually terse, presenting the basic details about lives, miracles, and famous sayings. The one she consults, however, reads more like a novel.

By contrast, scholars of Hinduism are comfortable with the term "hagiography" for *bhakti* saints. These have been characterized by extraordinary powers, reversals of conventional norms, and sometimes liberated, incarnational, or quasidivine status. In my own studies of two female Hindu saints, Āṇṭāḷ, a Tamil saint of the ninth century, and Ānandamayī Mā, a modern Bengali saint, I have found the following features: unusual or divine conception; extraordinary birth; extraordinary childhood; life stretched to eccentric boundaries; social conventions ignored; reversals; miracles; possession or dreams (a special conduit of the divine); homologization with the lives of other saints; and unusual death.[34] But by reading between the lines of their own works and of early hagiographies, I have detected clues to their real-life situations (*Sitzen im Lebin*)—especially when other kinds of evidence are available.

In this book, Pandharipande's presentation of the Maharashtrian saint Janābāī[35] reveals general features of the Hindu hagiographical genre I have just surveyed. Janābāī herself says "Blessed (indeed) is my birth," a point echoed by hagiographies that describe how her parents overcame lack of progeny by prayers to Lord Viṭṭhal. The Lord then appears in a dream to her father, telling him that he will have a daughter who will uplift her family through association with the guru Nāmadev. Next consider the "reversals" in her later years. Lord Viṭṭhal follows her when she washes clothes in the river. He comes and lies down beside her, "whispering the secrets of love." He turns out to be the real thief when she is accused of stealing a pendant. (This incident provides a context for the miracle that established Janābāī's status as a saint: when she is about to be hanged for stealing it, the tree melts into water.) Finally, the life of Janābāī exemplifies the genre by her homologization with the life of another saint. In this case, it is Nāmadev (the hagiography declaring that she entered a final meditative trance and "died" at the same moment as he did).[36] In any case, Pandharipande's discussion shows how Janābāī appropriates the genre for her own ends. She plays on associations of the word *dāsī* (servant), for example, because she is both a female servant in the secular sense of the term and a servant of the Lord in the religious sense (*dāsa/dāsī* being technical terms for a devotee). As a woman, she selects those aspects of the tradition that are feminine. She prefers to think of Viṭṭhal as a mother, for instance, even though motherhood is only one of his attributes. Indeed, it is as if she knows that she "fits" the genre or that the genre was created to fit her (as a way of giving the religion universal appeal). Through this genre, she can uplift other women: "[D]o not be depressed because you are a woman; saints and mystics are born in this form (of a woman) among the people!" Her ultimate act is to appropriate a superior status for herself. Nāmadev was just a saint, but she is the very incarnation of the Lord himself! In short, she has bested him by circumventing the status defined by male roles, such as being the founder of a sectarian path (*sampradāya*), a philosopher, or teacher. Pandharipande also notes the innovative aspect of sainthood and hagiography: "The saints by their very nature are innovators [because] they interpret the religious beliefs to make them relevant within the context of a particular time and the sociocultural reality."

Hagiographical details are imperceptibly intertwined with the historical ones of Muslim saint Sayyida Nafīsa, boosting her saintly status as a member of the Prophet's family. According to the story, her birth is extraordinary: she has the most beautiful face and an illuminated forehead. The Prophet later tells her father in a dream that she will have "a bright future filled with glory and miracles." Aside from the supernatural features reported in her "biography," there are clues of her real, high status in the community, by virtue not only of her birth but of her accomplishments as well. The story of her life, moreover, has a *Sitz im Leben* marked by personal tragedies: abandonment by her husband, and the death of her children.

Mayeski and Crawford raise a question: "Is Radegund the real hero of her own story or is the story so recast into the conventional Christian pattern that it becomes not individual at all, but a reinforcement of the accepted pattern of feminine behavior?" Looking for clues to her real life situation, they focus on her early status as queen and her noble upbringing; both subtly inform the conventional narrative. This saint makes decisions, persists to achieve her goals, and demonstrates courage and compassion. She destroys places of pagan worship, redeems captives, offers alms, refuses to listen to slander, feeds pilgrims, and washes the feet of the sick. Although some of these acts belong to the typical acts of a saint found in other Christian hagiographies, they are expressed here in an informal way. This, thinks Mayeski and Crawford, indicates her internalization of the model.

The lives of saints are connected not only to the literary genres of biography and hagiography, but also to public cult. Connerton thinks that memory of groups is conveyed and sustained by ritual practices in the form of commemorative performances involving habits and bodily automatisms. The story is re-enacted and re-presented in the metaphysical present, which develops a kind of mnemonic power. Re-enactments—more formalized, stylized, and repetitive than myths—at sacred sites become sacred cults. Continuity with the communal past is established by the economy of form/performance encoded in set postures, gestures, movements, and utterances. What is being remembered, then, in the sacred cult of a saint's life? It is memory of the religion's master narrative, what Connerton calls its "collective autobiography,"[37] sustained by the ritual performances of those who are habituated bodily to them. The past becomes the present, and the transmission of an embodied authority is expressed with ease and flow. It can remain latent or be invoked. When men appropriate saint's lives for public cults, they encourage formalism. This focuses on the body of the saint. Just as the body is the substratum of a saint's life and death, it is the substratum of collective memory in the form of ceremonial cults of the body. Women's connections with the bodies of saints are less formal, characteristic of their nonliturgical and more spontaneous religion (although men, too, participate in this type of religious expression).

Class and Sainthood

Female saints have come from all classes. Cahill observes that over half the Taoist women in her collection are of low birth, for example, and the focal points of local cults. The Hindu saint Janābāī is yet another example of a lower-class woman (by both caste and orphan status). But female saints have come from elite families, too. Consider Radegund, the Meroviangian queen who became a nun; Sayyida Nafīsa bint al-Ḥasan, a descendant of the Prophet who had connections with important officials in Egypt and other Islamic countries; the well-educated Dolce of Worms, daughter of a famous rabbi and wife of another one; and the Ch'an teacher Miao-tsung, daughter of a prime minister and wife of an important Sung official. The fact that many elite women become saints can be explained partly by the fact that they are more educated than other women, sometimes extremely well educated, and have high social status and political connections; for these reasons, they have access to the public realm. The fact that many lower-class women become saints can be explained in two ways. In some cases, they have worked in the public realm as laborers and have always had some freedom. In other cases, men might promote their saintly reputations as propaganda for the universality of their religions, using these exemplary women to attract other women and lower-class or marginalized people. In any case, the fact that female saints come from all classes suggests that women have appropriated whatever openings the religious traditions have offered or have created ones to serve their own spiritual interests.

The Political Significance of Sainthood

The political significance of sainthood has two dimensions. One is the connection to mundane political power through human connections. The other is the connection to supramundane power through spirituality (extraordinary virtue, for example, being acclaimed as magical power or a sign of being an intercessor).

The connection with mundane power is a feature of several saints discussed here. The Christian saint Radegund was a Merovingian queen. Mayeski and Crawford write of Radegund that she herself was a victim of the violent and coercive struggles for power that surged around her, threatening every goal she pursued. Even after becoming a nun, she continued to traffic in power (albeit for the welfare of her monastic community). On occasion, she stopped conflict between warring factions, using old but not forgotten political skills.

Miracle stories recall the supramundane power of saints. This power exists because saints are channels for, have contact with, or embody divine power. The latter enables them to intercede or work miracles. Miracle stories are an effective way of proselytizing. They promote the status of holy places and inspire pilgrimages. In Christianity, according to Mayeski and Crawford, "often the author of the miracle intends to demonstrate that the biblical story of salvation was continued in the 'later days' and new cultural contexts of the saints whose stories were narrated." Similarly, the life of the Hindu saint Janābāī was politically important, because it contributed to a general Maharashtrian revival with its inclusive message for all castes, women as well as men. This occurred because India had been ruled by the Muslims; the result had been low morale for Hindus, the rigidification of rituals, even the abandonment of Hinduism itself.

The Muslim saint Sayyida Nafīsa was not only a descendant of the Prophet's family via Ḥasan, she also married the great-grandson of Muḥammad's grandson Ḥusayn. Her marriage itself had political connections, because it reunited two major branches of the Prophet's family through the two sons of ʿAlī (who was, in turn, the son-in-law of Muḥammad). Politics entered the life of Sayyida, too, because the Sunni ʿAbbāsid Caliphs' persecuted the Prophet's family called the ʿAlids (who were Shīʿī). This forced some of the ʿAlids to leave Medina for Egypt, where members of the family had already relocated. The Egyptian ruling authorities were proud that the Prophet's descendants had made Egypt their new home, and gave great honors to them, including special accommodation to protect them from the masses of visitors clamoring for audiences with them. Once, when a tyrannical governor was making life difficult for the ordinary people, Sayyida asked him on their behalf to mend his ways. Her letter was effective, and the people were thankful. Later, the ʿAbbāsids attracted Sayyida's husband back to Medina by offering to him its governorship, but Sayyida stayed behind to care for her aged and ill father. She and her husband were never reunited. Politics continued even after Sayyida's death, when her husband wanted her body returned to Medina despite strong protests from the Egyptians. The account says that God intervened to keep it in Egypt.

Levering points out that early Ch'an in China was a marginal religion. It was willing to promote magic and miracles, albeit drawing on its own tradition of the supernormal powers created by meditation, as a way of competing with the more established religions. By the time it had become an elite religion during the Sung period (960–1276), it had diminished the importance of magic, miracles, and veneration of the "nondecaying" body of its founder or his relics; instead, it had focused attention on his words, just as the *sūtras* were enshrined as sacred objects. This miracle of speech, as it were, gave primacy to sacred words instead of sacred relics. Levering argues that Ch'an selected the more prestigious Confucian pole of Chinese culture instead of the Taoist one. As for the female saint she discusses, it might be no coincidence that she is the granddaughter of Su Sung, a prime minister of the Southern Sung dynasty (1086–1094). She had visited all the famous masters in Kiangsi and Chekiang, studying with them, going on retreats with them, and receiving their seal of awakening at a time when the lives of elite women consisted of marriage and bringing up children within the sequestered women's quarters. The high, social status of Miao-tsung (which gave her educational opportunities), along with her Buddhist education, was responsible for her excellent education, her literary accomplishments (sermons, poetry, and Buddhist verses left to posterity), and her leadership position as abbess of a famous Ch'an monastery for women.

The Taoist Tu Kuang-t'ing states that he writes about the lives of women for three reasons: 1) to preserve the precious history of his sect (the Shang ch'ing, or Supreme Clear Realm school) at a time of social turbulence; 2) to illustrate the power of women's faith in times of trouble; and 3) to glorify the T'ang dynasty, which was then losing the mandate of heaven. His political motive was to secure protection, even imperial favor, for his sect. When the T'ang fell, after all, he swiftly changed his political allegiance, now suggesting that the heavenly mandate had passed to Shu.[38] This suggests public recognition that the power of women's faith could protect the kingdom. The author focuses on saints of the two T'ang capitals, moreover, one in Szechwan and the other in the south. This, too, suggests political motivations.

Remembering the lives of saints can have political implications in connection with sacred geography. Relics, shrines, and tombs extend the power of saints and by extension the religion and its temporal powers. Drawing on the scholarship of Peter Brown, Mayeski and Crawford observe that the mobility of relics in the late Roman world resembled the shifting quality of relationships. Social distance between groups could be undone by gestures of grace and favor, and physical distance could be overcome by a rhetoric of unanimity and concord. The movement of relics from one region to another provided a kind of "spiritual aqueduct." The latter connected distant churches to Rome (the center and source of imperial identity), which upgraded local identity. Seen from this point of view, it is not surprising to find that Radegund was a passionate seeker of relics. She most wanted a relic of the cross on which Jesus had been crucified, because that would connect her church at Poitiers with the personal presence of the Lord himself. It would bring not only blessings in general, of course, but "the welfare of the whole fatherland and the stability of [Sigebert's] kingdom" in particular. That was because relics were thought to bring peace, eliminate evil, and promote harmony. With these potential benefits in mind, Radegund used every possible strategy: prayer, fasting, political intrigue, enlisting the aid of powerful bishops, and so on. In fact, she had a place of pagan worship burned, risking the ire of the pagan Franks. This act of vandalism by a Christian saint should not be surprising; many rulers have staked out their power by destroying the holy places of those they conquer and replacing them with the holy places of new, imperial religions.

Tombs are important sites in sacred geography, because they are conduits of the saintly power transferred to those who make contact with it. The tomb of Sayyida (remember, she herself had constructed it and then had fasted to death while reciting the Qur'ān) was important for the extension of Islamic sacred geography into Egypt. Her former husband wanted to return her body to Medina, but the Egyptians tried to prevent him from doing so by offering him money and interceding with the governor. Nothing dissuaded him, so the accounts say, until God himself intervened. He convinced her husband in a dream that she should remain there in the land of the Egyptians, because God "will cause mercies to descend on them by her *baraka*" (power). Perfume and praises to God filled the air.[39] Although, to my knowledge, there are no tombs of female saints in Hinduism (there are tombs of male saints, who are not cremated like other men and women, and Hindus visit the tombs of both Muslim women and men), there are shrines where Hindu women died heroic or self-willed deaths. Many of these shrines are built over the *satī* stones that mark the place where "good women" (the literal meaning of *satī*) performed self-willed deaths to follow their husbands.

Constraining Female Saints

Saints often present religious leaders with a serious problem. Many saints are individualistic or even eccentric. Sometimes, for whatever reason, they become very independent. The authorities soon begin to wonder if they are becoming too independent; that is, likely to foster renegade traditions. That is when they take preventive measures. Usually, they try to curtail the activities of these saints or to incorporate them into institutions. In short, they try to domesticate these saints, as it were, to prevent chaos. When renegade saints are women, male authorities often encourage them to return to their families. At the very least, they try to regulate the number of women choosing alternatives such as monasticism. Religions have developed many strategies for constraining independent-minded saints.

Rabbinic Judaism has been careful, for example, not to let the popular piety of women (or men) turn into countercultures that would undermine family life, the religion in general, or the authority of men. In some cases, Baskin says, men were allowed to pursue prolonged ascetic regimens. Women, on the other hand, were highly criticized for fasting and other acts of deprivation. Women were prevented from assuming religious leadership roles that would compete with those of men. In the history of Judaism, one woman did take on a leadership role: Hannah Rachel Verbermacher, the "Maid of Ludmir" (born 1815). She belonged to a Hasidic community, which, by definition, acknowledged both mystical and charismatic leadership. Bright, well-educated, wealthy, and pietistic, she refused marriage and lived alone in the study house she had built. After she gained a reputation for working miracles, writes Baskin, she "held court" there, conversing and lecturing to both men and women from behind a closed door. Reaction from the male Hasidic leaders of her region was uniformly negative, though, and pressure was successfully applied on her to resume her rightful feminine role by marrying. Although her several marriages were unsuccessful, they did result in the end of her career as a religious leader. As Baskin puts it, this is "the exception that confirms the rule." (But even the exception is not really an exception, because it was not allowed to continue, much less become a model for others.) Baskin mentions another intriguing example: a seventeenth-century document about the death of the Dolce of Worms. According to this revised version, she and her daughters were alone when they were killed by several murderous (gentile?) students. It was the rabbi's own students who caused an uproar to protect their teacher and brought help, not knowing at the time that his wife and daughters had been killed. Baskin suggests that men in the seventeenth century were uncomfortable with the idea that it was a woman who acted to protect the family by going for help despite being wounded; as a result, she was represented as a nameless and passive victim.

Other religions, too, have thwarted women's experiments with independent spirituality—even though these religions often began as reform movements, and reform movements that addressed women at that. A Hindu strategy was to honor but simultaneously marginalize any renegade group. Tantra, the most extreme of Hindu countercultures (possibly on its way to becoming a popular movement given its contribution to popular religious symbolism) and one of the few that esteemed women as gurus, was safely relegated to the margins of society as an esoteric cult.

One of the most common measures has been to suggest that a sex change was necessary in order for women to attain salvation. Some Mahāyāna Buddhist texts, for instance, say that this would be necessary, in either this life or another one, for women to become *bodhisattvas.* In real-life situations, women in several religions have tried to stop their menses (which has made them more like men). Female Taoist adepts, for instance, tried to do this through extreme fasting in order to make their bodies more like those of male adepts. Female Sufis did the same thing. Despite the flouting of convention by Sufis, the tradition of chastity among women remained strong. However, it now had a new raison d'être. Even in the early Sufi tradition, according to Hoffman, fasting by women was so severe that it often led to the inhibition of menstruation. Because this eliminated the need for some prohibitions in Islamic law, such as the one that forbade prayer by menstruating women, nonmenstruating women were considered the equals of men. Both male and female Sufis, moreover, internalized the heroic code of men: courage, self-denial, and generosity. All are captured in the term *muruwwa* (manliness). Mary, the mother of Jesus, considered a Sufi by Muslims, is said to have been the first *man* to enter Paradise. Female Sufis are often listed among the men (as was the famous Rābiʿ al-ʿAdawiyya). Although some

Sufi orders included or honored women, others denounced them, arguing that women among the Sufis would lead to immodesty or, even worse, moral laxness. Scandalized by Ibn ʿArabi's norm reversals, for instance, they debated whether women in paradise would have the same opportunities for closeness to God. These apologists returned to the post-Qur'ānic (cloistered) role of women. Women transcend the religious restrictions of their sex by transforming their femaleness into maleness. In this context, it is only fair to remember that some Sufi men take on femaleness (as have men in some Hindu bhakti religions such as the āḻvārs in medieval South Indian Vaiṣṇavism or Rāmarkrishna, a nineteenth century saint in Bengal). Men assume the psychology of women, and women suppress their physiology to become like men. The gap between the two sexes is virtually eliminated. Nevertheless these traditions have maintained nominal male dominance, despite advocating equality on the soteriological level.

One interpretation of why men constrain spiritual women is that they constrain any renegade group (including countercultural movements led by men) that threatens their grip on power and the cultural norms that uphold it. Another interpretation is that men are motivated by social need. Some effort must be made to maintain the reproductive system, which depends not only on women's physiological ability to bear children but also on their psychological willingness to be mothers. The interpretation usually favored by feminists, of course, is that men are motivated by malice. Men, they claim, want nothing more than to control or exploit women which is why the world religions have been called patriarchal.

Are Female Saints Relevant Today?

Since the Enlightenment, Baskin says, secular Jews have tried to eliminate the miraculous element of religion. This is true of some other religions as well. Moreover, in the modern period, secular societies have all but closed down the genre of sacred biography. This is not true of societies that are just now undergoing massive industrialization, modernization, and secularization, to be sure. In my study of the Hindu saint Ānandamayī Mā, for instance, I found that hagiography has been not just a way for society to maintain its collective spiritual memory, especially a noncanonical one, but also a way to transform society and shape the future. In this sense, the hagiographical genre has remained relevant (at least in non-Westernized circles) even toward the end of the twentieth century.

Describing Radegund, Mayeski and Crawford observe that "the pursuit of holiness grounds, refines and orients but does not destroy the self nor the possibilities of life and action. Radegund's story, retold and reclaimed anew, can shape a renewed understanding of the significance of the spiritual journey in the pursuit of one's deepest dreams, ambitions and desires." Mayeski and Crawford suggest that the stories of the saints can inspire women once they are restored to the historical record. Female saints show that women have taken charge of their own lives even within "patriarchal" societies.

The Problems of Definition and Category Revisited

My own working definition of a saint is "someone whose life as a whole has had an extraordinary (especially altruistic) orientation, whose death is extraordinary, and whose memory is preserved in narrative, cultic, or iconic/image form." Of course, as we have seen, "extraordinary" can mean something quite different in each religion. "Narrative" can vary in form, moreover, because it draws both from a genre and a real-life situation. Even the meaning of "genre" can vary. It might refer to either a biography or a hagiography. It might be an elaborate story, a few vignettes, or even a single episode iconically represented. The same is true of "memory." It might refer to a grandmother's telling, a public performance, a liturgical event, or a pilgrimage to a tomb. With this general definition in mind and in view of the comparative nature of this volume, I will next examine whether there are any patterns when the world religions are compared on this topic.

First a word on the relation of the extraordinary life to altruism. Why is altruism a key diagnostic feature? Both male and female roles, whatever the specific cultural details, have involved selflessness as parents, at the very least, for the sake of their children. The narcissism of infants must be directed outwards so that children can be socialized. This is a major way in which culture complements biology for human survival. Individuals must also act selflessly for their communities (although the ways can vary, especially in connection with gender). When the degree of selflessness voluntarily goes beyond "duty," it is called altruism. This makes the person extraordinary (and sometimes a saint) in the eyes of ordinary people. Some kinds of saints express their altruism by acting directly for family and society whereas others do so indirectly. The latter is more difficult to understand. These saints bypass (or flout) social and gender norms by performing extraordinary (miraculous or divine) feats or (in some religions) even incarnating the supreme deity. Paradoxically, by contravening familial and societal norms through *optional* or *prohibited* acts, they create an excess or even *plenum* of virtue by transgressing ordinary virtue. This becomes a source of power that can be tapped by ordinary people. In fact, this is like the *mother* goddess who has no children, yet is a *plenum* of power that can be redistributed to devotees to ensure fertility and fulfill other desires. This power makes the person charismatic. The fact that the power is individual rather than institutional contributes to its charismatic nature.

Besides altruism, an unusual death is a universal feature of sainthood, as the description of the lives of saints in this volume demonstrates. Because death is the most liminal, mysterious, and frightening point of human existence, it should come as no surprise that self-willing it is dramatic and powerful. Its locus classicus is martyrdom (a response to some external situation); its sequel or derivative is some form of self-willed death or, at least, unusual signs at the time of natural death that indicate an extraordinary passage. This is found across the world religions and characterizes all kinds of saints. Jews, Christians, and Muslims choose martyrdom rather than betray God or community; Buddhist *bodhisattvas* sacrifice their bodies to feed those in need (including starving animals, so the stories go); Ch'an Buddhist monks die in meditation and their bodies are physically preserved as material but "living statues." Taoist saints consume cinnabar and other drugs by which they seek physical immortality. According to the *Lieh-nü chuan* (*Biographies of Women*), Confucian women perform self-willed death to preserve the reputations of themselves or their families. The Buddhist work *Pi-ch'iu-ni chuan* (*Lives of the Nuns*) describes women performing self-willed death in honor of the Buddha, his law, and his order.[40] Hindu *yogis* bury themselves alive. The altruistic, saintly wife in elite Hinduism (called the "good" woman) is epitomized in the female form of self-willed death called *satī*, the self-immolation of a woman on the funeral pyre of her husband. This extraordinary act not only exemplifies wifely devotion and loyalty par excellence, therefore embodying Hindu *dharma* (a concept related to *ṛta*, which means cosmic and social order), it also generates excess merit. That eliminates all bad karma for both her and her husband. It makes possible rebirth in paradise or even enlightenment for both of them. In fact, this extraordinary act generates excess merit that can be transferred to the *satī*'s family and descendants, to anyone who witnesses the event, or to anyone who visits a temple built where she died. The lives of all the women in this book have had some extraordinary kind of death, at least as reported by the traditional stories.

One other general characteristic of sainthood is the dialectic of chaos and order. This dialectic informs the concept of sainthood, I suggest, because it, too, is basic to human life: chaos being represented by natural disasters or by human disease, death, and other catastrophes and order being represented by human cultures that make possible survival, group well-being, and so forth. Because of their deep significance for human life, awareness of both dimensions must be maintained to do justice to the phenomenon of being human.

With these three diagnostic features of sainthood—altruism, unusual death, and the dialectic of chaos and order in mind—I turn now to a discussion of four types of saints. I will first discuss types one and four at the two poles of my continuum.

The first type of saint exists when chaos prevails and order appears as a goal, an ideal, even an elusive sacred dimension (whence the cosmogonic myths that order chaos and give sacred meaning and purpose to life). Those who try to rescue people from chaos (which is always potentially present in human life and nature) are saints (in the sense of heroes, prophets, or founders of religions).

The fourth type exists when order has prevailed and become so routine that it is mundane. It must be shattered (at least temporarily in special contexts) to reveal again the sacred power of chaos. This type of saint is a virtuoso who ruptures order by turning the norms upside down in order to reveal the power of chaos. In Hinduism, for instance, several high-caste, female saints have pursued religious lives outside of marriage (though lack of official orders, or communities, has always made it problematic for them to pursue religious paths). Because that takes a great deal of courage, of course, it is considered heroic. And that, in turn, makes these women saints and virtuosos, despite the normative refusal to legitimate a spiritual life for women outside of marriage. We can reconcile this conundrum, both accepting the norm of marriage and denying it, by noting that the latter is a heroic test and thus itself an act that constitutes the passage to sainthood. Female virtuosos, for example, communicate with deities directly (often in a state of possession), spontaneously, and in the vernacular. Their spirituality is a powerful antidote to the formalism of official religion and attractive to many men and women alike. It should come as no surprise, then, to find female saints as miracle-workers and, in many religions, as intercessors. What might be surprising, however, is exactly how clever they have been to seize the spiritual initiative. They have promoted their own fame, built and consecrated their own tombs, and even claimed to be not merely saints but divine incarnations. In other words, precisely because of the lack of institutional roles in some religions, women have had greater opportunity to be flamboyant and free-spirited. This gives them an extraordinary power in the eyes of those who are constrained by norms *and institutions* (even those designed to upset norms). Moreover, these expressions of virtuosity (which can become virtually mainstream in due course) keep the canon open, so to speak, by democratic recognition of populist religious experiences, vernacular expressions of piety and spirituality, and appreciation of spontaneity. These have maintained the vitality of religious life.

In between these two types of saint are two other types that mediate between the poles. The second type comes close to, or actually embodies, the *virtues* by which a religion inspires the norms for family and social life and thereby ensures that the order envisioned or achieved by the first type of saint prevails. Virtues are fixed in normative roles, which have gender distinctions. For women, that traditionally has meant chaste maiden, wife, and mother (roles by which they have supported the patriliny).[41] For men, it has meant protection of, and provision for, the family (and by extension, clan and society). The saints of this type are those whose expression of virtues is more altruistic than that of ordinary people and who die in an extraordinary way.[42]

Also in between the two extremes is type three, the saints belonging to monastic orders or ascetic traditions that are quasi-institutionalized. These provide more routine (and safe) opportunities for rupturing order that has become too mundane than those of the virtuoso saint (the fourth type) who radically reverses order.

All these four types of saint participate in the dialectic of chaos and order but in different ways. The first creates order out of chaos. The second provides exemplary lives as ideals to inspire ordinary people to maintain order. The third offers orderly ways to rupture order to reveal anew the power of chaos. And the fourth creates chaos through reversal to destroy order. Put otherwise, my four types may be labeled: norm-discoverer, norm-preserver, routine norm-destroyer, and virtuoso norm-destroyer.

How does my definition of sainthood compare with those of other scholars mentioned at the beginning of this introduction? First, I agree with those scholars who think that comparisons across the religions yield patterns and insights on the nature of this phenomenon. Like van der Leeuw and Cohn, I think that the power created by the unusual death of the saint and its perpetuation in tombs, shrines, or relics is a diagnostic feature of sainthood. I am not as reductive as van der Leeuw, however, because I think the extraordinary life (characterized by altruism and the dialectic of chaos and order) is also important.

Scholars who analyze the category *sainthood* are themselves of two types. Those who distinguish the saint from other types (prophet, founder, ascetic, mystic, teacher, enlightened person, *bodhisattva,* and so forth) and those who understand the category *sainthood* as an umbrella category that subsumes other types—even though they recognize some overlap, which makes distinctions more a matter of emphasis than exclusive jurisdiction. To the former group belong van der Leeuw and Wach; to the latter Cohn, Hawley, and Keyes. I would place myself in the latter category, because I think that sainthood is the umbrella category because of its three diagnostic features: altruism (of two types: direct and indirect), unusual death, and the dialectic of chaos and order. To the extent that prophets, founders, mystics, and other religious figures have these three features (though they have other ones in addition), they belong to the category of saint. Not all religious figures would be included, however: priests, some teachers, and others (probably because their roles are even more routinized than those of my middle two categories and they are not characterized by an extraordinary death) do not belong to my category of saint.

My second and fourth types resemble the concepts of *imitable* and *inimitable* saints suggested by Cohn and Hawley. But I find that they do not do justice to the concept of *imitable* as norm or explain why it is worthy of sainthood by way of both extraordinary altruism even in the context of family and extraordinary death. In other words, their models of sainthood are derived mainly from the norm-destroyer model, especially the institutional variant that has well-defined spiritual paths (in Cohn's terms, the moral,[43] the intellectual, and the emotional) and the characteristic of charisma, which expresses the contact or union with chaos (the key characteristic for Keyes). None of these definitions, moreover, has captured the deep structure of sainthood as a general category.

Difference between Male and Female Saints

Is there a substantial difference between female and male saints? As noted at the beginning of this introduction, Cohn, the one scholar to have remarked on female sainthood, has observed that female saints are less common because the path is less accessible. When a path does exist, it is more rigidly or supernaturally defined and places greater emphasis on penitance, nurture, altruism, and finally purging the signs of female sexuality. Does this analysis hold true for the lives of the female saints analyzed in this book?

Cohn's analysis of gender differences is too focused on the concept of *path,* which characterizes my third type of saint (the routine norm-destroyer). Unlike Cohn, I think that the distinguishing features of female sainthood are more sociological than soteriological in nature. It is true that there are fewer accounts of female saints preserved in the public record. I agree with Cohn that one explanation for this is the absence of institutional paths or the lack of free choice to pursue them because of marriage as theoretically or functionally essential to the gender role definition of women in a number of religions. But this is only part of the explanation. In the case of female saints, I find more concern by women themselves over marriage. On the one hand, this includes the virtues[44] needed to sustain it and the trials involved (during marriage itself, the death of a husband, abandonment, and so on). On the other hand, marriage talk might be about how to avoid it. The prominence of discussions about marriage makes sense given the fact that most women's identity in the past was associated with marriage. Even those women in the past who defied the expectation of marrying (or remaining married) defined their identity in opposition to marriage much more often than men. (Men had a double identity, as it were, in both the home and the public realm which included authorized paths outside marriage.) There might be other reasons for fewer female saints being remembered in history. One is elite male dominance in the public space, including the writing of biographies and hagiographies and the choices they make for inclusion. Then, too, we no longer think of the many exemplary women within domestic contexts as saints, because talk of virtue has largely disappeared from modern and secular societies and the embodiment of feminine virtue, especially altruism, has been considered a problem for women instead of an ideal. Moreover, we tend not only to dismiss self-willed death as irrelevant to sainthood, even though the patterns detected here show that it is a key diagnostic feature, but also to think of these things with abhorrence. They are understood as either suicide or homicide—the expression par excellence of the problems that women face.

I agree with Cohn that the accounts of female saints place a greater emphasis than accounts of male saints on fasting. But, unlike Cohn I do not think that penitence is necessarily the issue. In India, for instance, fasting takes the form of *vratas* (vows creating power that can be used in various ways). Sometimes, women perform extreme vows to create a negative power, as it were, by which they can get others to do what they want. Take an example from Islam. Sayyida, the Muslim saint, repeatedly asked her husband to visit the tomb of Abraham, but to no avail; he lacked the time. "Her longing increased," writes Hoffman, "until Ishaq found that her gaunt body bore the marks of her intense longing and love." Then, she had her way. Of course, fasting is also important in the lives of male saints, especially if they are ascetics of some sort. But the topic does not seem to dominate their sacred biographies to quite the same extent. The accounts of female saints emphasize self-willed death, too. This topic might stand out simply because of its dramatic contrast with common stereotypes of women (their timidity, say, or their fickleness). Or it might be highlighted in comparison with men, who also performed these feats, only because not all female saints had tangible things that they left to society (such as books or new institutions) by which they would be remembered.

Like Cohn I have observed that descriptions of female sainthood do refer to caring for others, but it is difficult to know whether this is a distinguishing feature. Altruism is the raison d'être of both male and female saints. I would argue that it is the types of caring that are gendered, not the concept itself.

By default, Cohn implies that the stories of male saints refer more often to public and more differentiated roles related to learning and leadership. On initial examination this might be explained in connection with male dominance in the public realm. Prophets offer critical analysis of social problems, for example, and some move beyond critique to provide solutions or even new social visions. This is true of religious founders, of course, but also of reformers and philosophers who establish sects. Almost all of these are men, as are the teachers who convey the resulting spiritual insights, techniques, and paths for subsequent generations. But women as well have had differentiated and leadership roles. Christianity, Buddhism, and Taoism (and to a lesser degree Sufi Islam) have provided a separate space for women for learning and female leadership. This institutional life has, in turn, created cults based on the memory of female founders and saints. But even religions such as Judaism, Confucianism, and brahmanical Hinduism have provided women with separate spaces and some degree of autonomy and leadership precisely because of the now much maligned, sexual segregation. Moreover, exactly what does Cohn mean by *more often?* This allusion to statistics can be assessed in two ways. Because there are many more male saints in our records and many of them have been elite men with special roles, the global number of male saints as religious leaders would be greater than female saints of this type. But number might be understood in a different way if we examine the category of female sainthood to determine the number of female saints who are learned and leaders compared to the number of female saints who are not. Here in this volume the Christian,

Muslim, Buddhist, and Jewish examples have all been highly educated and have exemplified leadership (at least in female circles). Because this is a limited survey, the question should be researched further.

The study of individual female saints helps us to understand women's religious lives in the past. The translation of their works and the stories of their lives is one of the ways that scholars are recovering information about women hidden in various languages or obscure texts. These works are important not only for what they tell us about extraordinary religious women but also for the contribution that they make collectively for determining the concept of sainthood in general and the difference between female and male saints in particular. Learning about the lives of female saints, of course, also teaches us something about the world religions themselves and the civilizations of which they are an essential part.

Notes

1. In the preparation of this introduction based on the drafts of the chapters, I have quoted freely from the authors of this volume. I have not provided footnotes, however, because page numbers were not available at the time. Although I have drawn from the materials presented (and hope that I have presented them fairly), I alone must take responsibility for the general analysis that is found in this introduction.

2. All these saints lived in the first millennium C.E.

3. This method of mummification was probably developed by the Taoists. The Buddhist Ch'an monks adapted this. They were to die while sitting in meditation. Then they were wrapped in a cloth soaked with red laquer. When this hardened, the image was cast in their likeness and became their immortal remains (See R. H. Sharf, "The Idolization of Enlightenment: On the Mummification of Cha'an Masters in Medieval China," *Journal of the History of Religions,* 1 (1992) 23.

4. "Hagios" is masculine singular and *hagiai* is feminine singular.

5. Robert L. Cohn, "Sainthood" in Mircea Eliade, ed. *The Encyclopedia of Religion* (New York: Macmillan, 1989) 13: 1–2. The annual ceremonies occurred especially after the third century.

6. Cohn 1987, 1.

7. Gerardus van der Leeuw, English edition of 1933 German original, *Religion in Essence and Manifestation* vol. 1 (Gloucester, MA: Peter Smith, 1967), 214–238.

8. See Joachim Wach, *Sociology of Religion* (Chicago: University of Chicago Press, 1944).

9. John Stratton Hawley, ed., *Saints and Virtues* (Berkeley: University of California Press, 1987). Once again, this is most useful for the universalistic religions. For other definitions, see Richard Kieckhefer and George D. Bond, eds., *Sainthood* (Berkeley: University of California Press, 1988).

10. Charles F. Keyes, "Charisma: From Social Life to Sacred Biography," in *Charisma and Sacred Biography*, JAAR Studies, *Journal of the American Academy of Religion* ed. Michael A. Williams, 48. 3 and 4 (1982) 1–23.

11. The same is true, of course, for other religions—notably, Christianity and Islam.

12. The Talmud (like all later rabbinic sources) consists of two genres, as it were: *halakhah* and *agadah*. The former refers to legal discussions, the results of which are binding on all orthodox Jews; the latter refers to everything else. Included in this category are prayers, jokes, riddles, proverbs, theological debates and so on—*including accounts of miracles*. People, according to the rabbis, could be channels of God's power. Miracles, in any case, might have been created by God "in the beginning" (which is how the rabbis explained biblical departures from the natural order created by God).

13. The Hasidim are not marginal within the traditional Jewish community. Because they follow the *halakhah* rigorously, they are fully within the mainstream of orthodox Judaism, although they have adopted many distinctive practices *in addition*. Not surprisingly, they are often known as "ultra-orthodox" Jews. Because they institutionalized kabbalistic doctrines and practices, though, they can be considered representatives of the mystical tradition as well.

14. Also, human participation in the cosmic process begun by God at creation and to be completed by God in the Messianic Age.

15. The distinction of separate spheres for men's and women's religion can easily be taken too far, however, because, women do pray in the synagogue (and are required to do so on festivals) just as men pray at home or in private.

16. Men are certainly not discouraged from praying spontaneously, privately, and in the vernacular. And they often do in traditional communities. But their distinctive halakhic *obligation* is to pray liturgically, on behalf of the entire community, and in the sacred language.

17. At least some Sephardic Jews are familiar with the notion of vicarious atonement, according to Walter Zenner in "Saints and Piecemeal Superstition among the Jerusalem Sephardim," *Anthropological Quarterly*, 38:4 (1965): 201–217.

18. I thank Paul Nathanson for this observation.

19. The fact that tombs of postbiblical Jewish figures are found in Muslim countries (but, aside from those of Hasidic leaders not in Europe) suggests that there was more exchange between Islam and Judaism on this topic than between

Judaism and Christianity. Perhaps this is because Judaism and Islam shared certain religious ideas: both had strong monotheisms, for instance, whereas Christianity appeared polytheistic. Or perhaps it is because the political relations between Judaism and Islam and Judaism and Christianity have been very different. In any case, it should be remembered that Sarah, Rachal, Leah, and Rebecca all have tombs in Israel, and so visits to these sites would have predated Islam.

20. The rabbis have been extremely cautious, however, when it came to mysticism (which they associated, correctly, with disastrous messianic movements). Men are allowed to study esoteric texts, to be sure, but only if they have already mastered the authoritative exoteric ones, only if they are over forty years old, and so on. I thank Paul Nathanson for this comment.

21. Baskin citing Ada Rapoport-Albert, "On Women in Hasidism, S. A. Horodecky and the Maid of Ludmir Tradition" in *Jewish History: Essays in Honour of Chimen Abramsky,* eds. Ada Rapoport-Albert and Steven J. Zipperstein (London: Halban, 1988), 507.

22. Baskin begins her discussion by assuming that the notion of sainthood is characterized by the ability to perform miracles and to attain human perfection. With this definition in mind, she observes that Judaism has no concept of human perfection—which would undermine not only the notion of monotheism but also that of human finitude (because Judaism recognizes only two ontological categories: the human and the divine). Moreover, she opines that Judaism does not recognize miracles. These two observations would seem to make the general category of sainthood an anomaly in Judaism. The idea of female sainthood, she continues, would be a double anomaly.

In my opinion, this would be an unnecessary conclusion. Although Baskin starts her discussion by suggesting that sainthood in Judaism is an anomaly (which seems to reflect a non-Orthodox view of Judaism) and female saints a double anomaly (which is curious, because if the first anomaly is that there is no concept of sainthood, then by definition there would be neither male nor female saints). By the end of her discussion, though, she has made a case for saints in Judaism. Miracles are accepted, after all, in an authoritative source (nothing less than the Babylonian Talmud) and there is the notion of transferring power (through the good deeds of ancestors according to Zenner, "Saints and Piecemeal Superstition," 207). Moreover, the Hasidic movement, which began in the late seventeenth century, has drawn from the kabbalistic tradition and thus focused attention on mysticism and extraordinary people. And the Hasidim are anything but marginal in traditional, orthodox world. Besides, some Jews, especially in Islamic countries, have their own tradition of making pilgrimages to worship at the tombs of ancestors (where miracles occur or the powers of saints are transmitted). Finally, it is unnecessary to assume that saints represent human perfection; even Christianity has never gone that far, though Hinduism and some other religions have.

23. See also *Concept of Saint in Early Islamic Mysticism: Two Works by Hakim al-Tirmidhi* (Richmond, Surrey: Curzon Press, 1996) and Grace Martin Smith, ed., *Manifestations of Sainthood in Islam* (Istanbul: Isis Press, 1993).

24. For a useful background, see Reginald A. Ray, *Buddhist Saints in India: A Study in Buddhist Values and Orientations* (New York: Oxford University Press, 1994).

25. Anneke B. Muller-Bakker, ed. *Sanctity and Motherhood: Essays on Holy Mothers in the Middle Ages* (New York: Garland, 1995).

26. Paul Connerton, *How Societies Remember* (Cambridge: Cambridge University Press, 1989) 37.

27. See Thomas Hefferman, *Sacred Biography: Saints and their Biographers in the Middle Ages* (New York: Oxford, 1989) for the issue of genre in Christianity.

28. See Hsiang Liu, *The Position of Woman in Early China according to the Lieh nu chuan, 'The Biographies of Eminent Chinese Women'* (Westport, CT: Hyperion Press, 1981).

29. By the twentieth century, there were twenty-four collections.

30. Chinese Buddhism has other biographies called the *Lien-teng hui-yao,* the *Chia-t'ai p'u-teng lu,* and the *Su-teng hui-yuan* along with the *Sui-pi-chi,* 'a more casual collection of biographical matter and anecdotes').

31. Kathryn A. Tsai, "The Chinese Buddhist Monastic Order for Women: The First Two Centuries," 3–4, in Richard W. Guisso and Stanley Johannesen, eds., *Women in China: Current Directions in Historical Scholarship (Historical Reflections,* 8. 3 (1981) 1–21.

32. Tsai 1981, 5.

33. Tsai 1981, 14. See also Kathryn Ann Tsai trans., *Lives of the Nuns: Biographies of Chinese Buddhist Nuns from the Fourth to Sixth Centuries* (Delhi: Sri Satguru Publications, 1972) Appendix A, pp. 107–111).

34. Katherine K. Young and Lily Miller, "Ānandamāyī Mā and Modern Hinduism" in Dhirendra Vajpeyi, ed., *Boeings and Bullock-carts: Studies in Change and Continuity in Indian Civilization,* vol. 2: *Indian Civilization in its Local, Regional and National Aspects* (Delhi: Chanakya Publications, 1990).

35. See also G. Tulpule, "Janabai and Kanhopatra: A Study of Two Women Saints" in Anne Feldhus, ed., *Images of Women in Maharashtrian Literature and Religion* (Albany: State University of New York Press, 1996).

36. The poetic and hagiographic genres in this Maharashtrian tradition have deep similarities to Tamil genres, which had developed between the seventh and ninth centuries. These include the following: being playful with the Lord in role

reversals; being blessed to serve the servant of the Lord (in this case Nāmadeva); living only for the Lord and seeking refuge in Him alone; being lowly, helpless, and humble before him; repeating his name; alluding to his promise to marry and then not appearing (the concept of thief in Tamil cankam poetry from the first century B.C.E.) for which she threatens a public declaration of love (the āḻvārs' and nāyaṉārs' use of the cankam convention of riding the *maṭal*); seeing the Lord in various roles (as father, mother, lover, and child) and requesting the Lord to come soon because his devotee is dying. The almost identical use of these conventions (aside from the fact that the Marathi tradition is more *advaitic,* or nondualistic, in its ultimate expression) can be explained either by cultural contact or by the fact that both draw on an even older tradition than the Tamil, not an improbable hypothesis given the fact that the earliest Tamil poetic tradition seems to have had links with a larger megalithic tradition of the Deccan, where the shrine of Lord Viṭṭhal is located (that is, Pandapur). I am inclined to see a later Tamil connection for the *Vārkarī Pantha* (to which Janābāī belongs) originating in Karnataka (which had links with Tamil Nadu via Melukoṭe, a centre of Śrīvaniṣṇavism).

37. Connerton 1989, 70.

38. For another interesting discussion of female Taoist adepts see, Deborah Sommer, ed., *Chinese Religion: An Anthology of Sources* (Oxford: Oxford University Press, 1995) 205–210. An especially developed Taoist master was a woman named Sun Pu-erh (1119–1183). Her life, especially her intellectualism and pursuit of the highest path, was celebrated in a folk novel called *Seven Taoist Masters.* Her life represents the epitome of reversal motifs. She disfigures her face to eliminate the problem of beauty, leaves home to become a beggar and madwoman, and uses miraculous power to punish men who try to rape her. "Alone of all the Seen Perfected, Sun Pu-erh is the only one who radically immolates herself physically before achieving the Tao, which suggests the unique difficulties women encountered in religious practice" (206).

39. For other examples, see Zohra Khatoo, *Muslim Saints and Their Shrines* (Jammu India: Jay Kay Book House, 1990).

40. Kathryn Ann Tsai trans., *Lives of the Nuns: Biographies of Chinese Buddhist Nuns from the Fourth to Sixth Centuries* (Delhi: Sri Satguru Publications, 1972) Appendix A, 110–111.

41. This was the prevalent social structure in enduring, complex societies (that is, ones that have undergone state formation).

42. Both women and men have acted altruistically in the course of fulfilling their normative duties. In Judaism, for example, women work not only to care for their families, but also to provide financial support for the Torah learning of their husbands and sons. But the role of men as well is described in terms of ethics and

holiness; every bar mitzvah boy is told to grow up *l'Torah, l'hupah, ul'maasim tovim;* that is, to the *halakhah,* to marriage, and to good deeds (acts that go *beyond* the obligations imposed by *halakhah*) (I thank Paul Nathanson for this observation).

The traditional Hindu upper caste (especially brahmin) wife is another case in point. These women are to marry and are forbidden to divorce or remarry. The Hindu word for piety is *dharma.* From the verbal root *dhṛ,* it refers specifically to maintenance of social and cosmic order through normative roles. These have resulted in a highly regulated system of family life. Hinduism devotes a great deal of attention to the various roles of the householder (*gṛhastha*) and promotes the stability of marriage. Although orthodox Hinduism encourages ascetic paths to salvation for men, it tries unofficially to ensure that they do not compete with family life (the reproductive and intergenerational cycles) for the majority. Hinduism, like other religions, promotes selfless actions for the sake of society. In Hinduism, though, these are associated with identities defined by caste (or sex). The male warrior/ruler (*kṣatriya*), for instance, has a code of honor by which he pledges protection of the community and places his own life on the line to achieve this. Similarly, the servant vows loyalty to the death. As in Judaism, I would add, Hindu women of the brahmin caste support the learning of their husbands (though by household tasks, not by earning income). Occasionally their household labor is extended to meet the needs of their husband's live-in students as well. Feminine virtues are embodied in the concept of *strīdharma* (literally, the duties or righteousness of women). These include fasting or other acts of self-denial (*vratas*), ostensibly for the welfare of husband and family, though she too benefits. This behavior makes a woman *satī,* literally, a good woman. Furthermore, virtues are exemplified by epic heroines such as Sītā—wife, paragon of loyalty and devotion to her husband—portrayed in the *Rāmāyaṇa.*

43. This seems to be a misnomer given his description of it as ascetic rather than ethical.

44. The word "virtue" is derived from the Latin *virtus,* which originally meant manliness, strength, capacity, effective force or power, manly courage, and valor. And *virtus* is derived from *vir,* the word for "man." A link between masculine qualities and virtues can be found in the ideal that masculine qualities should be used for the sake of others and for society as a whole (thus, making physical or self-centred qualities into moral qualities by directing them to the other for the larger good). With urbanization, *virtus* became more internalized and nonphysical in concept. That made it applicable to women, too. In Christianity, the word "virtue" was generalized even further to refer to conformity to standard mores, responsibilities, duties, or any form of moral excellence (such as forgiveness, compassion, faithfulness, or chastity).

II
Dolce of Worms: Women Saints in Judaism

Judith R. Baskin

At first glance, a discussion of female sainthood in Jewish tradition appears anomalous on two counts. For one thing the idea of sainthood, in the sense that certain individuals are endowed with special qualities, such as miraculous powers, that set them apart from ordinary people, is all but absent in most mainstream forms of Jewish belief, which maintain a strict separation between divine and human attributes.[1] Rather, Judaism esteems most highly the human piety that stems from devout religious observance and study. While such piety may reach extraordinary levels in certain outstanding individuals, occasionally meriting the designation of "saintliness," the option of choosing a life characterized by such devotion is open to all Jewish males. However, while Judaism teaches that every man should dedicate his life to achieving ever higher levels of piety through obedience to God's commandments and study of the revealed word, such activities have not generally been deemed appropriate for Jewish women. Here is the second anomalous aspect of this essay's title: in official Judaism, before very recent times, women have been neither the shapers nor the exemplars of formal Jewish religious life and practice, and were, therefore, less likely to achieve reputations for saintliness.[2] Although women of outstanding piety have merited praise in every generation, they have been absent from the literary Jewish mystical traditions which have most highly esteemed pietistic spirituality. Jewish practice, however, has never been monolithic or without variations; female saints, and the veneration of such saints by Jewish women, have long been a feature of the popular religion of many Middle Eastern Jews.[3]

Women of outstanding piety who figure in postbiblical Jewish sources include Hannah, the mother of seven sons, whose story appears in various forms in Jewish Hellenistic, rabbinic, and medieval literatures.[4] This legend features a widow whose seven sons give up their lives to affirm publicly the truth of their religion. Hannah, who sees her seven sons slaughtered one by one because they will not bow down to idols, and then is killed in turn, becomes paradigmatic of the positive value of martyrdom for the sanctification of God's name.[5] And, as a symbol of the bereaved mother who will ultimately be comforted in the world to come, she also offers consolation to all who are oppressed. As the story is recounted in a tenth century work, the *Book of Josippon:*

> This woman was Hannah the Righteous and Pious who sent seven sons before her with joy and gladness of heart. . . . And afterward, she too went to the great light in happiness, and it is of her that the psalmist says: "As a happy mother of children" (Psalm 113:9).[6]

The story of Hannah celebrates the piety of a mother whose sons refuse to become apostates even at the cost of death; she is a paragon of the parent who is prepared to sacrifice her children as an act of conviction. As such she became, like the biblical Abraham, a model to other Jews of the demands and rewards of unquestioning faith and religious loyalty, especially in times of persecution and suffering.[7] It is instructive, however, that Hannah does not earn her renown based on her own learning or, indeed, on her own willingness to defend the truths of Judaism, but for supporting the steadfast devotion of her sons, even to the bitter end.

This essay will concentrate on an Ashkenazic model of female martyrdom and piety, the twelfth-century Dolce of Worms, through close examination of accounts of her life and death written by her scholarly husband, Rabbi Eleazar of Worms. Yet, although Dolce is characterized by her husband in these documents with the epithet, "saintly" (*hasidah*), the implications of this term are circumscribed, both by Jewish assumptions about the meaning of saintliness in general, and by the ramifications of Dolce's gender.

Saintliness in "Official Judaism"

Jewish tradition, as expressed in biblical and rabbinic sources, places the highest value on devoted obedience to the commandments God has revealed to Israel. Such faithful compliance is variously described as *kedushah* (sanctity), *tzedakah* (righteousness), and *hasidut* (piety or saintliness). Often these terms are used interchangeably as synonyms for all sincere efforts to serve God and to imitate God as much as is humanly possible. However, while stressing the imperative to emulate God and to act for the sake of God in all things, Judaism also maintains a constant distinction between the divine and the created. As the biblical writer Ecclesiastes proclaimed, "There is none righteous upon earth who does only good and does not sin" (Ecclesiastes 7:20). In the Jewish view, no human being, regardless of his or her virtues, can ever be regarded as without flaws or failings. Sainthood, as a definition of total human perfection, or of a person who possesses miraculous powers, is not a normative Jewish concept.[8]

Still, Judaism does make distinctions in the spiritual achievements of individuals. Solomon Schechter has defined individual holiness as "the highest achievement of the Law and its deepest experience, as well as the realization of righteousness."[9] He notes that individual holiness consists not only of imitation of God through obedience to the revealed precepts and statutes of Jewish law, which he characterizes by the Hebrew term *kedushah,* but also may have higher and mystical aspects best described by the term *hasidut,* which he translates as "saintliness." While *kedushah* concentrates on achieving closeness to God through fulfillment of all mandated commandments, *hasidut* aspires to a superior kind of holiness, supplementing and even correcting the law by going beyond what is required.[10] Thus, Schechter observes that the pious man or saint (*hasid*) does not wait for distinct commandments, but devotes himself with zeal and self-sacrifice to achieving a state of sanctity beyond the literal demands of the law. Accordingly, the *hasid* refrains even from actions that are permitted if he believes they are in any way ethically or ritually questionable.[11]

Biblical and rabbinic sources, moreover, do maintain the conviction that certain individuals, by virtue of their outstanding piety, can intercede with God on behalf of other humans, and may even perform miracles. Comments in the Babylonian Talmud, at Sanhedrin 65b and 93a, suggest that the righteous (*zaddikim*) could, if they desired, create a world, and similarly, that *zaddikim* are to be considered greater than the ministering angels. During the rabbinic period, a concept of vicarious atonement developed related to the belief that the good deeds of righteous ancestors served to benefit later, sinning generations. This concept of the "merit of the fathers" was elaborated in Jewish folklore and in Jewish mystical writings. As Walter Zenner writes, "such conceptualizations [once] existed throughout the Jewish world, but the anti-mystical reactions among European Jews since the Enlightenment have extinguished practices concerned with saints, except for the Hasidim [a pietistic movement which began in eighteenth century East Europe]."[12]

This conception of saintliness is closely linked to Judaism's mystical aspect, since the ultimate goal of *hasidut* is communion with God. As Schechter writes,

> This superior holiness, which implies absolute purity both in action and thought, and utter withdrawal from things earthly, begins, as a later mystic rightly points out, with a human effort on the part of man to reach it, and finishes with a gift from heaven bestowed upon man by an act of grace.[13]

Yet it must be emphasized that the essential first step on the Jewish mystical path is obedience and devotion to the commandments of the Torah. This can only be achieved through concentrated study of the divine word. Jewish mysticism, in almost all of its historic manifestations, is a highly intellectualized enterprise whose practice entails significant levels of both study and devoted observance and practice, in addition to a strongly developed spiritual propensity on the part of the mystical seeker. Virtually no women would ever have received the requisite educational background to undertake any Jewish version of the mystic quest and it is, therefore, not surprising that no mystical tracts or testimonies written by or attributed to a woman are included in the canon of Jewish mystical literature.[14]

Jewish Women's Religious Status

Traditional Judaism privileges and values the religious obligations and spiritual endeavors of men over the religious observance and spiritual efforts of women. The rabbinic Judaism that characterized most Jewish communities from the sixth through the eighteenth century of our era, and in many cases, beyond, ordained rigid separations between male and female roles.[15] Ideally, women's activities were to be confined to the domestic sphere of family life and economic endeavors on the family's behalf. In general, women earned cultural approbation by enabling their husbands and sons to fulfill religious obligations. Thus, Jewish women have historically been excluded from the paths of study and communal worship activity which led to religious authority and cultural esteem. Rather, through their domestic and economic activities, women made it possible for the men of their family to achieve in these areas. As a statement in the Babylonian Talmud at Berakhot 17a puts it, women earn merit "by sending their sons out to learn [Torah] in the Synagogue, and their husbands to study in the schools of the Rabbis, and by waiting for their husbands until they return from the schools of the Rabbis." This is not to say that women were totally excluded from religious life. While exempt from a large number of the ritual obligations incumbent on men, women were encouraged to pray and to perform several rituals specific to their sex. Women's prayers, however, were characterized as spontaneous and individual and could be offered in the vernacular language, as opposed to the mandated and ritualized public worship of men which followed a specific Hebrew liturgy.[16] Women might attend the synagogue, although they had no obligation to do so, but they sat apart from men and were not counted as members of the praying community.[17] Similarly, women's educational opportunities were far more limited than those available to males and rarely included instruction in the Hebrew language necessary for study of the sacred texts.

Given the exclusion of Jewish women from most communal religious experience and from involvement in intensive study before the modern era, it is not surprising that Jewish mysticism has been an essentially male endeavor. As Gershom Scholem has written,

> Both historically and metaphysically it is a masculine doctrine, made for men and by men. The long history of Jewish mysticism shows no trace of feminine influence. There have been no women Kabbalists; Rabia of early Islamic mysticism, Mechtild of Magdeburg, Juliana of Norwich, Theresa de Jesus, and the many other feminine representatives of Christian mysticism have no counterparts in the history of Kabbalism.[18]

While celibacy and monastic living allowed a large number of Christian women, and to a certain extent, also, some Muslim women, to cross gender boundaries and secure a place alongside men as the saints and mystics of both Christianity and Islam, rabbinic tradition forbade any access to such life alternatives for Jewish women.[19] Formal Judaism offered no adult avenues through which Jewish women could express their spiritual aspirations beyond marital devotion, maternal solicitude, observance of domestic Jewish rituals, and acts of charity to others. As Ada Rapoport-Albert has observed, despite a Jewish ambivalence towards asceticism in general, Jewish mystical circles sanctioned ritualistic practices for men, which could include prolonged periods of sexual abstinence. For women, on the other hand, such conduct was considered as "inherently false, hypocritical or self-deluding."[20] Jewish religious leaders criticized women who adopted such ascetic practices as fasting, prayer, and acts of personal deprivation. These signs of singleminded devotion to God were seen as a dereliction of a woman's primary duties to her husband and family, and were suspect, as well, even in the unmarried girl and the widow.[21]

Similarly, while some Jewish sects, in particular the early modern east European pietistic movement, Hasidism, which had a strong mystical aspect, have championed the belief that certain religious leaders are distinguished by outstanding spiritual qualities that include enhanced access to the divine, such *zaddikim*, "righteous ones," are all but invariably male.[22] The one apparent example of a woman who crossed gender boundaries to achieve religious leadership in a Hasidic sect on her own is, in fact, a story of female failure.[23] Hannah Rachel Verbermacher, known as "the Maid of Ludmir," was born in the Volhynian town of Ludmir in 1815. Extremely bright and unusually well-educated for her sex, she demonstrated exceptional piety, "praying with ecstasy three times a day, like a man." Rejecting marriage in order "to transcend the world of the flesh," Hannah used her sizable inheritance to build a study house in Ludmir where she lived in complete solitude. She soon acquired a reputation for saintliness and miracle-working, and became known as "the Holy Maid of Ludmir," attracting both men and women to her "court," to whom she would lecture from behind a closed door. Reaction from the male Hasidic leaders of her region was uniformly negative, and pressure was successfully applied on Hannah to resume her rightful female role in marriage. Although her marriages were unsuccessful, they had the intended result of ending her career as a religious leader, and Hannah ended her life in obscurity.[24] As Rapoport-Albert notes, the effort of the Maid of Ludmir to act as a *zaddik*,

> reflects a certain aspiration or yearning, which may well have been profound and could have found expression in reality for a while, at a grassroots level, in a Christian environment which was not, after all, unfamiliar with "holy maidens" and female saints. Nevertheless, it constitutes the perfect exception which confirms the rule whereby no woman could legitimately claim the full powers of spiritual leadership in Hasidism, any more than she could establish the legitimacy of such a claim at any previous stage in the development of Jewish mysticism.[25]

The "Little Tradition": Female Saints in Popular Judaism

The Maid of Ludmir, even in her lack of ultimate success, is a rare exception in Jewish history of a woman who competed on the same field with men, however briefly, for religious authority. Her battle was bound to be unsuccessful, for until the recent modern era, no form of official Judaism has accepted women as religious leaders. No one would deny, however, that Jewish women throughout the ages have found spiritual sustenance through a variety of rituals and customs. While these observances were always seen by Jewish leaders as ancillary to male needs, and as secondary in religious value to the Jewish practice demanded of men, they were and are of immense spiritual value to their practitioners.[26]

One such area of female ritual is connected with prayer and the development of liturgical language for women. Although women were always encouraged to pray in the vernacular, it was the invention of printing at the end of the Middle Ages that led to the widespread writing and publication of *tkhines,* supplicatory prayers for Jewish women in Central and East Europe. At least some of the authors of these prayers were women.[27] These printed collections of prayers in the vernacular (Judaeo-German or Yiddish), which women could recite at a variety of specified moments in their lives, often invoked the merits of the biblical matriarchs, Sarah, Rebecca, Leah, and Rachel, just as the Hebrew liturgy called upon divine remembrance of the merits of the fathers, Abraham, Isaac, and Jacob, on behalf of the Jewish people. Similarly, these prayers often called upon deceased female relatives to intercede for the petitioner. This excerpt from the seventeenth century *Shloyse she'orim* (*Three Gates*) of Sarah bas Tovim combines both forms of intercession:

> I take for my help the living God, blessed be He, who lives forever and to eternity, and I set out this second beautiful new *tkhine* in Yiddish with great love, with great awe, with trembling and terror. . . . May God have mercy upon me and upon all Israel. May I not long be forced to be a wanderer, by the merit of our Mothers, Sarah, Rebecca, Rachel, and Leah. And my own dear mother Leah pray to God, blessed be He, for me, that my being a wanderer may be an atonement for me for my sins.[28]

This particular collection of prayers also invokes the authority of meritorious women of the past in its complex description of a multichambered "women's Paradise"; in each chamber an outstanding female biblical figure presides over thousands of joyous women studying the divine word. Chava Weissler has noted that Sarah bas Tovim's work, which drew heavily on Jewish mystical writings translated into Yiddish, is unique in its vision of women in Paradise learning Torah, "the primary religious duty of Jewish men, from which women were excused or excluded," as well as in its portrayal of biblical women as powerful spiritual figures.[29] Sarah bas

Tovim concludes with a vision of the elevation of the most meritorious women of all:

> And the chambers of the matriarchs cannot be described; no one can come into their chambers. Now, dear women, when the souls are together in paradise, how much joy there is! Therefore, I pray you to praise God with great devotion, and to say your prayers, that you may be worthy to be there with our Mothers."[30]

In none of these texts is the word "saint" actually used in describing these influential women of the past, yet the assumption of their proximity to the divine, and of their ability to intercede on behalf of the supplicant is clear, and represents an aspect of Jewish women's popular religious practice just beginning to be explored.

The terms "saint" and "saintliness" are freely evoked, however, in the ritual customs of some contemporary Jewish women originally from Muslim countries. Susan Sered has described how Middle Eastern Jewish women in Israel see themselves as a link between the generations and as responsible for soliciting the help of ancestors in times of trouble.[31] Ancestors may be deceased relatives, or they may be sages and famous figures from the Jewish past; in either case, these ancestors have the status of saints. These saints, "being part human, part divine, cross the boundary separating spheres," and it is believed they can intercede with God on behalf of individual Jews or the Jewish people as a whole.[32] Sered writes that the channels of communication between the world of the dead and the world of the living can include dreams, prayers, and candle lighting, as well as visits to cemeteries and holy tombs. A pilgrimage to a tomb is considered particularly efficacious: "The tomb is not only a cult object, but also a place for the living pilgrim to meet the dead saint and make a pact with him."[33] Since it is not always certain that the dead saint will be inclined to offer aid,

> Gifts such as new curtains to cover a tomb, flowers, candles, and contributing money for the upkeep of the tomb encourage the saint to intercede. The women believe that by touching or kissing the tomb one can have some type of physical contact with the person inside the tomb, and they trust that the dead saint comes out of his grave at night (and possibly at other times) to bless objects, such as oil, that are left near the tomb.[34]

The gender of the saint whose tomb is visited does not seem to be a particularly relevant factor in the religious lives of the women Sered studied, although visits to the tombs of female saints are probably particularly connected with fertility concerns. In fact, there is only one tomb in Israel of a female Jewish saint, that of Rachel the matriarch, at Bethlehem,[35] although there are tombs of female Jewish saints, predominantly martyrs, which are popular Jewish women's shrines in other Middle Eastern countries. While visiting the tombs of saints is not a custom limited to women (it is also common among Middle Eastern Jewish men), Sered details the specifically female rituals that characterize women's acts of pilgrimage.[36] She notes that visiting tombs is perceived as giving women "the merit or right to ask the saints to intercede on behalf of their families," since this ritual, like most others these women perform, is "directed towards helping their loved ones."[37] She also notes that the tombs in Israel are under the control of the Ministry of Religion, which represents male, official Judaism, so that women's behavior is highly regulated: "At Meron and at Rachel's Tomb, groups of men praying the formal prayer service frequently tell the women to stop making so much noise. . . . While the tombs are undoubtedly female sacred space, there does not seem to be the strong sense of the 'female collective endeavor' that writers have noticed at shrines in other countries."[38]

Dolce of Worms and the *Hasidei Ashkenaz*

Dolce of Worms is an unusual figure in a number of ways, perhaps most strikingly in the quantity of information we have about her. She was from the elite, leadership class of medieval German Jewry, the daughter of a cantor and community benefactor and the wife of a major rabbinic figure, Rabbi Eleazar ben Judah of Worms (1165–1230). Dolce and her husband were also members of a small circle of Jews distinguished for their pietism. These *Hasidei Ashkenaz*, the German-Jewish pietists, had a particular religious outlook which had a significant impact on the Jews of the Rhineland, and on other communities in Germany and France. The main documents of this movement, written in the twelfth and thirteenth centuries, reflect the uncertain atmosphere in which Jews lived following the First Crusade of 1096, during which a number of Rhineland Jewish communities had been destroyed by Crusaders.[39] The *Hasidei Ashkenaz* produced many esoteric, mystical works, as well as a major volume reflecting their ethical concerns, *Sefer Hasidim*, (*The Book of the Pious*) which is also an important historical source for the study of everyday Jewish life in medieval Germany. As Ivan Marcus writes:

> *Sefer Hasidim* is a speculum of the society in which it originated. It contains allusions to knights and demons, princes and prices, grain profiteering,

> monastic practices, tensions in communal politics, Jewish-Christian debates, conversion in both directions, coin clipping, sexual promiscuity, local customs, women's occupations in weaving and moneylending, and a variety of other facets of medieval culture and life in medieval Germany.[40]

This volume is attributed to R. Judah the Pious (1140–1217), although some parts may have been written by Judah's father, R. Samuel b. Kalonymous *he-Hasid.* Some of the passages also bear close similarity in language and ideals to the introduction to the *Roqeah,* a legal work by R. Eleazar, who was Judah's most prominent disciple. R. Eleazar, who is also known as the *Roqeah,* may have written some of the passages in *Sefer Hasidim,* and could have been its editor, although there is no definitive evidence of this.[41]

The *Hasidei Ashkenaz* came into being, at least in part, out of the spiritual crisis generated by the catastrophic consequences of the First Crusade for so many Jewish communities. In Jewish theology such disasters were viewed as a reflection of divine disfavor which demanded individual and communal repentance and atonement. Thus, the major leaders of the Hasidei Ashkenaz agreed that the *hasid,* or pietist, whether as an individual or as part of a group separated from the rest of the Jewish community, must pursue a goal directed towards otherworldly salvation through singleminded devotion to divine demands. As Marcus writes, understanding God's "larger will" was the *hasid*'s main endeavor.[42]

> The Pietists held that when God revealed His will to the Jewish people at Sinai, He revealed only part of it explicitly and hid another part. German-Jewish pietism focuses on the effort of the Pietist to fulfill not only the explicitly revealed divine will, as expressed in Jewish law, but in addition to search out and strive to fulfill an infinitude of additional obligations imposed by God's implicitly revealed, or, hidden will.[43]

The pietists of this community, demonstrating a fervor unprecedented in Jewish history, imposed extra prohibitions and established numerous safeguards around what was already prohibited in order to fully discover and fulfill the divine will and in that way achieve personal atonement and atonement for the entire community.[44]

The *Hasidei Ashkenaz* were certainly influenced by popular Christian spirituality and religious thought, although to what degree is uncertain. Robert Chazan has demonstrated that "close analysis of the events of 1096 has revealed a set of Jewish communities socially integrated into the environment around them," and he shows that zealous

Jewish attitudes towards martyrdom, for example, must be seen in the larger context of the intense spiritual ethos of Christianity of the late eleventh and twelfth centuries which very much esteemed death in defence of one's faith.[45] Similarly, Joseph Dan has noted the sensitivity of medieval Jewish thinkers to Christian and Muslim criticisms that Judaism emphasized the physical enactment of religious practices rather than their spiritual meaning. He suggests that Jews were under constant pressure to prove that Judaism was a spiritual religion, which put primary emphasis on spiritual ethics and the spiritual meaning of ritual, beyond physical fulfillment of legal prescriptions.[46] Dan writes that "the discovery of the spiritual aspect of Judaism and its dominance over the physical aspect is the main subject of Jewish ethical literature in the Middle Ages," and that this is particularly the case for the German-Jewish pietists.[47] The profound ambivalence the *Hasidei Ashkenaz* felt towards Judaism's emphasis on the physical component of commandments, which included the requirement that all men procreate, can be said to reach its height in their attitudes towards women.[48] Medieval Christian convictions of the inherently carnal nature of human beings, the negative role of woman in man's fall, and the preferable option of celibacy for those who were capable of it, would have been known to Jews. In fact, Christian writers often criticized as evidences of carnality such Jewish sexual mores as virtually universal marriage, the availability of divorce, remarriage of widows and widowers, and marriage within limits of consanguinity forbidden by the Christian Church.[49] The special intensity of the German-Jewish pietists' uneasiness with women owes much to their exposure and apparent attraction to many of these negative attitudes about sexuality.

Certainly, in their mystical yearning to transcend the physical pleasures of the material world, the *Hasidei Ashkenaz* go beyond rabbinic norms in their displacement of women in favor of devotion to the divine, as the following passage indicates:

> The root of loving God is loving God with all your heart (Deuteronomy 6:4). . . . And the joy of this love is of such intensity and so overpowers the heart of those who love God, that even after many days of not being with his wife and having a great desire for her, in the hour that a man ejaculates he does not find it as satisfying as the intensity and power of loving God and finding joy in his Creator. . . . He must love the Creator with a great and strong love until he becomes sick because of his love, as the man who is love-sick for the affections of a woman and reels constantly because of his love, when he sits, rises, goes and comes, also when he eats and drinks. He neither sleeps nor slumbers because of this love. Greater than this should

> love of the Creator be in the hearts of those who love Him and they should be absorbed in it constantly, as we were commanded, "with all thy heart, with all thy soul. . . ." (Deuteronomy 6:4).[50]

To remove female distractions, *Sefer Hasidim* recommends that men hold extremely limited social converse with women, including their own wives: "Each one who wishes to return in repentance and achieve a status of piety . . . let him forsake . . . converse with his wife except while making love . . . and let this not be a burden upon him because of his love for his Creator."[51] Yet maintaining too great a distance from one's wife may also lead to sin, and therefore happy marital relations are also encouraged as a fence against the possibility of sexual temptation elsewhere. Eleazar of Worms himself advised that "One should avoid looking at other women and have sex with one's wife with the greatest passion because she guards him from sin."[52] Yet passion with women must always come second to passion for the divine.

The authors of *Sefer Hasidim,* and other *Hasidei Ashkenaz* writings saw potential sexual irregularities at every turn. Significant portions of *Sefer Hasidim* focus on male sexual violations with women who may be Jewish or gentile, single or married, of age or minors. Great attention is given to how atonement may be undertaken by male transgressors, and how repentance might be achieved.[53] How females might do penance for their sexual indiscretions, however, is not a subject that is considered. The result is that women are portrayed as objects of desire, or causes of sin, but not as sinners themselves in need of redemption. This apparent blindness to the possibility that women are also moral and spiritual beings may simply be indicative of medieval Jewish thinking about women; it might also stem from Judaism's understanding that a woman's primary duty is to enable her husband to fulfil his religious obligations. Were she herself to be involved in penances and repentance the entire life of her family would be disrupted.[54]

This is not to say that women are never represented positively in the writings of the *Hasidei Ashkenaz*. Generally, individual women who are part of the pietistic circle are depicted favorably. Pietists are advised to marry women who share their values, even at the cost of parental disapproval; some pious women are portrayed as more energetic in giving charitable contributions than their husbands. However, women are also associated with sorcery and witchcraft, and even the most pious women, simply by virtue of their sex, are seen to have the potential, however unwitting, to tempt a man to sin or sinful thoughts.[55]

Avoiding contact with women, however, was all but impossible for the German-Jewish pietists. It is well known that Jewish women of this milieu, as in medieval Jewish society in general, were active participants in the lives of their households. By virtue of their generous dowries and their own financial skills, they were essential to the family's economic sustenance. Often familiarity with money led women to take the initiative in business matters. Dolce, like other Jewish wives of her social world, supplied the whole of the family income, allowing her husband to devote himself to study and teaching. Such financial undertakings, which could be extremely complex, required literacy in the vernacular language and training in mathematics and bookkeeping skills.[56] As Kenneth Stow notes, these unique economic roles of Jewish women appear to have strengthened their hand as marriage partners. He suggests the strong and self-contained conjugal family units that resulted were essential for Jews because of the "necessarily limited nature of Jewish social and political institutions," and he sees such strong marital partnerships as a factor in the growth of the medieval bourgeoisie, of which Jews in Christian Europe were early exemplars.[57]

There is, then, a profound dissonance between the religious and mystic yearnings of German-Jewish pietist writers, who sought relief from the human relationships that distracted them from the closest possible communion with God, and the love and attachment they felt for the wives and children of their everyday lives. The contradictions raised by this duality of male engagement in both the quest of the spirit and the life of the body are among the factors that distinguish medieval Jewish mysticism from its Christian counterparts.

The Document

Eleazar of Worms, the Roqeah, is particularly known for his mystical writings. He was in many ways a transitional figure between earlier, more exclusivist visions of the German-Jewish pietist endeavor and those leaders who sought to reach out to the Jewish community as a whole. As Ivan Marcus, writes, "By putting his private penitential into his *Sefer ha-Roqeah* (*Book of the Perfumer*), a book of Jewish law and custom, Eleazar "normalized" a revolutionary form of Jewish atonement and thereby enabled it to be preserved and readapted by a variety of Jewish religious innovators and sects down to the present day."[58] Eleazar also left a number of other writings, both esoteric and personal, and these latter documents include two accounts, one in prose and one in poetry, of the murders of his wife Dolce, and their daughters, Bellette, and Hannah. Two extant manuscripts preserve both the prose and poetic texts.[59]

The better known of these two texts is the poetic elegy, based in part on Proverbs 31, the biblical description of the "woman of valor." This lament, which records numerous and poignant details of its subjects' daily lives, constitutes an important source for the activities of medieval Jewish women in general, as well as a moving tribute to Dolce and her daughters. While this elegy has been translated into English several times,[60] the Roqeah's prose description of the attack on his family circle, which precedes the poem in the two extant manuscripts in which the poem appears, is less well-known, and has not, to my knowledge, been translated into English or discussed by other scholars:

> In 4957, on the twenty-second of Kislev [15 November, 1196], after I, Eleazar the small and the lowly, had expounded Parashat "*V'yashev Ya'akov*" [the weekly scriptural reading, "And Jacob settled," Genesis 37–40] in safety, and I was sitting at my table, two marked men[61] came to us, and they drew their swords and struck my *saintly* wife, mistress Dolce. They broke the head of my elder daughter Bellette, and they struck my younger daughter Hannah in the head, and they both died. And they wounded my son Jacob from the crown of his head to half his cheek to his forehead. And they wounded my head and my hand, on my left side, and they wounded my students and my schoolmaster. Immediately the *saintly* woman jumped up and ran out of the winter quarters[62] and cried out that they were killing us. The wicked ones went out and cleaved her in the head from the windpipe to the shoulder, and from the shoulder to the waist, across the width of the back and her front, and the righteous woman fell dead. And I secured the door, and we cried out, until help should come to us from heaven. And I cried out over this *saintly* woman, praying for revenge. And thus it happened. For after a week they caught the murderer who killed her, and who killed my two daughters, and wounded my son, and they killed him. I was left in want of everything and in great affliction and overwhelming suffering.
>
> Before her murder, she purchased parchment for the writing of books. She supported me and my son and my daughters by [lending] other people's money. Because of my great sins she was killed, and my daughters. As God is my witness, she was put to much trouble so that I and my son might study. And woe is me concerning them! How much blood was spilled, and she was dying before my eyes! May the Holy One show us their revenge, and take pity on their souls, and have compassion on the bereaved survivor who remains, and on my son, and on all of His people Israel. Amen.[63]

This prose narrative not only tells us a great deal about Dolce and her activities, but also raises a number of questions about these horrible murders and their aftermath. Among the mysteries is the identity of the perpetrators of the attack on the family circle of the Roqeah, which included his wife, two daughters, at least one son, a number of students, and a junior teacher. The depiction of the attackers as Crusaders has raised a number of questions in earlier scholarship as to when and where the attack actually took place.[64] The political climate in Germany in this period very much militated against any kind of organized large scale anti-Jewish violence; nor is there any indication that Rhineland Jewish communities in 1196 perceived any threats from crusading hosts, as for example, had been felt by the Jewish community in Mainz in 1188 during the Third Crusade.[65] In fact, there was little crusading activity during 1196–1197 in Germany at all. Although the German Emperor Henry VI, who had also been crowned king of Sicily in 1194 following his conquest of Palermo, announced a new crusade in 1195, the primary activity was in Southern Italy where the crusading host began to assemble on the Apulian and Sicilian coasts in May and June, 1197. Part of the army was already en route from Italy to the Holyland when Henry died of a typhuslike fever in Messina on 28 September, 1197, and the crusading effort came to an end.[66] Were the two men who attacked the Roqeah's family crusaders planning to participate in this effort, who were passing through Worms on their way to Italy? Although the body of Henry's troops were with him in Italy, this is not impossible since the Crusade was also preached in Germany.

In the end, all that can be said about the two attackers in Worms is that if they were Crusaders they were individuals who had taken the cross on their own; they were not part of any crusading army passing through Worms, but were acting as individuals, out of hope of monetary gain. The Roqeah's home was almost certainly selected on account of the activities of Dolce, who functioned as a major banker and moneylender. It was likely that the miscreants believed they would find money or other precious objects in her home. They gained admission on some pretext, since the Roqeah gives no indication of violent entry, then, perhaps finding no valuable items or encountering resistance from Dolce, they attacked the family. I would stress, as well, that these attacks did not go unpunished. The Christian authorities, following the Emperor's mandate of protecting the Jews of his realm, quickly captured and executed at least one of the men.[67]

While the prose account concentrates on the events of the attack, and its devastating aftermath, the poetic eulogy recounts the range of endeavors of "the *saintly*"[68] Mistress Dolce in the form of a commentary on Proverbs 31, as the following excerpts demonstrate:

> *What a rare find is a capable wife* (31:10): Such a one was my saintly wife, Mistress Dolce.
>
> *A capable wife* (31:10): the crown of her husband, the daughter of community benefactors. A woman who feared God, she was renowned for her good deeds.
>
> *Her husband put his confidence in her* (31:11): She fed him and dressed him in honor to sit with *the elders of the land* (31:23) and involve himself in Torah study and good deeds.
>
> *She was good to him, never bad, all the days of* (31:12) his life with her. She made him books from her labor; her name signifies "Pleasant."[69]
>
> . . . *She was like a merchant fleet* [*bringing her food from afar*] (31:14) to feed her husband so that he might immerse himself in Torah. Her daughters saw her and *declared her happy* (31:29) *for her merchandise was excellent* (31:18).
>
> *She supplied provisions for her household* (31:15) and bread to the boys.
>
> How *her hands worked the distaff* (31:19) to spin thread for books. Vigorous in everything, she spun threads for phylacteries, and [prepared] sinews [to bind together] scrolls and books; she was as swift as a deer to cook for the young men and to fulfill the needs of the students.
>
> *She girded herself with strength* (31:17) and stitched together some forty Torah scrolls. She prepared meat for special feasts and set her table for all of the community.
>
> *Judging wisely* (31:18) she adorned brides and brought them [to the wedding] in appropriate [garments]. "Pleasant" bathed the dead and sewed their shrouds. . . .
>
> She sang hymns and prayers and recited supplications. . . .
>
> In all the cities she taught women, enabling their "Pleasant" intoning of songs.
>
> She knew the order of morning and evening prayer; she came early to the synagogue and stayed late.
>
> She stood throughout the Day of Atonement and chanted; she prepared the candles for Sabbaths and festivals. She honored those who devoted themselves to the study of Torah.
>
> *Her mouth was full of wisdom* (31:26): she knew what was forbidden and what was permitted. On the Sabbath she sat and listened to her husband's preaching.
>
> Outstanding in her modesty, she was wise and well-spoken. Whoever was close to her was blessed. She was eager, pious, and amiable in fulfilling all the commandments. . . . She was happy to do the will of her husband and

> never angered him. Her actions were "Pleasant." May the Eternal Rock remember her.
>
> May her soul be enveloped in the wrappings of eternal life. *Extol her for the fruit of her hands* (31:31) in Paradise.[70]

Of his daughters, Eleazar writes that, at the age of thirteen, his older daughter, Bellette had learned all the prayers and songs from her mother who was "modest and pious, 'Pleasant,' and wise":

> The maiden followed the example of her beautiful mother; she prepared my bed and pulled off my shoes each evening. Bellette was busy about the house and spoke only truth; she served her Creator and spun, sewed, and embroidered.

As for Hannah, he wrote that "She recited the first part of the *Sh'ma* prayer every day. She was six years old and spun and sewed and embroidered. She entertained me and she sang."[71]

These descriptions of the doings of Dolce and her daughters, which center on female occupations, allow us to use gender as one of the categories with which to analyze medieval Jewish social and religious life. This approach illuminates not only the cardinal role that Dolce played both financially and domestically in supporting the life of her family, but also reveals the very profound love the Roqeah felt for his wife and daughters. The epithets Eleazar uses in describing his wife, "pious" or "saintly" (*hasidah*), three times in the prose account and again at the very outset of the poetic eulogy, and "righteous" (*tzadeket*), tell us a great deal about the qualities for which women in her culture were most esteemed. While not perhaps "saintly," in conventional understandings of the term, Dolce is saintly in her husband's eyes because of her piety and the outstanding ways in which she fulfilled all of the obligations her community found appropriate for her sex.

In both accounts Eleazar describes Dolce as supporting her family financially; in the prose passage, this activity is specified as through "the funds of others," *cesef aharim.* This appears to refer to a form of the medieval economic practice of *commenda,* similar in some ways to the talmudic *'isqa* which has been described by Abraham Udovitch, and Haym Soloveitchik.[72] This practice is an arrangement whereby an investor or group of investors entrusts capital or merchandise to an agent-manager, who is to trade with it, and then return to the investor(s) the principal and a previously agreed upon share of the profits. The remaining share of the profit goes to the agent as a reward for his or her labor."[73]

This is why it appears probable that Dolce, as a moneylender of significant funds who likely held valuable objects left in pledge, was the focus of the attackers' hostility.

Nor were financial matters the only focus of Dolce's life. Her husband describes her as managing an extensive household, for not only was she responsible for caring for the needs of her husband and three or more children, but her ménage also included her husband's students and at least one junior teacher. She provided food and clothing for all of these individuals. Dolce also paid for hiring additional teachers and for the purchase of parchment from her earnings. It is interesting to see the centrality of books in R. Eleazar's household, and Dolce's physical involvement in their production. For not only was she able to buy the material on which books would be written, but she sewed books together from thread she had herself spun, and repaired torn books as well.

Moreover, Dolce's needlework skills were also of use in the communal domain of the synagogue. She is credited with preparing gut and sewing together the quite extraordinary number of forty Torah scrolls (the scroll containing the first five books of the Hebrew Bible which is used in synagogue worship and is symbolic of the revelation of the divine word to the people of Israel); she is also have said to have spun thread for other religious objects, and to have prepared candles for synagogue use. Historically, Jewish women have always made contributions to enhance the synagogue and its sacred objects. While prosperous women donated Torah scrolls for the service, oil and books for study, and left legacies for the upkeep of the synagogue, poorer women gave their needlework in the form of Torah binders and covers, and as curtains for the ark containing the Torah scrolls. These actions can be seen as female strategies for imprinting their existences on a realm of activity in which they were otherwise secondary.[74] As the wife of the rabbi, Dolce undoubtedly felt a special responsibility to provide for the synagogue's needs.

Nor were Dolce's contributions to the synagogue the fruits of her physical labors alone. The daughter of an elite family distinguished for its learning, Dolce, herself, was unusually well-educated. Certainly, all Jewish women acquired domestic skills in childhood. These included not only the rudiments of cooking, needlework, and household management, but also the rules of rabbinic Judaism applicable to home and marriage. Basic religious training was considered essential so that a woman would know how to observe dietary laws, domestic regulations pertaining to the Sabbath and festivals, and the other commandments relevant to her family life. But higher educational achievements, such as literacy in Hebrew, which was standard for Jewish boys, only rarely applied to girls, and then only to those from select families. Dolce, the daughter of a cantor who led synagogue prayers and singing, was an example of such an unusually literate woman.[75] In his poetic elegy, her husband reports that she was able to chant Psalms, as well as hymns and Hebrew prayers, and that she taught some of these to other women: "In all the cities she instructed women and sang sweetly, coming early to the synagogue and staying late." She is among several medieval Jewish women who are described as women's prayer leaders. Another such woman, from the thirteenth century, is Urania of Worms, whose headstone epitaph commemorates her as "the daughter of the chief of the synagogue singers. His prayer for his people rose up to glory. And as to her, she, too, with sweet tunefulness officiated before the women to whom she sang the hymnal portions." Medieval Worms, which had a separate room for women attached to the synagogue, may have had special traditions associated with women and worship.[76]

Dolce also took on other communal responsibilities relating to women, again in her prominent role as the rabbi's wife. She is described as adorning brides and bringing them to their wedding in honor. Beyond preparing and escorting the bride, Dolce, as a respected investment broker, may also have been involved in arranging matches and negotiating the financial arrangements which accompanied them. Similarly, Dolce is said to have bathed the dead and to have sewed their shrouds. These acts are considered particularly meritorious in Jewish tradition, and generally Jews had burial societies which took on these responsibilities, men caring for men, and women caring for women. Dolce, clearly, figured prominently in such essential activities connected with women in her community.

R. Eleazar stresses Dolce's piety (*hasidut*) in both the prose and poetic passages, stating that all of her actions were inspired by a desire to fulfill the divine will, the pietist's highest goal. Dolce is described as knowing what was permitted and what was forbidden according to Jewish law, and as always eager to learn from her husband's teachings.[77] She was able to go far beyond the ordinary woman in the extent and content of her religious devotions due to her unusual knowledge of the traditional Hebrew liturgy, and she was atypical, too, in the extent of her synagogue attendance. It would appear that Dolce was training her daughters to follow in her footsteps, since their father relates not only their needlework skills, but also their knowledge of Hebrew prayers and their melodies. In everything, as the Roqeah puts it in the poetic lament, Dolce was concerned to "fulfill her Creator's commandments."

Yet it is significant that R. Eleazar's final words of praise for Dolce in his poetic eulogy are that she rejoiced to perform her husband's will and never angered him. Here, R. Eleazar is expressing his fundamental agreement with the view of the thirteenth century R. Moses of Coucy who taught in his *Sefer Mitzvot Gadol,* that although "a woman is exempt from both the commandment to learn Torah and to teach her son, even so, if she aids her son and husband in their efforts to learn, she shares their reward for the fulfillment of that commandment."[78] Dolce, more than anything, is revered for having facilitated in every way the spiritual activities of the men of her household, and this is why her husband has not the slightest doubt of her overwhelming merit. The reward that R. Eleazar invokes for his beloved wife in the final phrase of the poetic lament, to be bound in the eternal light of Paradise, is a recognition of her deeds, upon which so many were utterly dependent. As Proverbs 31:31, on which his elegy is based, says, "Extol her for the fruit of her hands,/ And let her works praise her in the gates." Dolce's saintliness, the only saintliness available to a Jewish woman in her time and place, lay in her willingness to exult in the secondary and subordinate role her culture had assigned all females, and to bear the burdens of the everyday for the sake of God so that men might devote themselves to deeper understanding of the divine word.

The physical powerlessness of Jews, who were a barely tolerated minority in Christian Europe, often led to interesting cultural role reversals. Thus, Jewish society has tended to esteem the scholar as opposed to the man of physical strength and action, a persona largely forbidden to Jews in medieval Christendom. It is striking that in his description of the intruders' assault, R. Eleazar describes Dolce as the one who takes physical action when her household is attacked. Dolce is the one who manages to get out of her house in order to summon aid for her family; and it is she who dies a combatant's death, cut to pieces in the street by the marauders. Indeed, it could be said that in many ways Dolce's behavior as wage earner and defender of her family more comfortably fits with conventional Western notions of masculine rather than feminine characteristics.

While her husband showed no discomfiture in describing his wife's active role in supporting her family, and in coming to their defense, it seems that this strong portrayal of the Roqeah's wife was disquieting to later generations. Some of this apparent uneasiness over seemingly inappropriate female and male behaviors is resolved in an account of this event found in the seventeenth century *Ma'aseh Nissim* (1670), a collection of tales and short stories in Judaeo-German based on legends that arose around the city of Worms and its distinguished Jewish figures, attributed to R. Juspe Shammash (1604–1678) of Worms.[79] R. Juspe recounts the events surrounding the attack as follows:

> The godly man, the great rabbi, Rabbi Eleazar of Worms, lived in a house which was called *Das Hirschen Haus,* because on the door of the house was hung a sign depicting a deer; the house stood beside the lower gate on the Jewish street and reached to the city wall. In the winter the disciples regularly came to him to study two or three hours before dawn. On one occasion, a Thursday, when the disciples had come to him as usual, before morning light, and were studying the weekly portion with Rashi's commentary with him, several murderous students gathered with swords and with bows and with all kinds of weapons in their hands and ascended the wall of the city which was below [the Roqeah's] house, and made an opening in the roof of his house and broke through into it and killed the Roqeah's wife and her children. The Roqeah and the disciples heard a great cry in the house and hurried in great haste to hear what had happened. And when the Rabbi and his students attempted to climb up to the upper floor, one of the murderers stood with his bow and tried to kill the Roqeah with an arrow, but he missed his aim [target] and only wounded him slightly in his shoulder. When they saw this, the disciples hurried to the street and raised an uproar so that [people] would come to help them. But they still didn't know that the rabbi's wife and her children were murdered. When people came in response to their outcry, the murderous students fled on the road on the wall and from there they jumped outside the city.[80]

In this later revision, we find that the murders take place when no men are present. It is not Dolce who raises the alarm but the Roqeah's students. The Roqeah is wounded in pursuit of the aggressors. Thus, many of the aspects of the Roqeah's account in which Dolce's activities were so central and which might have caused discomfort to later readers from a perspective of appropriate gender behaviors are deliberately defused. It is interesting, as well, that this legend, which is so vividly specific in its sense of location, attributes the murders to students. This may be indicative of the situation of the Jewish community of Worms in the seventeenth century, since R. Juspa mentions wild gentile students who roamed the Jewish section of the city in other stories as well.[81] It may also indicate that no tradition attributing the murders to Crusaders existed in the seventeenth century.

In R. Juspa's rendition, Dolce's role in defending her family has been eliminated while her scholarly husband is portrayed in heroic terms. This diminishment of female achievement to the point of invisibility, or worse, is not unusual in Jewish tradition which evidences enormous discomfort with able women acting as independent entities, even when they act on behalf of their families or people. Among the learned women mentioned in rabbinic literature, for example, the most prominent is B'ruriah, the wife of Rabbi Meir. Her extraordinary scholarship and perception is cited several times in the Talmud. However, by medieval times her learning is seen as a warning of the foolishness of allowing women to study: according to Rashi, Rabbi Shlomo ben Isaac (1040–1105), the preeminent biblical and talmudic commentator of the Middle Ages, Beruriah ended as an adulterous wife and a suicide.[82] The depiction of Dolce in R. Juspa's tale as a nameless and passive murder victim is not quite so harsh a fate, but nevertheless illuminates the low status of women in Jewish hagiography.

I return, then, to the double anomaly I alluded to at the beginning of this essay: mainstream European Judaism of the Middle Ages had no saints and if it had, they certainly were not female. Dolce, martyred with her daughters, admirable in her piety, unusual in her learning, and exemplary as manager and support of her household, finds her place in Jewish tradition in her connection to her famous husband. She is remembered because of his heartfelt words in her praise, but she is lauded because of what she enabled him to do and to be. It is in this way that Jewish women of the past, however saintly, achieved renown.

Notes

1. Judaism is far from monolithic. The major ethnic subgroups among Jews include Middle Eastern Jews, Sephardim, who are Jews of Mediterranean origins, and Ashkenazim, whose culture developed in Central and East Europe. Within these major branches are numerous subdivisions based on variables including differing geographical and cultural influences, differing religious practice, and different modes of self-identification. The most relevant subdivision among Ashkenazic Jews for the current study is between Hasidism, a pietistic Jewish movement which began in eighteenth-century East Europe, and the rest of Ashkenazic Jewry.

2. The anthropologist, Susan Starr Sered, *Women as Ritual Experts: The Religious Lives of Elderly Jewish Women in Jerusalem* (New York, 1992), 6–7, distinguishes between "official Judaism," which has been defined largely by literate, male authorities, and the ways in which women have developed their own "little tradition" within and/or parallel to the "great tradition." She notes that most studies of women and Judaism "necessarily treat women as objects," and not as actors in their own right, because this is how they are portrayed in "official

Judaism." The lack of primary documents recording women's voices and concerns before the early modern period has meant that scholars have mostly been limited to representing "official Judaism" as the only Judaism. The contributions of anthropologists such as Sered remind us that Jewish women also had religious customs and traditions, many of which are now lost, which coexisted with the "great tradition" of Jewish men.

3. On this topic, see the following notes, 9–13. Jewish subgroups differ on sainthood. Unlike most Ashkenazic communities, Middle Eastern Jews and some Sephardim have a long tradition of venerating Jewish holy men, and even some women, as saints. Pilgrimages to holy places and the graves of holy men are a significant part of contemporary Jewish religious practice for these men and women, as is the belief that the saint can intercede between the supplicant and God. Similar beliefs and practices are held by the Hasidim within Ashkenazic Jewry, but generally not by other Ashkenzic Jews. See Walter Zenner, "Saints and Piecemeal Supernaturalism Among the Jerusalem Sephardim," *Anthropological Quarterly* 38:4 (1965): 201–217; and Norman A. Stillman, "Saddiq and Marabout in Morocco," in *Jews Among Muslim Communities in the Pre-Colonial Middle East,* ed. Shlomo Deshen and Walter P. Zenner (New York, 1996), 121–130. On Hasidism, see Samuel H. Dresner, *The Zaddik: The Doctrine of the Zaddik according to the Writings of Rabbi Yaakov Yosef of Polnoy* (London, 1960).

4. On Hannah and her seven sons, see Gerson D. Cohen, "Hannah and her Seven Sons in Hebrew Literature," in his *Studies in the Variety of Rabbinic Cultures* (Philadelphia, 1991), 39–60; and Robin Darling Young, "The 'Woman with the Soul of Abraham': Traditions about the Mother of the Maccabean Martyrs," in *"Women Like This": New Perspectives on Jewish Women in the Greco-Roman World,* ed. Amy-Jill Levine (Atlanta, GA, 1991), 67–81.

5. On *Kiddush haShem,* the sanctification of God's name through martyrdom, see Cohen, "Hannah and her Seven Sons"; and Jacob Katz, "The Martyrs," in his *Exclusiveness and Tolerance: Jewish-Gentile Relations in Medieval and Modern Times* (New York, 1961), 82–92. On the use of this story, in particular, as a model during later periods of Jewish martyrdom, see Robert Chazan, *European Jewry and the First Crusade* (Berkeley, CA, 1987), 112–113, 121, 149.

6. Cohen, "Hannah and her Seven Sons," 52, quoting from the *Book of Josippon,* Venice edition, 1544, Chapter 89, fol. 136, col. c ff.

7. On literary uses of figures like Abraham and Hannah as models for martyrdom during the Middle Ages, see Shalom Spiegel, *The Last Trial: On the Legends and Lore of the Command to Abraham to Offer Isaac as a Sacrifice: The Akedah,* trans. Judah Goldin (New York, 1967), particularly 3–16.

8. On the whole, reference works on Judaism and Jewish civilization do not have specific citations for the term "saint," or "saintliness." Useful discussions of desirable human behavior traits can be found in the *Encyclopedia Judaica* under

"Imitation of God," "*Kedushah,*" Piety and the Pious," and "Righteousness." The spiritual life in Judaism is discussed in the series of essays in *Jewish Spirituality I: From the Bible through the Middle Ages,* and *Jewish Spirituality II: From the Sixteenth Century Revival to the Present,* both edited by Arthur Green (New York, 1986, 1987).

9. Solomon Schechter, *Aspects of Rabbinic Theology: Major Concepts of the Talmud* (New York, 1909; rep. 1961), 199.

10. Schechter, 201.

11. Schechter, 209.

12. Zenner, "Saints and Piecemeal Supernaturalism," 207.

13. Schechter, *Aspects of Rabbinic Theology,* 217.

14. See below, pp. 43–44 for further discussion of the absence of women from Jewish mystical traditions.

15. For a bibliographic essay on the rabbis and the rabbinic period, see Eliezer Diamond, "The World of the Talmud," in *The Schocken Guide to Jewish Books,* ed. Barry W. Holtz (New York, 1992), 47–69. The Babylonian Talmud, the major legal and literary achievement of this era, assumed its final form in the area of Baghdad, Iraq, in the mid-sixth century. For analyses of the role of women in rabbinic Judaism, see Judith R. Baskin, "Woman as Other in Rabbinic Literature," in *Where We Stand: Issues and Debates in Ancient Judaism.* Judaism in Late Antiquity 3.2, eds. Jacob Neusner and Alan J. Avery-Peck (Leiden, 1999), 177–196; Judith Romney Wegner, "The Image and Status of Women in Classical Rabbinic Judaism," in *Jewish Women in Historical Perspective.* 2nd ed., ed. Judith R. Baskin (Detroit, MI, 1998), 73–100; Judith Hauptman, "Images of Women in the Talmud," in *Religion and Sexism: Images of Women in the Jewish and Christian Traditions,* ed. R. R. Ruether (New York, 1974), 184–212, who writes, 197, that in rabbinic texts, "A woman's prime function in life is to concern herself with man's welfare and to provide for his physical comfort"; and idem, "Feminist Perspectives on Rabbinic Texts," in *Feminist Perspectives on Jewish Studies,* ed. Lynn Davidman and Shelly Tenenbaum (New Haven, 1994), 40–61.

16. Rachel Biale, *Women and Jewish Law: An Exploration of Women's Issues in Halakhic Sources* (New York, 1984), notes that women were believed to have fulfilled their obligation to pray by making a personal address to God as they started the day. She writes, 20, that although women could choose to participate in the set prayers, this was not required; rather "women's prayers remained essentially private, personal, and spontaneous supplication."

17. For discussions of issues connected with women and synagogue worship, see *Daughters of the King: Women and the Synagogue,* eds. Susan Grossman and Rivka Haut (Philadelphia, 1992).

18. Gershom G. Scholem, *Major Trends in Jewish Mysticism* (New York, 1941; rep. 1971), 37. Scholem does not attribute the exclusively masculine character of Kabbalism to women's secondary social position or exclusion from talmudic

learning, but instead writes, 37, that "This exclusive masculinity for which Kabbalism has paid a high price, appears rather to be connected with an inherent tendency to lay stress on the demonic nature of woman and the feminine element of the cosmos."

19. Ada Rapoport-Albert, "On Women in Hasidism, S. A. Horodecky and the Maid of Ludmir Tradition," in *Jewish History. Essays in Honour of Chimen Abramsky,* eds. Ada Rapoport-Albert and Steven J. Zipperstein (London, 1988), 507.

20. Rapoport-Albert, 507.

21. See, for example, the Babylonian Talmud Sotah 22a where disapproval is expressed of women's involvement in religious devotions. The sixteenth-century Italian writer Abraham Yagel, who warns that women who engage in ascetic practices are flouting their obligations to God because they have abandoned their primary domestic responsibilities, is cited in Howard Adelman, "Finding Women's Voices in Italian Jewish Literature," in *Women of the Word: Jewish Women and Jewish Writing,* ed. Judith R. Baskin (Detroit, MI, 1994), 54.

22. On Hasidism in general, see Elliot K. Ginsburg's bibliographic survey in his article, "Jewish Mysticism," in *Schocken Guide to Jewish Books,* ed. Holtz, 195–200; and on the *zaddik,* see Arthur Green, "Typologies of Leadership and the Hasidic Zaddiq," in *Jewish Spirituality II,* ed. Green, 127–156. Rapoport-Albert, "On Women in Hasidism," 501, notes that although Hasidic tradition preserves descriptions of "various daughters, mothers and sisters (again, rarely wives) of the famous Zaddikim" who are said to have acted as leaders of Hasidic communities and to have adopted rigorous standards of personal piety, there is little written documentation about them. She does not doubt that some of these prominent women existed, but suggests, 502, that their authority was based on their connection to revered male leaders. She points out that the significant fact is that "Hasidism did not evolve an ideology of female leadership, any more than it improved the position of women within the family or set out to educate them in Yiddish."

23. Rapoport-Albert, "On Women in Hasidism," 506.

24. Rapoport-Albert, 502–503.

25. Rapoport-Albert, 506.

26. For an anthropological study of the ways in which one community of contemporary Jewish women live out their religious lives within an androcentric patriarchal culture in which "men write the laws and the prayers," and within which the normative Jew is male, see Sered, *Women as Ritual Experts.* Her observations about the ways in which this particular group of mostly illiterate Jewish women, who have no access to formal modes of worship or to positions of communal authority, are still able to create opportunities to sacralize their own concerns demonstrate likely ways in which Jewish women forged connections to the sacred in earlier periods of Jewish history as well. Similar issues are raised in the

essays in *Active Voices: Women in Jewish Culture,* ed. Maurie Sacks (Urbana, IL, 1995).

27. See Chava Weissler, "The Traditional Piety of Ashkenazic Women," in *Jewish Spirituality* II, ed. Green, 245–275, and idem, "Prayers in Yiddish and the Religious World of Ashkenazic Women," in *Jewish Women in Historical Perspective,* 2nd ed., ed. Baskin, 169–192.

28. Weissler, "Prayers in Yiddish," 185.

29. Weissler, 185–186; and see idem, *Voices of the Matriarchs: Listening to the Prayers of Early Modern Jewish Women* (Boston, 1998), 76–85.

30. Weissler, "Prayers in Yiddish," 185–186.

31. Sered, *Women as Ritual Experts,* 18.

32. Sered, 19; quote is from Stephen Gudeman, "Saints, Symbols, and Ceremonies," *American Ethnologist* 3:4 (November, 1976), 726.

33. Sered, *Women as Ritual Experts,* 20.

34. Sered, 21.

35. On the tomb of Rachel, see Susan Starr Sered, "Rachel's Tomb and the Milk Grotto of the Virgin Mary: Two Women's Shrines in Bethlehem," *Journal of Feminist Studies in Religion* 2:2 (Summer, 1986), 7–22.

36. Sered, *Women as Ritual Experts,* 114–120.

37. Sered, 120.

38. Sered, 117–118.

39. On the German-Jewish pietists/*Hasidei Ashkenaz,* see Ivan Marcus, *Piety and Society: The Jewish Pietists of Medieval Germany* (Leiden, 1981); Jacob Katz, "The Hasid," in idem, *Exclusiveness and Tolerance;* and Joseph Dan, *Jewish Mysticism and Jewish Ethics* (Philadelphia and Seattle, 1986), 45–75. On the controversial issue of the impact of the Crusades, see Marcus, *Piety and Society,* 150–151, n. 57. Israel Kamelhar, *Rabbenu Eleazar mi-Germaiza, ha-Roqeah* (Rzeazow, 1930), 11, identifies Dolce's father as Rabbi Eliezer the son of Jacob, a Kohen (hereditary priest) and a cantor.

40. Marcus, *Piety and Society,* 131.

41. "*Sefer Hasidim,*" *Encyclopedia Judaica.*

42. Marcus, *Piety and Society,* 23.

43. Marcus, 23.

44. Ibid., 26; on vicarious atonement, see Marcus, 93.

45. Robert Chazan, *European Jewry and the First Crusade* (Berkeley, CA, 1987), 195–196. For a summary of scholarly discussion on the kind and degree of Christian influence on the *Hasidei Ashkenaz,* see Marcus, *Piety and Society,* 6–10.

46. Dan, *Jewish Mysticism,* 59.

47. Ibid.

48. For further discussion of this issue, see Judith R. Baskin, "From Separation

to Displacement: The Problem of Women in *Sefer Hasidim*," *Association for Jewish Studies Review* 19:1 (1994): 1–18.

49. Kenneth R. Stow, *Alienated Minority: The Jews of Medieval Latin Europe* (Cambridge, MA, 1992), 207–208.

50. *Sefer Hasidim*, ed. Reuven Margoliot (Jerusalem, 1964), Bologna version, paragraph 14; translation from Sholom Alchanan Singer, *Medieval Jewish Mysticism: Book of the Pious* (Northbrook, IL, 1971), 11–12. There is no complete translation of *Sefer Hasidim* into English.

51. *Sefer Hasidim*, ed. Margoliot, Bologna version, paragraph 29.

52. Eleazar of Worms, *Sefer Ha-Roqeah Ha-Gadol* (Jerusalem, 1968), Hilkhot Teshuvah, no. 20, p. 30.

53. Marcus, *Piety and Society*, 41–52.

54. Baskin, "Problem of Women," 4–5.

55. Baskin, 2–4; on the connection of women and witchcraft, see p. 18.

56. On medieval Jewish women, see Judith R. Baskin, "Jewish Women in the Middle Ages," in *Jewish Women in Historical Perspective*. 2nd Edition, 101–127; and Ivan Marcus, "Mothers, Martyrs, and Moneymakers: Some Jewish Women in Medieval Europe," *Conservative Judaism* 38:3 (Spring, 1986): 34–45.

57. Kenneth R. Stow, "The Jewish Family in the Rhineland in the High Middle Ages: Form and Function," *The American Historical Review* 92 (1987): 1008.

58. Marcus, *Piety and Society*, 17.

59. The accounts of the murder are extant in two sources: a single page of parchment that has been incorporated as folio 30 into Hebrew MS Michael 448, which is in the Bodleian Library in Oxford, and three pages in Hebrew MS Oppenheim 757, folios 25–27, a compendium of medieval Hebrew poetry, also in the Bodleian Library; they are listed in Adolf Neubauer, ed., *Catalogue of the Hebrew Manuscripts in the Bodleian Library and in the College Libraries of Oxford (Oxford, 1886–1906)*, 762, 798. An introductory scribal statement above the passage in Heb. MS Michael 448 states that the page was copied from the manuscript of Yacob of Gunzberg, which in turn was copied from the Roqeah's autograph manuscript. The page contains not only R. Eleazar's prose description, but also the poetic eulogy in memory of the slain female members of his family. The poetic eulogy in this version ends "*Baruch ha-Shem l'olam, amen amen.*" In the other version, Bodleian Heb. MS Oppenheim 757, the poetic elegy ends with an additional verse beginning, "*Kamah, v'kamah.*" This latter poem, in which the Roqeah laments the deaths of all of his sons and daughters is generally assumed to have been written at a later date; it does not appear in Heb. MS Michael 448. The exact relationship between the manuscripts has yet to be determined. The Oppenheim collection of manuscripts was purchased by the British Museum in 1829, while the Michael collection was acquired in 1848. The earliest transcription of the

prose passage was published by Solomon ben Ephraim Blogg, *Aedificium Salomonis* (Hanover, 1831), almost certainly from the page that became part of Heb. MS Michael 448. The Hebrew texts of both the prose and poetic passages are reproduced in Kamelhar, *Rabbenu Eleazar mi-Germaiza,* and in A. M. Haberman, ed., *Sefer Gezeirot Ashkenaz ve-Zarfat* (Jerusalem, 1945). I believe that both transcriptions are based substantially on Heb. MS Michael 448, although Haberman may also have consulted Heb. MS Oppenheim 757.

60. For translations of all R. Eleazar's writings connected to Dolce's life and death see Judith R. Baskin, "Dolce of Worms: The Lives and Deaths of an Exemplary Medieval Jewish Woman and Her Daughters," in *Judaism in Practice: From the Middle Ages through the Early Modern Period,* ed. Lawrence Fine (Princeton, 2000). Other translations include Marcus, "Mothers, Martyrs, and Moneymakers," 41–42; H. Ben Sasson, "The Middle Ages," in his edited collection, *A History of the Jewish People* (Cambridge, MA, 1976), 523; excerpts from the shorter poems in memory of Bellette and Hannah appear in T. Carmi, *The Penguin Book of Hebrew Verse* (New York, 1981), 387–388.

61. The word describing the attackers in Oxford, Bodleian Library Heb. MS. Oppenheim 757 is *m'sumanim,* which I have translated as "marked men"; it is a medieval Hebrew designation for Crusaders because their clothing was "marked" with a cross. In Oxford, Bodleian Library Heb. MS. Michael 448, the first reference to the attackers is unclear. Elsewhere, in both texts, the word *m'tuavim,* "wicked men," is used to describe them.

62. It is not exactly clear what the Roqeah means by "winter quarters," literally "the winter house." Perhaps during the winter months most of the rooms in which the family ordinarily lived were closed off because of the difficulty of heating them, and family life took place in one or two ground floor rooms.

63. This translation is based on the printed text in Haberman, *Sefer Gezeirot,* 164, with reference to Kamelhar, *Rabbenu Eleazar,* 17, and to photocopies of both manuscripts in the Bodleian Library, Oxford. I have translated as "saintly" the Hebrew word *hasidah;* it could equally be rendered as "pious," or as Ivan Marcus translates it at the beginning of the poetic elegy, "pietist," indicating Dolce's inclusion in the *Hasidei Ashkenaz* pietist community.

64. The identification of the intruders with Crusaders has led some scholars to place the event somewhere else, either earlier or later, at times of known Crusader persecutions of Jews. Eleazar's other poetic references to the deaths of all of his children, as well as a poem of lament, attributed in an acrostic to an "Eleazar ha-Katan," led Leopold Zunz, *Literatur der synagogalen Poesie* (Berlin, 1865), 317, 320, to link this attack with persecutions the Roqeah experienced in Erfurt in 1214, and to assume that Eleazar's son, Jacob, whom he describes as wounded in the 1196 attack, died as a result of his wounds. A reference in Eleazar's *Sefer HaHochmah* to the death of a son in 1217 also led some to place the attack at that

time. Heinrich Graetz, *Geschichte der Juden,* 6. vol. (Leipzig, 1861), 6:275, follows Zunz in identifying the attackers as Crusaders, and in the assumption that Eleazar's son Jacob died of his wounds, although he sticks to the 1196 date when he speaks of three of the Roqeah's children being killed, writing: "Wild crusaders committed even less justified excesses in Worms; they stormed into the house of a peaceful Talmudist, Eleazar ben Jehudah, killed his wife, Dolce, under gruesome conditions, his two daughters, his son, and his students that were studying the Talmud. They took everything he had (plundered his belongings) and they left only the naked life to the unhappy husband and father." Graetz's version of events, which wanders quite far from what Eleazar actually says, is cited by a number of other writers of Jewish history, including Adolf Neubauer and Moritz Stern, *Hebraische Berichte über die Judenverfolgungen während der Kreuzzüge* (Berlin, 1892), a collection of Hebrew sources on the Crusades.

65. On the government's commitment to protect German Jews during the Third Crusade, which began in 1188, see Robert Chazan, "Emperor Frederick I, the Third Crusade, and the Jews," *Viator* 8 (1977): 83–93. At the beginning of 1188, during the preparations for the Third Crusade, the majority of the Jews of Mainz felt cause to flee to Munzenberg, the castle and town of the imperial ministerial Kuno. But those Jews who remained in Mainz were also protected against their enemies by Frederick I and Henry VI. As Chazan notes, 84, at that time, the "authorities were committed to the maintenance of public peace" and to averting serious violence by the thousands of crusaders who were gathered in Mainz, threatening the Jewish community there. He writes, 90–91, that according to the Hebrew eyewitness account of R. Moses ben Eliezar, the brother-in-law of the Roqeah, who remained in Mainz, the Emperor Frederick I declared that "anyone who attacks a Jew and wounds him shall have his hand cut off. Anyone who kills a Jew will be killed." Rabbi Moses further records that the emperor sent both oral and written communications that the imperial officers "guard the Jews carefully, even more so than they had done heretofore." The Hebrew text of Rabbi Moses' account, in a letter to the Roqeah, can be found in Haberman, *Sefer Gezeirot,* 162–164.

66. On these events, see Karl Hampe, *Germany Under the Salian and Hohenstaufen Emperors,* trans. Ralph Bennett (Totowa, NJ, 1973; based on 8th edition of 1943) 226, 228; and Horst Fuhrmann, *Germany in the High Middle Ages: c. 1050–1200,* trans. Timothy Reuter (Cambridge University Press, 1986), 180–186.

67. Throughout the twelfth century, the Hohenstaufen emperors were determined to protect the urbanized Jews of their realm, who increasingly supported themselves almost wholly on the profits of moneylending, with welcome financial benefits for the crown. Horst Fuhrmann, *Germany in the High Middle Ages,* writes, 84, that this trend was established during the reign of Henry IV: "At a general

assembly held in Mainz in 1103 a peace was proclaimed for the Empire which was to be valid for four years. The ordinance laid down mutilations and death sentences for those who broke the peace, regardless of their rank, and specifically included the Jews under its protection." As Gavin Langmuir, *Towards a Definition of Antisemitism* (Los Angeles, 1990), 140–141 has written, "In return for a large share of the profits, kings and princes were willing to protect Jews and their moneylending, despite ecclesiastical admonitions to the contrary; as a result Jewish lenders in northern Europe reached their greatest prosperity around 1200."

68. Marcus, "Mothers, Martyrs, and Moneymakers," 41–42, translates *hasidah,* rendered here as "saintly," as "pietistic."

69. The Roqeah uses the Hebrew, *ne'imah,* "pleasant," here, and twice more in the elegy, as a play on the meaning of Dolce's name. Dolce, also transliterated Dulcia, Dulzia, Dulcie, is of Latinate origin, based on the adjective *dulcis,* "agreeable, pleasant, charming, kind, or dear." Medieval Jewish women often had vernacular rather than Hebrew names. Of Dolce's two daughters, one had a vernacular name, Bellette, the other a Hebrew name, Hannah.

70. This translation appears in full in Baskin, "Dolce of Worms." Printed versions of all the Hebrew texts can be found in Kamelhar, *Rabbenu Eleazar,* 17–19, and Haberman, *Sefer Gezeirot,* 165–166.

71. This translation also appears in full in Baskin, "Dolce of Worms."

72. Abraham Udovitch, "At the Origins of the Western *Commenda:* Islam, Israel, Byzantium," *Speculum* 37 (1962): 198–207; and Haym Soloveitchik, "Concerning the Date of the Composition of *Sefer Hasidim*" [Hebrew], in *Culture and Society in Medieval Jewry: Studies Dedicated to the Memory of Haim Hillel Ben-Sasson,* ed. M. Ben-Sasson, R. Bonfil, J. R. Hacker (Jerusalem, 1989), 383–388, particularly 384–385. On medieval Jewish women's moneylending in general, see Baskin, "Jewish Women," 104; and Marcus, "Mothers, Martyrs, and Moneylenders," 39.

73. Udovitch, "At the Origins," 198.

74. On Jewish women's contributions to the synagogue, see Baskin, "Jewish Women," 101–102; and Cissy Grossman, "Womanly Arts: A Study of Italian Torah Binders in the New York Jewish Museum Collection," *Journal of Jewish Art* 7 (1980): 35–43.

75. On medieval Jewish women's education, see Judith R. Baskin, "Some Parallels in the Education of Medieval Jewish and Christian Women," *Jewish History* 5:1 (1991): 41–51. Learned Jewish women would almost certainly have been daughters of elite Jewish families, unusual in wealth or in scholarship, or in both. As noted previously, p. 11, Dolce's father, R. Eliezer ben Jacob, was a cantor.

76. The inscription on Urania's tombstone is cited in Israel Abrahams, *Jewish Life in the Middle Ages* (1896; rep. New York, 1969), 26. On Jewish women who led women's prayers in the synagogue, see Emily Taitz, "Kol Ishah—The Voice of Woman: Where Was It Heard in Medieval Europe?," *Conservative Judaism* 38:3

(Spring, 1986), 46–61; and idem, "Women's Voices, Women's Prayers: Women in the European Synagogues of the Middle Ages," in *Daughters of the King: Women and the Synagogue,* ed. Susan Grossman and Rivka Haut (Philadelphia, 1992), 59–71. On the Worms synagogue, see *Encyclopedia Judaica,* "Worms."

77. Learned women such as Dolce were sometimes asked to offer testimony on Jewish legal matters, but it was understood that the information they gave was valuable only because they were transmitting the practice of their husbands or fathers. As one medieval scholar, Isaac of Dampierre put it, they were "the daughters of the prophets and leaders of the generation and we may rely on their custom." See Baskin, "Parallels," 51, n. 46.

78. Moses of Coucy, *Sefer Mitzvot Gadol,* positive commandment 12.

79. The anecdote from *Ma'aseh Nissim* is recounted in Kamelhar, *Rabbenu Eleazar,* 17, n. 8; it may also be found in Shlomo Eidelberg, *R. Juspa, Shammash of Warmaisa (Worms): Jewish Life in Seventeenth Century Worms* (Jerusalem, 1991), 64–65 (in English), and 66 (in Hebrew). R. Juspa was the sexton and scribe of the community, and *Ma'aseh Nissim* was based on the ancient manuscripts of the Worms Jewish community and on oral histories of the community elders (Eidelberg, 11, 13). R. Juspa would almost certainly have had access to the Roqeah's original account of the attack, preserved in a manuscript in the Worms synagogue, as well as to a manuscript of customs of the Worms Jewish community, compiled by his predecessor Judah Liwa Kirchheim, in which the Rokeah's prose account was recorded almost verbatim. Kirchheim is discussed in Eidelberg, and his version of the murders appears in Appendix A, 91–92.

80. The translation is my own, based on the Hebrew translations in Kamelhar and Eidelberg.

81. Eidelberg, *R. Juspa,* 65.

82. On B'ruriah, see Wegner, "Image and Status of Women," in *Jewish Women in Historical Perspective,* ed. Baskin, 81–82, and Rachel Adler, "The Virgin in the Brothel and Other Anomalies: Character and Context in the Legend of Beruriah," *Tikkun,* November/December 1988, 28–32, 102–105. On denigrations of other outstanding women in rabbinic sources, see Hauptman, "Images of Women," 197–208.

III

Reclaiming an Ancient Story: Baudonivia's Life of St. Radegund (circa 525–587)

Marie Anne Mayeski
with Jane Crawford

Introduction

If the feminist author and literary critic, Carolyn Heilbrun, is right when she affirms in *Writing a Woman's Life,* that it is not the *lives* of people who have gone before us, but their *stories,* that make them models and exemplars,[1] then St. Radegund, a sixth-century Merovingian Queen, became an exemplar for widely diverse groups of people from her own day to the twentieth century. The historical events of Radegund's life are a tangle of violence. Her context is the internecine struggles of the early Merovingians, struggles that were domestic and political at the same time. Her family was virtually obliterated in a battle of revenge waged in 531 by Clothar, then king of the Franks, against her uncle, the ruler of the Thuringians; she was taken from the battlefield by Clothar and raised to be his future wife, one of the six wives and at least one concubine that Clothar took to his bed. Though she was his wife for about ten years, she bore him no children and left him after he killed her last remaining brother in 550. She retired to one of the villas, at Saix, that belonged to her by dowry rights and stayed there about eight years until, as Baudonivia narrates, she heard a rumor that the king wished to reclaim her wifely presence. At that moment she fled to Poitiers, negotiating, through Bishop Germanus of Paris, the endowment by Clothar of an excellent convent there. For Radegund, the convent at Poitiers was never to be entirely a refuge; it remained caught up in the continuing narrative of domestic and political violence. The Visigothic princess, Galswinth, passed through on her way to the marriage that ended in her being murdered by her husband and his paramour. Chilperic's daughter, Basina, sought refuge there from her marriage to Reccared; after Radegund's death, she led an uprising against the new abbess that had to be mediated by a gathering of local bishops. Plunder, rape, and murder marked the entire region around Poitiers throughout Radegund's life and after her death, and her ties of kinship with many of the principals in the political drama brought her into the heart of the struggles. Out of this tangled web of violence and disorder, the story of Radegund as victim, Queen and nun, her various biographers weave their stories of Radegund the saint.

The story of the battle in which almost all of her family was slaughtered was told in poetic form, probably by Venantius Fortunatus with her own collaboration. Fortunatus was her friend, a poet, hymnist, and later, Bishop of Poitiers; he wrote a full-length biography celebrating her achievements as Queen and saint. Gregory of Tours, the comprehensive historian of Merovingian aristocrats, also documented her role in politics and church history in several texts, including the *History of the Franks*.[2] One of the nuns in her convent, who had known her well, added her account of Radegund to that of Fortunatus,[3] consciously stressing the monastic holiness she exemplified after she separated from her husband, King Clothar. Much later, Radegund became the patroness of Jesus College, Cambridge, and her life was written in English by Henry Bradshaw to demonstrate the virtues which she exemplified for that scholarly community.[4] While her continuous efforts to make peace in the Touraine were ultimately frustrated, the French government made her feast a national holiday in 1921, in fulfillment of a vow taken during the First World War and thus reclaimed the political implications of her life in a new story.[5] Thus Radegund's appeal has been wide and enduring, her story told many times.[6] The various texts indicate the adaptability of her story to various communities of readers. What kind of sanctity, what kind of exemplar, do they find in this woman's life? Is the story capable of yet another adaptation? Can it be read by women today who seek to find in her story access to their own and to the ultimate story of salvation? In the following essay, I will focus on the story as told by Baudonivia, in the hope that out of that woman's narrative will come a story that is meaningful to other women.[7]

Radegund's Saintly Character in Social Context

I am aware, as I read Baudonivia's account, of two criticisms that Heilbrun makes about biographical narratives of women; both seem particularly pertinent to accounts of the life of Radegund. On the one hand, Heilbrun raises the possibility that Radegund's choice of the convent at Poitiers may have made her stereotypically feminine in her quest for safety and thus robbed her of real autonomy and achievement. Heilbrun says that, "safety and closure, which have always been held out to women as the ideals of female destiny, are not places of adventure, or experience, or life. Safety and closure (and enclosure) are, rather, the mirror of the Lady of Shalott. They forbid life to be experienced directly."[8] The fact that Radegund's convent was never really safe does not rob Heilbrun's criticism of its force. It may be that in *choosing* enclosure, Radegund made an internal choice that invalidates her story for women today; it may be that, in portraying the beauty of that choice and Radegund's fidelity to it, Baudonivia further vitiates her story.

Heilbrun's second criticism has to do with the way in which women have consistently been required "to put a man at the center of one's life and to allow to occur only what honors his prime position. Occasionally women have put God or Christ in the place of a man; the results are the same: one's own desires and quests are always secondary."[9] This is a far-reaching criticism indeed. If allowed to stand, it means that no commitment to the divine plan and to transcendent reality is sufficient to validate a woman's story, a female saint's narrative. Rather, that story must be tested by the criterion of personal "desire" and "quest." Dynamics such as these will always be difficult to discern in the lives of saints that were written precisely to edify according to the pattern accepted by the Christian ethos. Does Radegund's story, as narrated by Baudonivia, tell of her own desires and quest? Is Radegund the real hero of her own story or is the story so recast into the conventional Christian pattern that it becomes, not individual at all, but a reinforcement of the accepted pattern of feminine behavior? Those questions underlie my analysis of Baudonivia's text.

Baudonivia gives us the story of a woman who struggled to attain control: of her self, her life, and the social and political environment in which her life's drama was played out. Baudonivia tells us that she "inherited nobility," a reflection of the ancient idea that nobility obliges, that aristocratic blood commits a person to play a social and political role that cannot be ignored without serious jeopardy. Baudonivia's statement that Radegund *adorned* her nobility with faith indicates her understanding that faith cannot excuse one from the political and social obligations of birth and status; faith is the fulfillment of the natural superiority conferred by blood and enables those who have the *right* to rule the *ability* to rule rightly. Faith does not entirely substitute heavenly goals for earthly goals; rather it subsumes earthly goals (and therefore political and social action) into a transcendent understanding of human life and society. It gives direction to one's political activity, but it does not excuse one from the obligation to act politically. Therefore, the specific virtues that Baudonivia attributes to Radegund are those appropriate to Radegund's social status and have political significance; she describes specifically Radegund's obedience, political vigor, and generosity.

Radegund is first praised for her "obedience to God's servants"; by this virtue, Radegund accepts her true situation in the theoretical structure of Merovingian society. As a Christian queen, she is to further the development and influence of the church, obeying church leaders in all that pertains to the spiritual well-being of the realm. Baudonivia illustrates this kind of obedience with an anecdote. On route to a banquet and adorned with all her worldly display, Radegund comes upon a place of pagan worship. She orders it burned, displays great personal courage in facing the violent reaction of the pagan Franks and remains there until "the opposing sides had made peace." It is, perhaps, a distasteful story to modern readers, but Baudonivia's point of view is clear: Radegund has defended the rights of the Christian faith, even at personal risk to herself, and, not content with destroying an evil, has persevered toward a greater good in making peace. Second, Baudonivia affirms that Radegund is "energetic in redeeming captives." Again, her political position makes her capable of righting the wrongs of society, and her obligation is to use her power to do everything she can to alleviate the suffering of those who suffer the misfortunes of political warfare.

Third, Radegund is "profusely generous with alms to the needy." This too is a Christian aristocratic obligation in the world; generosity in almsgiving had been a commonplace of spirituality from the beginning. But Baudonivia describes Radegund as convinced "that anything that the poor received from her was their own in reality"; this reflects a complex understanding of goods and property that was developed by some of the earliest theologians in the classical period. For theologians like Clement of Alexandria (second-century A.D.) the earth was created by God for the benefit of all of humanity; he describes the true purpose of ownership succinctly: "Goods are called good because they do good, and they have been provided by God for the good of humanity."[10] Those who were given an abundance of material possessions by the Lord were obliged by that same Lord to see to their equitable distribution. Indeed, for some of the classical early Christian authors, ownership itself, not to say the possession of an excess of goods, constituted a kind of robbery. John Chrysostom regarded the very existence of private property as the consequence of an unjust act in the past. In this view, almsgiving becomes restitution, as Ambrose makes clear: "Not from your own do you bestow upon the poor man, but you make return from what is his. For what has been given as common for the use of all, you appropriate to yourself alone."[11] Baudonivia attributes a variation of this patristic theology to Radegund the Queen, making her "profuse generosity" an act of political and social justice. These are the virtues, this the character, which Baudonivia attributes to Radegund as Queen. They are intrinsic to her identity in a way that her role as wife is not. For Baudonivia says that "she played the role of a wife." She implies that to be wife to Clothar was a function that Radegund was content to fulfill, for a while at least, but that her social and political obligations were conferred by blood (not marriage) and, therefore, were constitutive of her very self. We anticipate, therefore, that they shall somehow be manifest, even within the confines of the convent life she chooses.

Baudonivia records her movement toward a cloistered existence in two stages.[12] First, Radegund removes to one of her own villas; there she presumably gives herself more seriously to the interior life, the life of personal discipline and contemplation. That, at least, is implied both by Baudonivia's use of the word "conversion" (a technical word for the personal commitment to the religious life) and by the vision that Radegund has during this interim period. Ascetical literature often records that those who begin an intense spiritual journey have a mystical experience designed to confirm their commitment and to entice them more deeply into the realms of the spirit. Radegund's vision of herself on the knee of "a man-shaped ship" is of this pattern and prepares her for the next step. While at the villa, Radegund hears a rumor that the king wants her back as his wife. This provokes a deeper commitment to a life of her own and her second move to Poitiers where she founds her monastery.

In making this move, she intensifies her personal asceticism, wearing a hair shirt as well as increasing her fasting and prayer vigils. Perhaps she desires to make herself less desirable to the king; perhaps she is simply reinforcing her strength of will so that she can resist his blandishments. Baudonivia says that, at this point in her life, she "scorns to rule" in a worldly way, though her subsequent activity demonstrates her willingness to carry on what she sees as the true political activity of a queen; according to Baudonivia "she [also] rejected the sweetness of marriage," surely an ironic comment, though perhaps unintentional on Baudonivia's part. In any event, she continues to marshall human forces to enact her own will. She sends her last bit of finery to a well-respected recluse; in return she requests his prayers in support of her intention, another hair shirt and, most importantly, information from the Holy Spirit about the outcome of her conflict with the king. In her world view, such envoys may be sent to the world of the divine, just as spies are sent to human rulers. John the recluse gives her a promising response and she begins her negotiations with the king, enlisting a powerful Bishop and a Duke to persuade him to build a monastery for her. Even when she has succeeded in creating her own world at Poitiers, however, she is not yet free from the power of the king and, once again, she has recourse to powerful mediators, this time Germanus, the Bishop of Paris. His intervention finally persuades King Clothar to leave Radegund in peace.

Carolyn Heilbrun notes how critical the issue of power is in women's biographies and autobiographies. She points out that while the acquisition and use of power is central to the biographies of men, authors of the lives of women and, often the women who are themselves the subjects of such narrated lives, are often deeply troubled about a woman's relationship to power. But in medieval saints' lives the issue is more complex than can be explained by gender alone. The hagiographical tradition repeatedly documents the tension between spiritual power (considered real power in the world of the saints) and human (political) power which, ideally, implements the divine will, but is, in reality, more often in conflict with that will. Access to *real power* is achieved through the abnegation of political power and by humility. Through all the conflicts that Radegund must negotiate in order to create and maintain her monastery, she experiences the tensions and dilemmas within the dynamics of divine and human power for one who would be both saint and queen.

In Baudonivia's account, Radegund rejects the earthly power that was hers as queen, and, when she founds the monastery, she refuses to be its Abbess, "reserving no authority of her own in order to follow the footsteps of Christ more swiftly. . . ." At the same time, Radegund uses her aristocratic power and personal prestige to achieve her designs; she invokes the influence of powerful bishops and magnates, sending gifts and gracious words to the Bishop of Paris "secretly," as any canny politician would. She does not hesitate to call on heavenly power to support her aims, a power that, in the spirit of the times, she considers more devastating than any army. Though not an Abbess, she assumes a leadership role in the formation and education of the nuns and when she desires relics for her convent, she appeals to bishops, King Sigebert and even the emperor to give her what she wants. Her attempt to acquire a relic of the true cross was, in fact, a quest for social and political prestige for her own convent as well as for a source of spiritual riches for all who would come there. Heilbrun gives her own definition of power: "[It] is the ability to take one's place in whatever discourse is essential to action and the right to have one's part matter."[13] Radegund willingly seeks precisely that kind of power, political and spiritual, and uses it without hesitation.

In narrating Radegund's life as a nun, Baudonivia clearly has recourse to the commonplaces of the hagiographical tradition and to catalogs of monastic virtues that were already standardized in her day. She notes, for instance, Radegund's devotion to prayer and vigils; she also describes the way in which the aristocratic woman identifies with the poor: feeding pilgrims from her own table, washing the feet of the sick with her own hands, eschewing her maid, good food, a feather bed, and the soft garments of the wealthy. As Baudonivia notes, Radegund made herself "a pauper for God," an accepted strategy by which the wealthy traditionally sought divine favor. In the list of Radegund's virtues, along with patience, charity, prudence, and fervor of spirit, Baudonivia particularly emphasizes Radegund's dedication to the study of scripture. She repeats in several places that Radegund read the scriptures incessantly and, when she was forced to take a little rest, had the Psalms continuously read to her. Though devotion to scripture was also a hagiographical commonplace, Baudonivia testifies to its reality in Radegund's life by relating a little story in which the queen, wishing to hail the portress, calls out "alleluia" instead of the nun's name. Her mind is so thoroughly filled with biblical texts that they slip out inappropriately in ordinary conversation. Although biblical literacy was the ideal promoted by the monastic life, its embodiment in the life of Radegund is, in the sixth century, worth noting. The possibility of learning for women, still confined primarily to convents, was one of the things that made the choice of the cloister attractive. The Christian ethos affirmed the importance of biblical literacy for a religious faith rooted in a sacred text; yet that literacy, and consequently the full experience of faith, was generally accessible to women only in the monastic situation. The choice of a cloistered life was, among other things, a choice to live at the heart of the world of the spirit.

Much of what Baudonivia relates about Radegund's life in the convent at Poitiers indicates the quality of her relationship with others. She notes that Radegund would not speak or listen to slander—surely a measure of her great self-control given the political and familial struggles around her; instead she insisted that the sisters pray for those who persecuted them. Her prayers were for the lives of *all* the kings who were engaged in warfare all around her and she prayed "for their stability." She well knew that the devastations of war fell most heavily on the land itself and the general population and that therefore political "stability" rather than the success of one warring faction over another was the most important outcome. Though she prayed and did penance to this end, she also engaged in the exercise of her political and spiritual power in pursuing it. Baudonivia tells us that she wrote to all the kings as soon as she heard of bitterness beginning to arise among them; obviously she kept her ear to the ground, as it were, and may have engaged spies so that she could forestall conflicts at their inception. "And, likewise, she sent to their noble followers to give the high kings salutary counsel so that their power might work to the welfare of the people and the land." By "noble followers," Baudonivia refers here to the magnates who acted as royal counsellors, an institution of political and moral importance much commented on under the Carolingians but already significant in Merovingian times. Radegund is attempting to bring her moral vision to bear on the political struggles of the various kings, not directly, but through the established lines of political advisement. Baudonivia attributes great success to her efforts although history records that the peace she helped establish was quite transitory.

With the other nuns, a community of women voluntarily assembled, Radegund established relationships of loving and mutual support. Baudonivia states explicitly that the community was accepted by her in place of the royal relatives she had left behind; Baudonivia quotes her as saying often, "Daughters, I chose you." She seems to have understood the teaching of the New Testament that for those who follow Christ in faith, blood ties become a metaphor and model for kinship freely chosen and rooted in spiritual realities. With this community, she willingly shared all that she had and was. Although she had wine cellars of her own (as she seems to have had the possibility of a maid, a feather bed, and clothing appropriate to her status), she used them only with the permission of her abbess and only for the needs of others. To them, she offered "undiluted wine," a phrase that has biblical resonance suggesting wisdom, joy, and the vitality of life itself. Baudonivia records that Radegund eagerly served the needs of everyone in the community and "washed the feet of all with her own hands. . . ." This is an echo of the Johannine story of the Last Supper in which Jesus models the new relationship between those who follow him and become his family. The concrete action of washing feet becomes for Radegund, as it had for Christ, the external manifestation of her inner affection.

Besides attending to the physical needs of the sisters she had gathered around her, Radegund was also solicitous for their education and formation. Baudonivia records that she would question any "servant of God" who visited Poitiers, seeking wisdom in the spiritual life. Her status gave her the privilege of entertaining such guests. Before she passed on such wisdom to others, however, she tested it in the crucible of her own experience. Only then would she distill her experience into words that became more meaningful for having first been exemplified in the life of the queen. Experience was, also, the hermeneutical key to her interpretation of the biblical texts. She bade her sisters search for the meaning of the scriptures "in the mirror of [their] souls." The texts were authoritative only in so far as they illuminated, and were illuminated by, the experience of life. Her monastic spirituality was not a slavish following of rules but a careful and discerning interpretation of her own life in the light of the wisdom of the tradition and of the shared understanding of the community. Heilbrun suggests that it is precisely in the exchange of stories between groups of women freely assembled that authentic women's stories can arise. "I do not believe that new stories will find their way into texts if they do not begin in oral exchanges among women in groups hearing and talking to one another. As long as women are isolated one from the other, not allowed to offer other women the most personal accounts of their lives, they will not be part of any narrative of their own."[14] If Radegund did succeed in crafting her own narrative, in shaping her own life, then it was in large measure the result of the community of sisters with which she exchanged her own story and her own dreams and out of which was born Baudonivia's narrative of her life.

After Radegund's death, Baudonivia sought to assess the legacy that she began to see more clearly in hindsight. A touch of humanity graces her narrative here; she notes that the sisters did not always respond fervently to the founder's admonitions during her lifetime. It is only in retrospect (and, especially, in the turmoil after her death) that they appreciated fully the wisdom of her leadership. Not surprisingly, Baudonivia emphasizes the way in which Radegund shaped the religious and community life of the convent at Poitiers. Though Radegund had probably adopted the Rule of Caesarius of Arles in founding her monastery, it was a very flexible instrument, as religious rules remained for several centuries. Under that Rule, the insight and wisdom of the founder and early abbesses gave to each foundation its individual character. Baudonivia lauds Radegund particularly for the way in which she promoted the spiritual and intellectual formation of the community. She notes that Radegund ordered reading during meals, insisted on reading and "incessant daily preaching" along with prayers and almsgiving to combat "slovenliness" and to obviate ignorance as an excuse for mediocrity. No mention is made of who is to do the preaching, but the biographer records, in several places, that Radegund herself preached, even while she was asleep! Presumably then, it was the nuns themselves, at least those with authority and wisdom, who were to preach to and teach the others. Certainly, Baudonivia sees Radegund as the convent's protective force, a kind of spiritual shield that stands between the convent and all outside threat. She records that Radegund frequently bestowed a nightly blessing upon the monastery, signing it with the sign of the cross; through that blessing, she expelled any evil that gathered around the place. On one occasion, demons were seen fleeing from the blessed sanctuary and, on another, a night bird that disturbed the rest and prayers of the sisters was banished by a blessing in her name. These stories are but exemplifications of the kind of spiritual protection that Baudonivia attributes to the guiding presence of Radegund.

Miracles and Relics: Instruments of Power

The stories suggest that two other, and related, elements in Baudonivia's account of Radegund require comment. One is the element of miracles and the other Radegund's aggressive pursuit of relics. This is not the place to discuss the extensive play given to miracle stories in the lives of saints and many other medieval texts; that theme has been well-treated by Benedicta Ward in *Miracles and the Medieval Mind.*[15] Ward explains the teaching of Augustine that she believes laid the foundation for the medieval understanding. Augustine believed that such miracles happened in order to move the human mind to awe and reverence for God. According to Augustine, miracles were connected to the natural world, not contradictory to it; they occurred because the human mind had grown habituated to the more common miracles of creation itself and were no longer moved by them. Augustine encouraged the publicizing of miracles, particularly those associated with saints, because he believed that they stimulated the faith of those who believed and confounded those who did not. Ward affirms that miracles were central to the world view of the Middle Ages; it was universally accepted that the miraculous was "a basic dimension of life. The bounds of reality included the unseen in a way alien to modern thought."[16] This does not mean that miracles were simply retold reverently and without secondary purposes on the part of the author. Indeed, Ward discusses monastic miracles as "propaganda," publicized to promote the importance of shrines and inspire pilgrimage. Often the narrator intends to demonstrate through the miracle that the biblical story of salvation was continued in the "later days" and new cultural context of other saints.

Seen against this complex horizon, the purpose of Baudonivia's miracle stories becomes a bit more clear. For the most part, they are designed simply to show Radegund's sanctity, to demonstrate that she has been seized by the saving power of God to such fullness that she can now mediate that power to others. They are also part of the attempt of those who admire her to promote her own places as sacred shrines. The matron Mammezo is healed at the oratory Radegund established even though the saint is still living and is not present at the shrine. Posthumous miracles attest to the healing power to be found at the basilica that is her burial place. Baudonivia makes clear these intentions when she exclaims, "how bountiful and rich is the mercy of God that makes His own fold stand in awe of Him and seeks out the places where He may show His power to the faithful as the giver and dispenser of virtues." Her words echo Augustine's thought.

The odd little story of Vinoberga, a convent housemaid, is also, perhaps, designed to increase "awe" and, as Augustine hoped, "confound" those who do not believe. Vinoberga "rashly dared to presume to seat herself" in Radegund's "high seat," and is punished by a fire that burns, without consuming, "for three days and three nights." Is she rash and presumptious because, as a housemaid she takes the chair of the foundress, an aristocrat? Is this a story about status? Perhaps the author wishes to teach that, while the mighty may forgo earthly status through humility, such status may not be ignored by the lower classes with impunity. Or does the housemaid's action indicate her lack of faith in Radegund's sanctity? If so, she thereby impugns, not Radegund, but the power of God and is punished, appropriately, by the fire that symbolizes both God's transcendent presence and the purification required of all those who seek it. In either case, Radegund saves Vinoberga from her penalty; if Vinoberga's fault was a lack of faith in Radegund, her "conversion" is signified by her prayer to that saint for relief. If her sin is arrogance, then she is well-purified by the fires. As Baudonivia says, "Such a punishment [not the miracle itself!] made everyone cautious and more devout."

This story also directs our attention to the special concern for afflicted women that we see in many of Radegund's miracles. Besides the stories of Mammezo and Vinoberga, two other stories bring women supplicants to the foreground. The last miracle story that Baudonivia tells is about two women who come to the basilica of St. Hilary where abbots have gathered to celebrate the vigils of his feast. They stand out among a large group of demoniacs assembled there because they are "gravely infested" and rave violently, to the point of shaking the building. The narrative details reflect the tendency to view women as vulnerable to demonic influence and dangerous instruments of demonic power. Baudonivia specifically notes that the women are not healed at the shrine of St. Hilary; they follow the monks and abbot to Radegund's basilica where her power is invoked and they are cured. For Baudonivia, this is a sign that Radegund's power and sanctity are equal to those of the regional patriarch, since some of the possessed group are healed at both shrines. She does not affirm, though she suggests by the way she tells the story, that this female saint has particular power to effect the healing of women.

Finally, Baudonivia notes that Radegund's funeral procession is attended by "female serfs," each of which carries a candle bearing her own name. When a debate ensues over the placement of those candles, one of them flies out of the hand of the *boy* (to whom they have been handed over at the gravesite) and to the feet of the dead saint. This decides the issue and the name of the woman, Calva, whose candle it was, is recorded for all posterity. As a miracle story, it is slight. As a story about status and gender, both of which Baudonivia carefully details, it is intriguing. Though men are in charge of the burial rites (bishops preside and male servants take control of the candles once they arrive at the chosen site of St. Mary's Basilica), it is female serfs who have the privilege of processing in front of the bier. Do they represent the nuns who are prevented from this honor by the rule of enclosure? Do they represent Radegund herself who, in humility, renounced her royal status to become "a pauper for the Lord?" Peter Brown in *The Cult of the Saints*[17] has examined how processions to the graves of the martyrs in the Late Antique empire allowed the Christian community to restructure itself in the marginal ground of the cemetery. There, women, the poor, the crippled and dispossessed jostled the arms of the wealthy and aristocratic, "on terms equal in everything but status."[18] All had equal access to the power of the holy ones, an experience of human solidarity that was unavailable anywhere else. Baudonivia's narrative suggests a similar experience that is rooted in the life and holiness of Radegund.

Baudonivia's interest in narrating miracles as signs of Radegund's sanctity is matched by Radegund's own concern to bring significant relics to Poitiers. Recent solid scholarship has greatly illuminated the meaning and importance of relics, of their transfer from one place to another and of the installation ceremonies that solemnized their arrival. Benedicta Ward connects the tradition of miracle narratives to the development of relic-bearing shrines. Peter Brown, quoted earlier, situates the early devotion to relics within the late antique Roman culture of client and patron relationships. Having explored the way in which the posthumous *presence* of the saint was held to be accessible to the devout through shrines and relics, Brown explains that "if relics could travel, then the distance between the believer and the place where the holy could be found ceased to be a fixed, physical distance. It took on the shifting quality of late-Roman social relationships: distances between groups and persons were overcome by gestures of grace and favor, and the dangerously long miles of the imperial communications system were overcome by a strenuously maintained ideology of unanimity and concord."[19]

The arrival of relics from Rome often signified the connection between the new and distant Germanic church to its center and source, a kind of spiritual aqueduct between the Roman head-waters and the new fields of the Lord, waiting to be watered then harvested. In his *Ecclesiastical History* the venerable Bede records the pattern as it affected the Anglo-Saxon churches. The translation of relics both conferred status on the new church and required it to transcend its tribal understanding of itself. Once a local shrine possessed relics of a saint from "outside," it had to begin to think of itself as "Roman," that is, as part of a larger universe of communities. Brown particularly underscores the way in which the cult of relics in Merovingian Gaul was celebrated with what he calls a "studiously all-inclusive ceremonial." Using texts from Gregory of Tours, Venantius Fortunatus and Victricius, authors who are also among our sources for the life of Radegund, Brown describes how "the festival of a saint was conceived of as a moment of ideal consensus on a deeper level. It made plain God's acceptance of the community as a whole: his mercy embraced all its disparate members, and could reintegrate all who had stood outside in the previous year."[20]

It is within the context explored by Brown that Radegund's aggressive pursuit of relics makes the most sense. Baudonivia records that it was while she was still at Saix that "she *determined* . . . to collect relics of all the saints [emphasis mine]" and when she entered her monastery she continued to gather "a great multitude of the saints" from all four corners of the earth.[21] The acquisition of relics is, for Radegund, a lifelong commitment and her interest was in the most universal representation possible; her search culminates in her efforts to acquire a relic of the true cross. This relic would most firmly link the church at Poitiers with Rome and, thereby, with the whole world; it would also bring the personal presence of the redeeming Lord and universal savior to Poitiers in a particularly powerful way. To acquire it, therefore, Radegund brooks no obstacle. To acquire other relics, she had prayed, fasted, and begged. To possess a relic of the true cross, she takes counsel with King Sigebert, importunes the emperor, and when thwarted by the citizens of Poitiers who do not seem to want the relic, she fasts, wails, keeps vigil, and again appeals to the king who sends a royal warrior to achieve Radegund's desire. In describing Radegund's efforts on behalf of relics, Baudonivia emphasizes that she acts as both queen and as pastor. She repeatedly parallels Radegund's pursuit of the relic of the cross with that of St. Helena.[22] When thwarted, she does not exemplify any of the meekness with which she seems to have served everyone in her monastery; Baudonivia says "her spirit blaz[ed] in a fighting mood" and she exhibits all of the fierceness of a royal Thuringian in getting her way.

For her, the presence of the cross in Poitiers will ensure not only great religious blessings but "the welfare of the whole fatherland and the stability of [Sigebert's] kingdom," as she said in her petition to the king. Brown has shown how the cult of holy relics served both political peace and social inclusiveness. Therefore, bringing the cross to Poitiers is simply another way in which Radegund works assiduously for the peace of the people over whom she has never ceased to be queen.[23] When the relic finally is enshrined in her own monastery, Baudonivia calls her "this best provider, this good shepherdess." In facilitating the dispensation of divine power, Radegund has exercised her own power, at once royal and pastoral. Her power and that of the relics represented a particular form of justice, well understood in the Merovingian world. As Brown says, Christians in Gaul "turned the celebration of the memory of the martyrs into a reassuring scenario by which unambiguously good power, associated with the amnesty of God and the *praesentia* of the martyr, overcame the ever-lurking presence of evil power."[24]

The ambivalence toward power in Baudonivia's text has already been noted. She praises Radegund for eschewing the worldly power of a queen, yet portrays her as completely the queen in her aggressive pastoring of her flock at Poitiers. She describes how, in humility, Radegund foregoes the role of Abbess, yet praises her for giving the sisters rules and admonitions, leadership and teaching. Perhaps Brown's analysis of relic rituals and Radegund's fierce pursuit of relics help us understand this ambivalence. Radegund was herself a victim of violent and coercive power; her entire life was caught up in the various familial and dynastic struggles for power that surged around her, threatening every goal she pursued. It is not hard to understand how she might wish to renounce such power. But Radegund seems to believe that destructive power is only put to flight by alternative power, a divine power that is mediated through persons who work and struggle in accord with grace and wisdom. She tried to exercise such power herself, forming her community and bringing her powers of persuasion to bear on her kin and associates. In the use of that power, she was both gentle and firm. But she also wanted to bring divine and just power into her world through mediators more efficacious than herself. To that end, she collected her relics not gently, but fiercely, not just through persuasion and example but by marshalling the forces of kings and their envoys. Radegund was not, I think, ambivalent about power as such, but her experience had taught her the viciousness of coercive power and the dangerous hold power can acquire over those who would wield it.

Let me conclude by returning to the feminist critique that Carolyn Heilbrun raises. Can we identify with any assurance what Radegund's goals and desires were? This is difficult since we do not have access to Radegund save through Baudonivia whose purposes were, at least to some degree, hagiographical. If we prescind from the miracles, we can find a pattern in Radegund's actions as narrated by Baudonivia. She chose to provide a space where women were respected and protected, where they could escape the predatory designs of male rulers and pursue the treasures of intellect and spirit. Jo Ann McNamara has insightfully pointed out that one of the many socially important "roles" that convents played in the early middle ages, was that of "a shelter for abused and helpless women."[25] In providing that safe haven, Radegund was ready to use all the worldly power she possessed as well as the spiritual power she could acquire by sanctity and the collection of relics. She was not content to create only a safe physical space, but established an ordered environment where learning and wisdom could be honed through specifically feminine experience, where the established tradition could be recast through "oral exchanges" in a community of women voluntarily assembled. Undoubtedly Radegund wanted "a room of her own," but her sense of royal obligation, more central to her identity than the roles of wife, mother or nun, led her to establish a room for others as well. She espoused a public life, not merely private comfort. She created "safety and closure" to be sure, but her safe and enclosed space continued to be the venue of "action," "experience" and "life," for her and for many of those who joined her. The dramas enacted at Poitiers were part and parcel of the political and social action of the Merovingian world.

Were these goals and desires any less her own for being also part of the religious ethos of the time? No one escapes the influence that conventional and current ideology plays on personal choices and vocational commitments. The Christian ethos dictated the shape of power and the forms of political and public action in the Merovingian world. Radegund assumed power as she understood it and played her public and political role according to the terms dictated by the social realities of her culture. Her exercise of power fits very well Heilbrun's own definition. She did "take [her] place in whatever discourse [was] essential to action," at least in the discourse that was essential to her own life and to the lives of those who were important to her: her own and other royal families, her nuns and the people of Poitiers. That it mattered is the burden, I think, of the miracle stories and is also seen in the way kings, bishops, abbots, saints, and other powerful people took seriously her participation in the discourse.

Did Radegund "put God or Christ in the place of a man" and thereby rob herself of her own desires and autonomy? Curiously enough, Baudonivia, a (presumably) holy nun writing of the holiness of a beloved mentor, does not give us any insight into the role God or Christ played in Radegund's life. She does not talk of her prayer or her spiritual wisdom but of her desire and energy in pursuing them. She describes briefly her ascetical practices but situates them precisely within the context of the particular goals Radegund is pursuing. In fact, she rarely mentions God or Christ at all; Radegund's relationship with the divine is assumed as the foundation of her holiness. What Baudonivia does insist upon is the impact of that holiness (conventional or idiosyncratic as it may have been) upon her character and her choices. She describes a woman who displays a great deal of autonomy and persistence in following her desires, fierce courage in the face of opposition, compassion in leadership and strength throughout. Radegund remains what she was by temperament and nature, a woman of action, a queen shaped by violence, a leader committed to the public good as she understood it. That is how Baudonivia understands the consequences of putting God or Christ at the center of one's life: the pursuit of holiness grounds, refines, and orients but does not destroy the self nor the possibilities of life and action. Radegund's story, retold and reclaimed anew, can shape a renewed understanding of the significance of the spiritual journey in the pursuit of one's deepest dreams, ambitions, and desires.

Notes

1. Carolyn G. Heilbrun, *Writing a Woman's Life* (New York: Ballantine Books, 1988) 37.

2. *De gloria confessorum,* c. CIV; *De gloria martyrum,* c. V; *Historia Francorum,* 1. IX, 39 and 42; III, 4–7; VI, 29.

3. *Monumenta Germaniae historica,* Scriptorum rerum Merovingicarum, II:377–397. Both Fortunatus' and Baudonivia's lives have been translated into English by Jo Ann McNamara and John E. Halborg with E. Gordon Whatley in the

anthology *Sainted Women of the Dark Ages* (Durham and London: Duke University Press, 1992).

4. E. Briand, *Histoire de s. Radegunde, reine de France, et des sanctuaires et pélerinages en son honneur* (Poitier: Parigi, 1898).

5. McNamara et al. 93, n102.

6. Rene Aigrain, *Sainte Radegunde* (Paris: Librairie Victor Lecoffre, 1918) notes and evaluates the many authors of the lives of this saint.

7. Of Baudonivia's life, Aigrain writes that "without it we would know nothing or next to nothing about that which gives life to St. Radegunde, her individual countenance, her particular charm, nothing of the resistance to Clothair, nothing of the cult of the relics, the apparitions, the last moments" (viii). Suzanne Fonay Wemple affirms that "Baudonivia . . . introduced female values and ideals into hagiography. [She] replaced the ideal of the asexual female saint, the *virago,* whose greatest accomplishment was the imitation of male virtues, with a heroine who relied on female attributes to achieve spiritual perfection." "Female Spirituality and Mysticism in Frankish Monasteries," *Peaceweavers: Medieval Religious Women* (Kalamazoo, MI: Cistercian Publications, 1987) 44.

8. Heilbrun 20.

9. Heilbrun 20–21.

10. *Quis Dives Salvetur* 14.

11. *De Nabuthe* 11.

12. Baudonivia may be aware of that primary source of ascetical biography, Athanasius' *Life of Antony of Egypt* c. 357. Athanasius describes Antony's move toward perfection in terms of two geographical withdrawals. First, Antony moves from Alexandria to the tombs outside the city, then to a cave at much greater distance from civilization.

13. Heilbrun 18.

14. Heilbrun 46.

15. (Philadelphia: University of Pennsylvania Press, 1987).

16. Ward 33.

17. (Chicago: The University of Chicago Press, 1981). See also Patrick J. Geary, *Furta Sacra: Thefts of Relics in the Central Middle Ages* (Princeton: University of Princeton Press, 1978).

18. 45.

19. Brown 89.

20. Brown 99–100.

21. Note how clearly Baudonivia speaks of the relics as conferring the personal and living presence of the saint.

22. For a thorough development of this theme, see Jo Ann McNamara, "Imitatio Helenae: Sainthood as an Attribute of Queenship," *Saints: Studies in Hagiography,* ed. Sandro Sticca (Binghamton, NY: MRTS, 1960) 51–80.

23. Neither the importance of Radegund's miracles nor belief in her special protective power in the region of Poitiers ceased with the end of the Middle Ages. Jean Filleau in *La Preuve Historique des Litanies de la grande Reyne de France, Sainte Radegonde* (Poitiers: Abraham Mounin Imprimeur et Libraire, 1943), 207–213, details the continual protection of the saint. In 1450, she helps Poitiers defend itself against the English and a procession is instituted to honor this protection. In 1569, her tomb inspires the soldiers of Poitiers to withstand the assault of 50,000 Calvinists. In 1643, it was proposed that Radegund be made patroness not only of Poitiers but of the whole kingdom and be honored by appropriate observances on her feast day.

24. Brown 101.

25. "Living Sermons: Consecrated Women and the Conversion of Gaul," *Peaceweavers: Medieval Religious Women,* Lillian Thomas Shank and John Al Nichols (eds.) (Kalamazoo, MI: Cistercian Publications, 1987).

Secondary Works Cited

Aigrain, Rene. *Sainte Radegunde.* Paris: Librairie Victor Lecoffre, 1918.

Briand, E. *Histoire de s. Radegunde, reine de France, et des sanctuaries et pélerinages en son honneur.* Poitiers: Parigi, 1898.

Brown, Peter. *The Cult of the Saints.* Chicago: University of Chicago Press, 1981.

Filleau, Jean. *La Preuve Historique des Litanies de la grand Reyne de France, Sainte Radegonde.* Poitiers: Abraham Mounin Imprimeur et Libraire, 1943.

Geary, Patrick J. *Furta Sacra: Thefts of Relics in the Central Middle Ages.* Princeton, NJ: University of Princeton Press, 1978.

Heilbrun, Carolyn. *Writing a Woman's Life.* New York: Ballantine Books, 1988.

McNamara, Jo Ann, and John E. Halborg with E. Gordan Whatley. *Sainted Women of the Dark Ages.* Durham and London: Duke University Press, 1992.

McNamara, Jo Ann. "Imitatio Helenae: Sainthood as an Attribute of Queenship," *Saints: Studies in Hagiography* Ed. Sandro Sticca. Binghamton, NY: MRTS, 1960.

———. "Living Sermons: Consecrated Women and the Conversion of Gaul," *Peaceweavers: Medieval Religious Women.* Kalamazoo, MI: Cistercian Publications, 1987.

Nichols, John A., and Lillian Thomas Shank (eds.). *Peaceweavers: Medieval Religious Women,* Vol II. Kalamazoo, MI: Cistercian Publications, 1987.

Ward, Benedicta. *Miracles and the Medieval Mind.* Philadelphia, PA: University of Pennsylvania Press, 1987.

Wemple, Suzanne Fonay. "Female Spirituality and Mysticism in Frankish Monasteries," *Peaceweavers: Medieval Religious Women.* Vol II. Kalamazoo, MI: Cistercian Publications, 1987.

Book II To the Holy Ladies, Distinguished by the Grace of Kindnesses, to the Abbess Dedimia and All the Glorious Congregation of the Lady Radegund, from Baudonivia, the Humblest of All

You enjoin me to perform a task no less impossible than to touch heaven with a finger, that I should presume to say something about the life of the Holy Lady Radegund, whom you knew very well. But that task ought to be given to those who have a well of eloquence within themselves, because anything entrusted to them is explained fully with a flowing song. But on the other hand, those who are of limited learning do not have an abundance of eloquence through which they are able to refresh others or to relieve the poverty of their own aridity. Such (people) not only [do not][1] strive to say anything, but also, if anything is enjoined upon them, are afraid. This I recognize in myself, I who am of insignificant mind and have little eloquence of understanding, since as much as it is useful for the learned to speak, so it is useful for the unlearned to keep silent. For the former know how to discuss great things from small, but the latter do not know even how to produce small things from great; and therefore, that which is sought by some is feared by others. I am the smallest of all the small ones whom she raised from the very cradle as a handmaiden at her own feet. So that I may touch on her famous work of great service, not fully but having grasped a part, as long as I am the herald of her glorious life for the ears of her flock, although not with worthy eloquence, but devoted all the same, and so that I might comply obediently with your most friendly wishes, I seek to be helped by your prayers, since I am more devoted than learned. We will not go over again the things which the apostolic bishop Fortunatus composed about her blessed life, but those things which he passed over because of their length. For just as he himself explained in his book, "May a meagerness about the virtues of the Saint be sufficient, lest an abundance be despised; nor may it be considered too brief, when her greatness is recognized from a few things." Therefore, with Divine Power, whom blessed Radegund was eager to please on earth and with whom she reigns after her earthly life, as my inspiration, I try to approach those things which she did and to include a few things about her many miracles, not with polished expressions, but in a peasant's way. Here ends the prologue.

Here Begin Her Virtues

1. Therefore, no one should be ignorant of the life of Blessed Radegund, as it is contained in the first book, or about her royal origin or position, nor about her conduct while she was living with her earthly prince and husband, the glorious King Clothar. Her noble seed sprang from royal stock, and what she took from her noble birth, she adorned more with faith. A noble queen wed to an earthly prince, she was more heavenly than earthbound. But in the short time of their union, she conducted herself as a bride in the appearance of a wife, so that she might serve Christ more devotedly. She did in a lay purpose what she herself wished to imitate: the holiness of her spirit already anticipated the arrival of her future conversion, while under the secular habit she formed the example of sanctity. She was chained by no fetter of this world, but bound to the obedience of the servants of God. She was concerned for the redemption of prisoners, and generous in gifts to the needy, for she believed that whatever a poor man received from her was his own.

2. While she was still with the king, in worldly dress, her mind was intent on Christ. I speak with God as my witness, to whom, with silent voice, hearts confess, and from whom, although the tongue is silent, the conscience hides nothing, because we say what we have heard and we give testimony to what we have seen. She, having been invited to dine with the matron Ansitreda, was making her journey accompanied by her worldly attendants, in a long and extensive train. There was a pagan shrine, which was worshipped by the Franks, at a distance of one mile from the blessed Queen's route. When she heard that there was a temple there, tended by the Franks, she ordered it to be burned by her servants; she thought it was unjust that the God of heaven was despised and the Devil's doings worshipped. When they heard this, the Franks and their whole community tried to defend the temple with swords and sticks, and with every devilish shout, but the Holy Queen, unmoving, persevered. She held Christ at her breast; she sat on her horse and did not move forward, and before the temple was burnt to the ground, while she was praying, the people made peace among themselves. After this, everyone, marvelling at the courage and constancy of the Queen, blessed the Lord.

3. Afterwards, with the help of Divine Power, she left the earthly king, because her vows required it. While residing at her villa at Saix, which the king had given her, in the first year of her conversion she saw in a vision a ship, in the shape of a man. On all his limbs people were sitting, but she was seated on his knee. He said to her, "Now you are seated on my knee, but soon you will have a habitation in my heart." Grace was shown to her, which she was to enjoy. She related this vision secretly to her faithful companions, with the promise that no one would know this while she lived. How cautious in conversation, how devout in every act! In prosperity, in adversity, in happiness, in sorrow, she was always calm. She did not break herself down in adversity, nor exalt herself in prosperity.

4. While she was still at the villa, there was a rumor that the king wanted her back again. He was grieving at having suffered a grave loss, in that he had permitted such a queen, such a great queen, to leave his side. Unless he got her back, deep within himself he did not wish to live. When she heard these things, the most blessed one, very much frightened, handed herself over to be tortured further and put a hair shirt on her tender body. Moreover, she chose the torture of hunger, and staying awake all night, she totally immersed herself in prayer. She despised the throne of the fatherland, she overcame the sweetness of marriage, she shut out worldly affection and she chose to become an exile, so as not to wander away from Christ. She still had with her a "felte" from the royal regalia, which was fashioned from gold and made with gems and pearls. It was worth about a thousand gold solidi, and she sent it, through a nun named Fridovigia, whom she had near her with her faithful companions, to the venerable Lord John, who was shut up in the fortress at Chinon, so that he would pray for her that she would never have to return to the secular world, and that he would send her a hair shirt, with which she might diminish her body. He sent her a haircloth wrap from which she made herself both an inner and an outer garment. She also asked that if the above-mentioned man should hear anything from the Holy Spirit about her situation, for which she was afraid, that he would inform her. If the king wished this, she preferred to die before being joined again to an earthly king, because she was united in the embrace of the Heavenly King. And so the man of God spent the whole night in vigils and prayers, with the inspiration of the Divine Spirit upon him. On the next day, he sent word to her that this was indeed what the king wished, but that it was not permissible to God, and that the king would be punished by the judgment of God before he took her again as a wife.

5. After this statement, the previously mentioned Lady Radegund, her mind intent on Christ, with God as her inspiration and fellow-worker,

built a monastery for herself at Poitiers by arrangement of the glorious King Clothar. The apostolic bishop Pientius and the Duke Austrapius quickly made the structure with the Lord's order. The holy Queen, rejecting the false enticements of the world, entered into it rejoicing. There she would collect the ornaments of perfection, a great gathering of maidens for Christ, the never-dying bridegroom. When an Abbess had been elected and established, just as if she and her power had been subdued, Lady Radegund turned over everything to her, so that she might hurry unencumbered in the footsteps of Christ, and build up more for herself in heaven, by as much as she subtracted from herself in the earthly life. Certainly her holy association soon began to glow in the act of humility, in the fruitfulness of charity, in the splendor of chastity, and in the richness of fasting. So she turned herself over to the heavenly bridegroom in total love, so that embracing God with a pure heart she might realize Christ as a dweller within her.

6. But envious of the good, the Enemy of the human race did not cease to pursue her; she shrank from doing his will even while she was in the (secular) world. Now she had learned through messengers what she feared, that the glorious king, with his very excellent son Sigobert, had arrived at Tours, on the pretext of offering devotion, (but) so that he might reach Poitiers more easily, in order to take his queen.

7. When she learned this, the blessed Radegund wrote legal letters, with divine witness, to the apostolic Lord Germanus, Bishop of the city of Paris, who was with the King at that time. She sent these secretly, with gifts and eulogies, through her agent Proculus. And when the man of God read them, he prostrated himself in tears at the feet of the King, before the tomb of Blessed Saint Martin. With divine witness, just as had been revealed to him in the letters, [he begged] the King not to go to Poitiers. Thus the king, filled with sadness, realized that this was the petition of the blessed Queen. Led by repentance, rethinking[2] his evil counselors and judging himself unworthy, because he did not deserve to have such a queen any longer, he prostrated himself before the precinct of the holy Martin, at the feet of the apostolic Germanus. He asked that Germanus seek a favor for him from blessed Radegund, that she pardon him because he had sinned against her with evil counsellors. Thence divine revenge soon[3] punished them: just as Arrius, who, fighting against the Catholic faith lost all his intestines in a flux, so also did it happen to those who acted against the blessed Queen. Then the King, fearing the judgement of God because his Queen did the will of God rather than his, while she was with him, asked that Germanus quickly come there. Thus the apostolic lord Germanus, arriving in Poitiers, entered the monastery and

went into the chapel dedicated to the name of Queen Mary. There he prostrated himself at the feet of the blessed Queen, begging a favor for the King. And she, rejoicing that she was snatched from the jaws of the temporal world, kindly granted it and prepared herself for the service of God. Now she prepared to follow Christ, whom she had always loved, wherever he went, and with devoted spirit she ran to him. Therefore, intent on such things, when an order of vigils was added, she made herself the guardian of her body, as if of a prison, for the night vigils. And although she was merciful to others, she became the judge of herself; she was pious to the rest, severe to herself in abstinence; generous to all, but restrained for herself, so that exhaustion by fasting was not sufficient, unless she triumphed over her body.

8. Thus occupied with these enthusiasms through all measure, just as was revealed in the first book, she easily deserved to devote herself to God alone. Then, however, dressed with stronger arms, without ceasing in the prayers, the vigils and the lessons (literally, important reading), she herself served food to travellers at the table, and she herself with her own hands washed and cleaned the feet of the sick. She did not permit a servant to give comfort to her, because she, in her devotion, ran about to fulfill service. Moreover, she shut herself up in such arduous severity of abstinence, that as far as bodily weakness permitted, she did not need earthly food, so intent was her mind on God. Indeed, after she had put on the religious habit, she built a punishing little bed for herself; at no time did a soft pillow support her. Nor did the elegance of linen lay over her, but she housed her tender limbs in ashes and a hairshirt, for all her clothing. The earlier book has told much about the rigor of her abstinence and servitude. She made herself such a pauper for the sake of God that she offered an example to others. She did not have a sleeve, which she put on her arm, except that she made two gloves from her own leather boot; yet she conducted herself as a pauper in such a way that the Abbess did not know it. For who could explain her patience, her charity, her fervor of spirit, her discretion, her kindness, her holy zeal, her yoke of meditation day and night on the rule of the Lord? When she seemed to cease from meditation on the psalms or from praise, a reader, one of the nuns, did not cease to read to her. The praise of God did not leave her heart or mouth to this degree: once she saw the doorkeeper of the monastery, Eogunda by name, passing by in a certain place, and when she wished to call out to her, shouted "Alleluia" in place of her name. This she did a thousand times, but never did any slander come out of her mouth, never a lie, never anything said badly of anyone. And not only did she not disparage anyone, but she did not hear detraction with patience.

She always prayed for the persecutors and taught others to pray. She loved her flock, which she, full of desire for God, had gathered in the name of God, so much that she did not even remember her parents or that a King had her as his wife. Frequently she would say before us, "You I have chosen as daughters. You (are) my light, my life, my rest and my total happiness—you, my young plantation. Work with me in this world, whence we may rejoice in the future world. With complete faith and hearts full of affection let us serve the Lord; in fear, in simplicity of heart let us seek Him, so that with confidence we may be able to say to Him "Grant, Lord, what you have promised, because we have done what you commanded."

9. Never did she impose a task which she herself had not done before. From wherever a servant of the Lord had come, she inquired carefully in what way he served God. If she learned anything new from him, which she herself had not done, immediately, with all eagerness, she imposed it upon herself. Afterwards she showed the congregation as much by example as she taught them by word. When the reading of psalms aloud to her had stopped, her reading never ceased, not by day or by night, not even when she refreshed her body a little bit. While the lesson was being read, she, having care for our souls with pious concern, used to say, "If you do not understand what is being read, why is it that you do not diligently look in the mirror of your souls?" Because although perhaps it was presumed to ask this out of some irreverence, she, with pious concern and motherly affection, did not cease to explain what the reading contained for the salvation of the soul. Just as the bee, visiting different kinds of flowers, makes its honey, so she was eager to pluck the spiritual flowers from these whom she invited. Whence she brought forth the fruit of good work for her followers just as for herself. And when at night she seemed to snatch even one hour of sleep, the lesson was always being read. The reader, feeling herself drooping with sleep, thought that she (Radegund) rested for a little bit, and stopped reading. But she, her mind intent on Christ, just as if she said "I sleep and my heart is vigilant," said, "Why are you silent? Read, don't stop!" And when midnight made the hour for rising, although she had completed the whole cycle of prayers, and had not yet been to sleep, already prepared she arose from bed rejoicing in the service of the Lord, so that she might say with confidence, "In the middle of the night I arose to confess to you, Lord." For frequently she seemed to sleep and to say a psalm in sleep itself, so that thus rightly and truly she might say, "The meditation of my heart is always in your sight." Moreover, who could ever imitate her desire for charity, by which she loved all men? These virtues shone in her: modesty with frank-

ness, wisdom with simplicity, severity with gentleness, learning with humility, and finally a spotless life, a blameless life, a life always steady to itself.

10. She made herself so alienated from her own property that if she wanted to give some wine to her sisters, she would not presume to touch that from her own cellar herself. When this was known, the venerable Abbess gave her a cask of eight measures, which she entrusted to the blessed cellarer, Felicity, for dispensing. She dispensed from this vintage all the time, every day, whenever the holy one ordered her; it never diminished, but always remained the same. When the new wine came, which filled the cellar, she believed that the cask filled itself. The barrels and casks ran out before this one, which did the will of the saint in all things. The Lord fed five thousand men with five loaves and two fishes, and His servant, whenever she saw poverty, refreshed people from this small amount for a whole year. She was always solicitous about peace, and thoughtful about the health of the country. When kingdoms were moved among themselves,[4] because she esteemed all kings, she prayed for the lives of all of them, and she taught us to pray unceasingly for their stability. When she heard that there was bitterness among them, she was very fearful, and she sent one kind of letter to one, another to another, so that they would not bring arms and war against each other, but rather confirm peace, so that the fatherland would not perish. Similarly, she sent to their nobles, that they should administer health-giving plans for the exalted kings, so that while they reigned their people and country should be rendered more healthy. She imposed constant vigils on her flock, and she taught them with tears that they should pray unceasingly for them (the kings). But who can explain in words what kind of punishment she inflicted on herself?

And, with her intercession, peace among the kings, mitigation of war, and safety for the country was present. Understanding her mediation, they praised the blessed name of the Lord. How ever she obtained victory concerning the peace of kings with the King of heaven, the more she, as a devotee, readily adapted herself to God and sold herself to the service of everyone. Not caring what kind of allegiance she made, she desired to fulfill servitude totally. She washed the feet of all with her own hands, cleaned them with her veil and kissed them. If it had been permitted, she would not have resisted wiping them with her hair, for similarity to Mary. Whence, for these so immense kindnesses, which were conferred on her by divine gift, the Lord, the giver of virtues, made her more famous by miracles in France. There, where once she was seen to rule, He prepared a heavenly kingdom for her rather than an earthly one. She built an oratory for herself, near the borders, where, whenever she stole herself away from the king, she always invoked the God of heaven. There the benefits of God are offered to one invoking her name, whose prayer was constant.

11. After she had shut herself up in the monastery, a matron, Mammezo by name, got a big cinder in her eye while she was making a journey. Then one voice, one cry, one lament was in her night and day, that the Lord should show his faithful one to her. Even though she was not there in the flesh, the kindly one was present to one invoking her name. The Lord put it to her in a thought (or feeling) that she should go to the oratory of Radegund and believe that she would be saved by her invocation. Then, when the woman, full of pain and supported by the hands of her servants, could scarcely be led to this oratory, she threw herself on the pavement and began to cry out, "Lady Radegund, I believe that you are full of the virtue of God, whose will you have done more than men's. Good Lady, full of piety, have mercy on me, pray for me, that my eye should be restored to me, because my soul is afflicted with grave torture and pain." Thus she, who alone transferred the sorrows of all onto herself while she was still alive, kindly listened to the invocation of her name. With God's mercy, through her intervention, the pain fled, health returned, and she regained her healthy eye, which she thought she had lost when she was feeling only pain. She, who for many days had not taken food or seen the light of day, returned safe to her home, on her own two feet, with no one supporting her, and she is still giving thanks to God even to the present day.

12. Let there be added another miracle in praise of Christ, who makes His own cause fear in others. Vinoberga was one of her servants, who, with bold daring, presumed to sit in the chair of the blessed queen after her death. When she had done this, she was stricken by the judgment of God, and she caught fire, so that everyone could see the smoke arising from her and going on high. She made a statement before all the people, confessing that she had sinned, and that she burned because she had sat in the seat of the blessed one. After she suffered from continuous fire for three days and three nights, she shouted loudly, "Lady Radegund, I have sinned. I have done badly. Be kind, and cool my limbs, which are burned by this torture. You, with your generous mercy, full of glory in good works, you who pity all men, have mercy on me." The whole population, seeing that woman in such great punishment, prayed for her, as if she (Radegund) were present (because wherever she is invoked by faith, she is present), saying, "Good lady, spare her! Don't let the wretched one die with such great torture." Thus the most blessed one listened kindly to

the prayers of everyone, and quenched the blazing fire. Safe and sound, the girl returned to her home. And thus the punishment of that one made everyone cautious and devout.

13. While she was at her villa at Saix, with devoted and faithful spirit, her mind intent on Christ and full of devotion, she desired to have relics of all the saints. At her request, the venerable Presbyter Magnus arrived, with relics of Lord Andrew, and of many others. These were placed on the altar, and when she had passed a devoted night of vigil, according to the rule, and had prostrated herself in prayer, a brief sleep came over her. God declared to her that her wish was fulfilled, saying to her: "Be aware, blessed one: not only these relics, which Presbyter Magnus brought, are here, but as many as you have collected in the villa Athies, all these have come here too." When she opened her eyes, she saw a most splendid man, who had told this to her, and rejoicing, she blessed the Lord.

14. After she entered the monastery, she gathered a great number of saints (that is, relics) by the most faithful prayers. This the East witnesses, and the North, South, and West confess, because from everywhere she obtained the precious gems, which paradise has hidden in heaven. By her very devotion, as many came as gifts as by her prayers. She entrusted herself to be joined with these by incessantly meditating and by singing hymns and psalms. Finally, concerning the Lord Mammas the martyr, information reached her that his holy limbs rested at Jerusalem. Hearing this, she drank it in avidly and thirstily. Just as a person with dropsy, who increases his thirst by as much as he drinks in, so she, moistened by the dew of the Lord, burned more. She sent the venerable presbyter Reoval, who then was of this world and who still survives in body, to the Patriarch of Jerusalem, asking for a token of blessed Mammas. The man of God received him kindly, and declared the question to the people, seeking the will of God. On the third day, after he had celebrated mass, he approached the tomb of the blessed martyr, with all the people. In a loud voice, he bore witness in full faith of this kind, saying, "I ask you, confessor and martyr of Christ, that if the blessed Radegund is a true handmaiden of Christ, may it be made known to the nations by your power. Grant that, concerning your token, the faithful soul may get what it asks." When the prayer was completed, all the people answered "Amen." He approached the holy tomb, always pronouncing his faith in the blessed one, and touched the limbs [to find out] which one the most blessed one would order him to give to the petition of Lady Radegund. He touched each finger on the right hand, and when he came to the little finger, it detached itself from its own hand at his gentle touch, so that it might

satisfy that desire of the queen and fulfill her wish. The apostolic man sent this finger to blessed Radegund with worthy honor, and from Jerusalem to Poitiers praise of the Lord always sounded in her honor. What do you think? With how burning a spirit, with what faithful devotion, expecting the prize of such a great token, did she deliver herself over to abstinence? But when the blessed queen had received this heavenly gift, she rejoiced with all alacrity, for an entire week, with all her flock, she devoted herself to vigils of psalms and fasting, blessing the Lord because she had deserved to receive such a gift. Thus God does not refuse His faithful who ask. Frequently and sweetly, as if in a figure of speech so that no one could understand, she used to say, "The one who cares for souls must boldly fear praise from everyone." But nonetheless, as much as she wished to avoid this, more and more the Giver of virtues desired to reveal to all the one who was faithful to Him, so that whenever a sick person, imprisoned by whatever illness, called upon her, he received his health (again).

15. The illustrious man, Leo by name, was called to the synod by the apostolic men Bishops Leontius and Eusebius. While he was making his journey, his eyes were clouded by a heavy fog and covered with a mist of blood. He would not have seen the way at all if he had not gone on sustained by his servants. He entered the monastery of the blessed one, where he, devoted to her, had handed over his daughters to be servants of the Lord, and he went into the oratory dedicated to the name of Lady Mary. After the prayer was given, he prostrated himself, full of faith, on top of the hair shirt of the saint, courageously calling upon her. He laid there for a long time, until the pain left, the darkness was put to flight, and the coagulated blood led itself away with the help of the veins. And with clear eyes, he who had come sustained by the hands (of others) went away healthy. He received (his) sight from the hair shirt of the Saint; happy and unharmed he walked to the synod where he had begun (to go). The whole synod heard this later, when he himself told it, and returning from there, he explained this to us with his own mouth. This very devotion to her made him lay[5] the foundation of a basilica for Lady Radegund, and then he gave 100 solidi to build its building. Who can count how many sick have been returned to health by invoking her? Who, therefore, ever saw her and believed her to be an earthbound person? By the God of heaven I speak faithfully and truly, because thus always was her countenance, resplendent with spirit in the eyes of all, so that not unworthily what was going on within was apparent on the outside.

16. After the relics of the saints had been collected, if it could have

been done, she would have asked the Lord Himself, from the seat of His majesty, to dwell visibly here. Although the carnal eye does not see Him, the spiritual mind, attentive with unceasing prayers, contemplates Him. But because the Lord does not deprive those who walk in innocence of good things, and who seek Him with their whole heart, mind and spirit, just as this blessed woman did, divine clemency showed itself to be kindly to her, in whose heart He rested day and night. Thus, just as blessed Helena, imbued with wisdom, full of the fear of God, and glorious with good works, she sought to salute the wood where the ransom of the world had been paid for our salvation, so that He might snatch us from the power of the devil. Thus, she might applaud it, when it was found, with both hands, and when she recognized that it was the Lord's cross that had raised the dead when it touched them, with knee bent to the ground, she might adore the Lord, saying, "In truth you are the Christ, the Son of God, who came into the world and saved your captives, whom you had created, with your precious blood." What Helena had done in the East, blessed Radegund did in Gaul. And because she did not wish to do anything, while she lived, without advice, she sent letters to the most excellent king Lord Sigebert, by whose power that country was ruled. (She requested) that he should permit her, for the safety of the whole country and for the stability of his kingdom, to seek (a piece of) wood from the cross of the Lord from the Emperor. He very kindly offered approval for the petition of the holy queen. She, full of devotion and burning with desire, did not send gifts to the Emperor, because she had made herself a pauper for God. Rather, with continuing prayer, with the company of saints whom she unceasingly kept on invoking, she sent her messengers. But she got what her prayers sought, so that she might glory that she had the blessed cross of the Lord, decorated with gold and gems, and many relics of saints, which the East had, residing in one place. At the petition of the saint, the Emperor sent legates with gospels adorned with gold and gems.

But when the wood where the salvation of the world had hung, reached the city of Poitiers, along with its congregation of saints, the priest of the place, with all the people, wished to welcome it with devotion. Then the Enemy of the human race acted through his lieutenants, so that they would reject the ransom of the world, and not wish to receive it into the city, so that blessed Radegund might lie under tribulations. They were appropriating one thing for another, in the Jewish order, which is not ours to explain. They themselves saw; God knows who are His. But she, with fervent spirit and flashing mind, again sent to the most kindly king, because they did not wish to receive salvation in the city.

Meanwhile, until[6] her messengers returned from the lord king in Tours in his monastery of men which he built so that he might save himself, there she commended the cross of the Lord and tokens of saints, accompanied by the chanting of priests. The sacred cross suffered no less injury through hatred than did the Lord, who was summoned and recalled by a faithful runner before the guards and judges, and patiently bore every unkindness, so that what he had created would not perish. In what great torture she placed herself, in fasting, in vigils, in profusion of tears! With her whole flock she was in sorrow and grief until the Lord looked down on the humiliation of his handmaiden, and put it into the heart of the king, that he should do right and justice in the midst of the people. Thus the devoted king, through his faithful companion Justin the illustrious, sent to the apostolic lord Eufronius, the bishop of the city of Tours (saying) that he should place the glorious cross of the Lord and the reliquaries of the saints in the monastery of Lady Radegund with worthy honor. And this was done.

The blessed one rejoiced with joy with her whole sanctuary, and she took herself and this good gift from heaven, perfectly given to her flock, which she had gathered for the service of the Lord. For she sensed in her spirit that after her passing they would have too little. Although she gloried with the king of heaven, whence she could help them, this best provider of the heavenly gift, this good governess, would not ever leave her sheep. She sent the ransom of the world (consisting) of the token of Christ, which she had sought from a faraway region, for the honor of the place and the salvation of her people in her monastery. There, with the coworking of the strength of God, the powerful minister of heaven, the blind receive their sight, the ears of the deaf are opened, the tongues of the mute return to their duty, the lame walk, and the demons are put to flight. What more? Whoever comes in faith, held by whatever disease, his health returns through the strength of the holy cross. Who could say how great and what kind of gift the blessed one conferred on this city? Wherefore, whoever lives in faith blesses her name. For to the most excellent royal lords and the most serene queen, Lady Bronichild, whom she loved with dear affection, and to the holiest churches and their priests she entrusted her monastery with divine witness.

17. After she received this heavenly gift, the blessed one sent her messengers to the emperor, to give thanks; she sent the previously mentioned presbyter with the others, and with a simple garment [as a gift]. When they were returning, the sea began to be driven by waves, where they experienced many dangers, evidently winds and tempests such as they confessed that they had never seen before. For forty days and forty

nights their ship lay under danger in the midst of the sea. Then, despairing of their lives, having death before their eyes, they made peace among themselves, because the sea wished to swallow them. Seeing themselves in great danger, they raised their voices to heaven, shouting and saying, "Lady Radegund, save your servants—while we are obeying you, may we not perish by drowning. Free us from the danger of death, because the sea is now ready to swallow us while we are still living. Whenever you have been invoked in faith you are merciful; have mercy on us now and help us lest we perish." To these voices in the middle of the sea a dove came, which flew three times around their ship. While the dove was flying on its third turn, in the name of the Trinity, which the blessed one always loved in her heart, the servant of the blessed queen, Banisaios by name, stretched out his hand and plucked three feathers from its tail. When he touched the sea with these, the tempest calmed.

At the invocation of the name of the blessed Radegund the dove that appeared returned her servants from the door of death to life, and a great tranquility was made in the midst of the sea. And they, crying out in a loud voice, said, "You have come, good lady, full of piety, to rescue your captives so that they would not drown in the waves." At the invocation of her, not only her own men but all were freed through the virtue of Lady Radegund herself. The ones who were freed from death brought the very feathers here, framed, and, having promised, gave them to holy places. Whenever she is invoked, she listens kindly. If a fever-ridden person or one having pustules or gripped by whatever illness cannot come to her by reason of the long distance intervening, a candle lit in her name will dispel all fever. Who can say how much she loved her flock? Not if the plectrum moves on (the string of) my tongue with a hundred sounds could it suffice. She established that, while they dined, the lesson should always be read, so that not only would the jaws accept food but also the ears might hear the word of the Lord. Whatever she taught others or whatever she did herself, she always did everything for God. Whatever she prohibited from being done she herself avoided doing; everything in enthusiasm for God and nothing carnally did she do or taste. And because she never wished to be lazy about the work of God, she insisted also on prayer, reading, almsgiving, and preaching incessantly all day long, so that there would be no one who would excuse herself out of ignorance.

18. Finally, she had such a great gift in herself, by the generosity of divine grace, that by imitating the Lord in spirit wherever she went, she followed the teacher of humility, who descended to earth from His heavenly seat. After the flock secluded itself for rest, she stayed up all night in prayer and saved the monastery by (making) the sign of the cross with her

holy right hand. One time when the blessed one was making that sign, one of her sisters saw a thousand demons in the form of goats, standing on top of the wall. When the saint raised her blessed right hand with the sign of the cross, that whole multitude of demons was put to flight and never (re)appeared.

19. In a similar fashion, while she stood before her cell at night, always repeating the office in her heart and mouth—for the perpetual praise of God resounded in the depths of her heart privately—there was a nocturnal bird, which is not pleasing to men, screeching and making a nuisance of itself in a tree in the midst of the monastery. One of those standing with her said to her, "Blessed Lady, if you wish I will drive out the bird in your name." She said to her, "If it is harmful, go in the name of the Lord, nonetheless making the sign of the cross over it." She went and said to the bird, "In the name of our Lord Jesus Christ, Lady Radegund orders you, if you have not come from the side of God, to go away from this place and not presume to sing here within it." Just as if it had heard the word issued forth from the mouth of God, the bird took flight and never (re)appeared. Rightly the birds and the beasts obeyed her, because she never neglected to obey the command of the Lord. And if sometimes she wished to rest because of illness, with a vigilant spirit she would say, as if in warning, (to the one who was) reading the psalm, "Come, speak." It is doubtful to no one that either she was saying the psalms spiritually with the saints, or certainly that sleep did not overcome her.

Her mind was so intent on Christ, that frequently, even (while) positioned in sleep, she was preaching about the future judgment and eternal reward, and having awakened, she used to say to us, "Gather, gather the Lord's wheat, because truly I say to you, it will not be long that you gather it. See what I say: Gather, because you will be seeking that time; truly, truly you will be seeking those days and greatly you will be desiring them." Although then our laziness accepted this lukewarmly, now we prove that what she said has come to pass. That prophecy was fulfilled in us. "I will send famine on the earth, famine," she said, "not of food and water, but of hearing the word of God." May the preachings/predictions which she established be recited; nevertheless that unceasing voice ceased, the desirable warning, the sweet disposition. Oh God, good sculptor, who could ever explain what kind of face, what appearance, what persona she had? But it is punishment to recall this. In truth we humble ones desire the learning in her, her form, face, personality, knowledge, piety, goodness, and sweetness, which she, especially among the rest of mankind, had from God.

20. How holy was her life! How pure and sweet her aspect! Before

the year of her departing, she saw in a vision a place prepared for her. A young man, very rich and very handsome, came to her, and having youthful age as it were, spoke to her with a soft touch and flattering conversation, and she, jealous of herself, rejected this flattery. He said to her, "Why, fired with desire, do you seek me with so many tears, do you petition me with groans, do you demand with prayers poured forth, do you suffer with such great torture for me, who always helps you? You, precious gem, know that you are the first jewel in the diadem on my head." There is no doubt that He, to whom she while living in the flesh gave herself in total devotion, visited her, and showed to her the glory which she would enjoy. But she told this vision secretly, with oaths, to two faithful enough followers, that they should tell no one while she still lived. And there are still many things, great enough, which we pass over because of prolixity, lest our long-windedness cause weariness in our hearers rather than showing elegance of speech. How much we recall about her love, her nourishing, her charity, her preaching, about all her entirely holy association! We are tortured, and sorrowing with swollen eyes, we seek such great piety, but we do not find what we have lost. Oh how harsh a condition has happened to unhappy us! Oh most pious lady, may you obtain from God in heaven that you lead before you the sheep which you gathered. May you, following the Good Shepherd, turn over your flock to the Lord!

21. Now we come to her glorious passing, which we cannot speak of without an abundance of tears. The tears flow from the deepest core and the groans burst forth, but they find no place of consolation while we weep. If we say less about her faithful devotion, then we sin more. Up to the day of her departure (literally, transition) she never ceased to fulfill the office,[7] and she retained in her heart what she began, because it is not he who begins, but he *who perseveres right to the end who himself will be saved.* When her holy little body came to the end of life, drawing out a long martyrdom for the love of the Lord, all the blessed ones gathered, grieving around her bed, weeping and wailing and striking their breasts with hard fists and stones. They raised their voices to heaven, crying and saying, "Lord, do not permit us to suffer such a grave loss! You are taking our light! Why do you leave us in darkness?" And because when she wished to do something very powerful, she always chose to do it on the birthday of the Lord, so her glorious transition happened in this way: early in the morning of the Ides of August,[8] that is, the thirteenth day of the month, her eyes were closed and ours were darkened.

22. Alas for us, because we have sinned our hearts are afflicted in sorrow; we weep and we cry, because we did not deserve to have you with

us longer. That very morning, when such a great evil touched us, when one voice, one lamentation, and one shout penetrated heaven, the stonecutters who were working on the hill heard an angel speaking in the air. One said to the others, "What are you doing? Send her here." Because these voices reached the ears of the Lord, the angels, who were carrying her, answered and said, "It is already done." What shall we do? Paradise has received her, where she glories with the Lord. We believe, because she does not separate us from herself, that she wishes to please Him herself, with whom she reigns. Therefore we must not weep at such a thing, but tremble at it. Indeed, we have lost our lady and mother in the present age, but we have sent her ahead, interceding in the kingdom of Christ. Indeed, she has made wonderful joy in heaven, but left intolerable grief on Earth for us.

23. When her holy spirit traveled from this world to Christ, there was not a priest of the place there. A messenger went to the apostolic man Lord Gregory of Tours, Bishop of the city, and he came. And what he saw with his eyes, while present, before he buried her, concerning her virtues, he inserted in the book of miracles that he composed. When he came to the place where her holy body was lying—a thing which he himself told afterwards, weeping on his oath—he saw an angel in the form of a human. Her face was gleaming like a rose or a lily. Thus he trembled and was struck by fear; just as a devout man, full of God, he stood before the presence of the blessed mother of the Lord. The priest of the place was awaited, so that they might bury her with appropriate honor. The whole congregation was singing psalms, standing around her bed; when the psalming quieted a little bit, there was an intolerable lamentation. For three days the priest was awaited, because he was going around the neighborhood, but because he did not come, the previously mentioned apostolic man, faithful in charity (perfect charity sends fear away) buried her with worthy honor in the basilica founded in the name of Holy Mary, where the sacred bodies of the virgins from her monastery are buried.

24. While her holy body was being carried under the wall with psalms, because she had instituted that no one, while living, should go out of the doors of the monastery, her whole flock was standing on the walls, lamenting, so that their lament overwhelmed the psalms themselves. They gave back tears in place of the psalm, groans instead of chanting, moans instead of the alleluia. They, gravely bearing her absence, asked on high that the bier on which the blessed one was being carried should pause beneath the tower. But so that the Lord might declare his faithful one in the midst of the people, there, where the holy corpse paused, he caused a blind man to see. He who had not seen the

light of day for many years, received his sight; he who had come, led by the hand, went to the holy tomb behind the bier, with no one supporting him, seeing as if he had never had difficulty with his eyes, and even to this day sees clearly.

25. May another miracle not be overlooked. When the bishop buried her, he did not put the cover in place before the local priest came. The free women who carried the candles before her were all standing around the tomb. To each one he gave her own candle with her own name engraved on the candle, and according to regular order, each one gave the candles themselves to the servants. There arose an argument among the people; some were saying that the candles themselves ought to be placed in the holy tomb, while others were saying no. While that was going on, one of the candles jumped from the arm of the boy who was holding all of them, flew high in the air above the whole population, and put itself into the holy tomb, at the feet of the blessed one, and declared what was uncertain. Looking at the name of whose candle it was, the name of Calva was found. Seeing this, the bishop and all the people, marveling at the virtue of the blessed Radegund, blessed the Lord. After her passing, who can count how many worthy things were done, how many people were freed from demons, how many suffering from fever were made healthy?

26. Coming from Burgundy with the apostolic man Leifastus, the bishop, was his abbot, named Abbo. While he was in the city of Poitiers, he suffered a terrible pain of the tooth. Day and night there was one voice, one pain in him. He was hoping that death would come to him, so that he might be without such great pain. He, inspired by divine mercy toward himself, asked that he might be led toward the basilica of the saint. When he entered there, he threw himself on the ground before the holy tomb, with faith. Having death before his eyes, with his teeth he caught hold of the pall on top of the sacred tomb. He had not taken food for seven days nor had he been able to be refreshed with sleep; but with this bite sleep came, the pain went away, and healthy he returned to his lodging. Afterwards many knew this, since he himself referred to it when he confessed that he had been called back from the doors of death by the virtues of Lady Radegund.

27. And because it is the custom for the other monasteries nearby to celebrate the festival of the blessed Hilarius with vigils up to midnight, after midnight each abbot returns to his monastery with his brothers to celebrate the office. While they were keeping the vigil in the basilica of the blessed priest for the entire night, the possessed ones shouted. Among them the Enemy seriously afflicted two women; one especially

was reveling so much that the whole basilica trembled with her shouting. After the venerable man Arnegisselus, the abbot of the basilica of the blessed queen, went out with his monks, going to his own basilica to fulfill the office, which she had loved enough, they heard the very woman come shouting after them. Having entered the basilica, with loud cries they supplicated Lady Radegund to spare them. One of them was the more seriously afflicted, since at that time the worthless spirit had been flagellating her for fifteen years. Then, it is said, at dawn, the raging enemy left the vessel he had invaded. The other one was freed at the third hour (terce) before the door of the basilica itself, and after that the very wicked enemy could not harm them. How generous and rich is the mercy of God, which makes His own to fear; the giver and dispenser of virtues Himself seeks places where He can show His power through His faithful ones. Some were freed at the basilica of the holy man but others were directed to the basilica of Lady Radegund, so that, as her graces were equal, thus her virtue should be shown equal(ly).

28. If one is ill, even despairing of his life, if the guardian of the sacred tomb itself dips the lower cloth into a chalice of water and gives the cup to the fevered one, does not the disease disappear immediately and sleep come as he drinks, lying before her holy tomb? By the generosity of Christ, in all days in the name of the Lord Himself Jesus Christ, many worthy acts are done here, whence she departed. We also worship (her), in whose spirit we have confidence, with faithful devotion and due earnestness on the earth; we rejoice and proclaim that she shines in heaven, with Himself present, who with the Father and the Holy Spirit lives and reigns for ever and ever. AMEN!

—Translation by Jane Crawford

Notes

1. This negative, found in some variant manuscripts, is necessary for the sense.
2. Or "repudiating," MS. alternative.
3. Lit.: from the present.
4. Or "made war on each other."
5. Lit.: *percutio,* strike.
6. Reading *dum,* a MS. alternative for *quod* printed in my text.
7. Or, "run the race."
8. A Wednesday, *quarta feria.*

IV

Muslim Sainthood, Women, and the Legend of Sayyida Nafīsa

Valerie J. Hoffman

Praise be to God, who bestowed the robes of the honor of His graces on His saints (*awliyā'*), for which they praise Him. He has set them apart by His love, and established them in His service. They diligently keep their prayers and supplications to His presence. He has manifested their ranks in sainthood, and those who take precedence are those who are drawn near, and to whom the gates of His presence are opened and the veils of distance removed from their hearts. They are taught by Him, and He treats them kindly by His love, and has kept them safe from their opponents. "Indeed, on the friends of God there is no fear, and neither shall they grieve" (Qur'an 10:62). He has enlightened their inner vision by His favor, and has purified their inner selves (*sarā'ir*), and has shown them the guarded secret. He has protected them from others, and has veiled them from the eyes of the profligates, because they are brides, and criminals do not see the brides. If one of the saints of God passes them, they consider him a heretic or madman. You see them looking at you without seeing. Among them are those who deny the miracles of the saints, and those who belittle their spiritual stations, and those who slander them to their opponents, and those who oppose their spiritual states, and who delve ignorantly into their sayings and mock them.

---

*Some of the material in the first section of this chapter reproduces portions of Chapter 4 of my book, *Sufism, Mystics, and Saints in Modern Egypt* (Columbia, South Carolina: University of South Carolina Press, 1995).

> God mocks them . . . Glory to the One who drew people near to Him and chose them for His service. They do not depart from His gate. Glory to the One who made them stars in the heaven of sainthood, and made them guides for the people of the earth. Glory to the One who permitted them into the presence of His nearness, while the deniers are kept away. The saints are blessed in a paradise of nearness, while the deniers are tortured in a hellfire of banishment and distance (Shaʿrānī n.d., 1:2–3).

Sainthood in Islam

These words, written at the beginning of one of the most popular Sufi books in the Arabic language, a sixteenth-century biographical dictionary of saints written by an Egyptian mystic, articulate many of the components contained in the concept of sainthood (*walāya,* or *wilāya*) in Islam. A *walī* (pl. *awliyā*ʾ) is a "friend" of God, one who has been brought near to Him, granted special favor enabling him to be diligent in worship, purify his soul of its base passions, and receive mystical illumination. The author quotes the one Qur'anic passage employing the word *awliya*ʾ in this sense—a favorite passage, embroidered onto the cloths covering the sepulchres of saints, or engraved on a plaque by their tombs. The Qur'anic passage continues: "Those who believe and are pious will have good news in this world and the next. There is no substituting the words of God. That is the mighty victory" (10:63–64). The "good news" given to the friends of God in the next world is the reward of Paradise; in this world, according to a saying attributed to the Prophet Muḥammad (a *ḥadīth*), it is a sound vision of the spiritual realm (Māhir 1971, 57– 58).[1]

There is no pope or other religious body in Islam authorized to canonize a saint, and the entire phenomenon of sainthood, as it has been traditionally understood, has become controversial in recent times, as Muslim reformers have targeted the traditional veneration of saints as a

---

I present a more extended discussion of women and sainthood in Islam, particularly concerning the ideas of Ibn ʿArabī and Sufi attitudes toward sexuality, in Hoffman-Ladd 1992a. A much more detailed discussion of that topic and the broader issues of women in Sufism and the Sufi Orders, particularly in Egypt, is presented in Chapter 8 of my book, *Sufism, Mystics, and Saints in Modern Egypt.*

form of idolatry. Nonetheless, the concept of sainthood forms an essential component of popular Islam throughout the Muslim world. A saint is anyone—man, woman, or child—who is popularly recognized as having an especially close relationship with God. While some saints are of international reknown, others are of only local importance. The idea of sainthood developed in Sufism (Islamic mysticism), which is the foundation of popular Islam, though not all those reputed to be saints were followers of the Sufi way. Nonetheless, the seven stations of the Sufi path, leading the devotee in stages of discipline from repentance to gnosis, are known as the "stations of the saints" (*maqāmāt al-awliyā'*). The author of a favorite manual on Sufism, al-Qushayrī (died 1072), quotes the famous Sufi theoretician al-Junayd (died 910) as defining the *walī,* first, as someone whose affairs are taken over by God, and, second, as someone whose worship of God is constant, without any defect of rebellion. Both qualities are necessary for someone to be a saint (Qushayrī 200–201).

A favorite divine saying (*ḥadīth qudsī*),[2] after an initial stern warning, describes the condition of a saint:

> Whoever harms one of my saints on earth, I have proclaimed war against him. A servant draws near to Me with nothing better than the fulfillment of his religious obligations, and he continues to draw near to me by performing supererogatory deeds, until I love him. When I love him, I am his hearing with which he hears, his seeing with which he sees, his hand with which he strikes and his foot with which he walks. Were he to ask [something] of Me, I would surely give it to him, and were he to seek refuge in Me, I would certainly give it to him. I hesitate in nothing I am doing so much as I hesitate to take the spirit of my believing servant, because he hates death, and I hate to harm him, although [death] is inevitable (Ibrahim and Johnson-Davies 104–105).

Although the "believing servant" could describe a vast multitude of Muslims, popular interpretation of this ḥadīth limits its application to those holy persons who are considered particularly close to God, so that their prayers are answered, and whose subjugation of their passions and fleshly desires has been so complete that their spirits have become in some sense united with God, as this ḥadīth indicates. They are the ones who are indicated by the Qur'anic verse in which God addresses Satan, saying, "You have no power over My servants" (15:42).

Some people become saints after years of arduous discipline through ascetic practices, self-control, and the constant, repeated practice of recollecting God through reciting one or more of His ninety-nine

Most Beautiful Names. Finally God favors them with a mystical "opening" (*fatḥ*), revelation, or divine disclosure (*tajalliyāt*). They live in a state of nearness to God, often experiencing intense joy, and serve as the perfect channels of God's grace, blessings, and guidance to humanity. They become *shaykhs,* Sufi masters, counselors, and guides. Other people, however, come into sainthood suddenly in a single flash of mystical light that overwhelms their intellects and leaves them in some sense mentally impaired. Such people are *majdhūb* (plural, *majādhīb*), and serve as God's spies and policemen on the earth, but are useless as counselors or guides. They are, in fact, best avoided. It is this perspective on the nature of the divine-human encounter that allows lunatics and eccentrics to be popularly regarded as saints.

One twentieth-century Egyptian shaykh described the saints as resting in a state of equanimity in the presence of God, indifferent to their physical circumstances, rejoicing in nothing but God. Under divine protection, the saint is preserved (*maḥfūẓ*) from error (Raḍwān 1986, 35, 34, 35). This protection of the saints is seen as less absolute that the prophet's immunity (*ʿiṣma*) from error. Qushayrī wrote that the saint who is truly a saint must be in a state of superior spiritual awareness, whereas the person who opposes the law of God in any way is deceived. The saint's state of "preservation" does not mean that he cannot commit an error, but that he will not persist in sin (Qushayrī, 201, 276).

While the Sufi definition of sainthood may depend mainly on inner, and deeply personal, spiritual attributes and an attitude of separation from the world, the average person knows a saint by his or her ability to work miracles, dispense blessing, and function in an intercessory capacity for those in need. The ability to work miracles (*karāmāt*) is a necessary attribute for a saint. Saints communicate with each other and with their disciples over great geographical distances, they can "read hearts," tame and talk with wild beasts, speak any language, discern whether food was ill-gotten, banish evil spirits, heal diseases, procure passports, provide transportation, and cut through bureaucratic red tape, among other things. The ability to appear in more than one place at a time is commonly attributed to various saints, who are witnessed preaching in two different villages at the same Friday noon prayer, or breaking the Ramaḍān fast in two different locations at the same time, or performing the pilgrimage in Mecca while never leaving their home village. Shaykh Aḥmad Raḍwān of Egypt (d. 1967) reportedly used to say that a saint is not a saint until he can appear in forty places at a single time. While some saints engaged in contests of miracles to demonstrate their superiority, Shaykh Abū 'l-Wafā al-Sharqāwī (d. 1961) said that miracles are the menstrual blood of saints, from which they must cleanse themselves in order to enter God's presence, and that public display "breaks the back" (*al-ẓuhūr yuqsim al-ẓuhūr*).[3]

Yet however much popular expectations of usefulness may govern recognition of a person as a saint, the Sufis insist that one important element of sainthood is its hiddenness. The greatest saints, in particular, are hidden among God's servants, and may be serving in very lowly and inconspicuous capacities in society. They may even be despised by the general population. The fourteenth-century Sufi author, Ibn al-ʿAbbād al-Rondī (d. 1390), said that God hides the saints from the masses as a mercy, because a person who knowingly opposes a saint and does not obey him will come under divine wrath. For this reason, some of the gnostics are known by no one (Raḍwān, 35). This hiddenness poses problems: can a saint know he is a saint? What happens if a saint divulges his sainthood? The first question was much discussed by medieval Sufi authors, who were divided on the issue. Contemporary Egyptian Sufis, however much they might agree that the saints are hidden from the recognition of ordinary people, believe it is inevitable that a saint, as a gnostic (one who "knows"), knows that he or she is a saint, although such an individual must regard this as a pure grace from God, without any pride in one's self.

However, a gnostic will always be recognized by other gnostics, and the saints enjoy a communication between them that requires no words or geographical proximity. The saints, in fact, function on two levels, or, one could say, they live in two parallel worlds, an exoteric world in which they dwell with their bodies and interact with other humans in ordinary ways, and an inner world of visions, contemplation, revelations, and communication without words. The death of the body in no way impedes the ability of saints to communicate with the living, as is abundantly clear from tales both old and new. Ibn ʿArabī (1165–1240) wrote that it is entirely unnecessary for saints to meet in their bodies or correspond to each other, and that they do so only as a matter of custom (Sharqāwī 89). The fact that many Sufis have attributed their spiritual knowledge to instruction given through visions by saints either dead or alive, is adequate indication of the continued validity of this type of communication. It may take place through dreams, but it often takes place in the waking state as well.

The hiddenness of the saints, as we have already stated, is thought to be a mercy for ordinary people, because of the danger of opposing a saint. "The saint's anger," said Shaykh Aḥmad Raḍwān, "is the anger of God, and has effect in heaven and on earth." The person who opposes or hates God's saints "dies without the religion of Islam." This is because of the saint's identification with God, as indicated by the previously quoted ḥadīth in which the saint's hearing, sight, tongue, leg, and hand become tantamount to the hearing, sight, tongue, leg, and hand of God. "So whoever draws near to a saint in this state has drawn near to God, and whoever serves him has in reality served God, and whoever hates him has hated God" (Raḍwān, 27, 39). For this reason, the baraka or spiritual power of the saint, which is often defined as "blessing," can just as easily be a curse. As von Grunebaum wrote:

> The popular saint is as quick to harm as he is to help. The baraka is a force which is provoked only with some risk. . . . Thus, depending on whether travelling saints are well- or ill-received, they will cause fountains to spring or dry up, rivers to change their course, or earthquakes to occur. Saints may even openly compete to demonstrate their own superior power or engage in (often distasteful) predictions about the end and the burial place of their "colleagues" (von Grunebaum 1972, 83).

There are many stories of shaykhs who angered Aḥmad al-Badawī and were stripped of their spiritual stations or otherwise punished until they repented and apologized to him (Sharqāwī 207–208). Even today, people tell stories of cars breaking down when their drivers refuse to turn in at the crossroad to Ṭanṭā to honor him with a visit. Yet on most occasions, it is thought that the saint does not intend the harm suffered by his or her enemies.

The saints, both living and dead, play an important role in the lives of the Sufis and of ordinary individuals. The tombs of dead saints are transformed into shrines, perhaps a humble white-washed domed structure, but often attached to a mosque. Sometimes mock tombs are erected to honor a saint whose body is buried elsewhere. The sepulchre, in Egypt called the *tābūt,* is located in the center of the shrine, draped in thick green cloth denoting relationship to the Prophet. The cloth is decorated with the names of the first four Caliphs and Qur'anic verses, often in glittering gold. On top of the cloth, the saint's personal copy of the Qur'an, or another copy, is placed, as well as a turban, blossoms, and handkerchiefs and other items left by visitors. The *tābūt* is usually surrounded by a *maqṣūra,* a high gridwork made of wood or brass, which constitutes a barrier between the faithful and the tomb. The *maqṣūra* is often reinforced by glass, sometimes tinted green, and might be decorated with small colored lights and plaques bearing the name and dates of the saint, or Qur'anic verses. Above the tomb there is a dome denoting the opening toward heaven. If the location of the shrine had not been indicated during the lifetime of the saint by the building of a shrine in anticipation of the saint's body, it is indicated after death either by a vision or by the body itself pulling the pallbearers to the burial site preferred by the saint. Saints' shrines are believed to be places where prayers are most readily answered. Pilgrimage to certain shrines are believed by their devotees to have the same spiritual worth as the hajj, the pilgrimage to the Kaʿba in Mecca that is required of all Muslims.

While Sufis may go to shrines as a regular expression of their devotion, other visitors go to shrines in order to feel peace in their turbulent lives, to seek a place of refuge from their problems, and to appeal to the intervention of the saint. Saints' shrines are perceived as places of mercy for the oppressed, as much as they are places of power.

Visitors to the shrines greet the saint upon entering, just as they would greet a person who is alive. They recite the *Fātiḥa* (the seven-verse opening chapter of the Qur'an, which is a prayer often compared to the "Lord's prayer" in Christianity) on behalf of the saint, both as a courtesy and in hopes of attracting blessing on themselves. Proper etiquette calls for praying two *rakʿas* (cycles of prayer), but in the crowded conditions of visitation days this is often impossible, and in fact is rarely done. Visitors cling to the *maqṣūra,* kissing it, rubbing it and then rubbing their faces in order to transfer some of the saint's baraka to their own bodies. The holiness of the saint radiates out to the surrounding space, conferring holiness on ordinary objects, such as water, candy, or perfume, that are distributed by pious visitors at the shrine. Visitors circumambulate the tomb, absorbing the holiness, fervently muttering prayers all the while. Although Sufi leaders who defend saint shrine visitation stress that the faithful pray not to the saint but to God by virtue of the saint's baraka, the saint is nonetheless directly addressed in verbal petitions and letters, and visitors might make a vow to sacrifice an animal and distribute the meat or some other food to the shrine visitors and the poor if their prayers are answered. Such sacrifices take place outside the shrine. In Egypt, the Sufi ritual of *dhikr* (recollection of God's Names) may be performed both within and outside a shrine on the saint's visiting day or moulid. Visitors also sometimes sing songs of praise to the Prophet and his family. Visiting the shrine places the visitor in direct contact with the holy power inherent in the divine light passed down from the Prophet to his descendants. Some visitors choose to bask in this holy presence by sitting by the shrine, whether reading the Qur'an or simply sitting. Others, particularly women, sit along the outside wall of the shrine for the same reason.

The saints are not all equal in stature, but are ranked according to function and proximity to God, in a hierarchical structure. At the top of the saintly hierarchy is the *quṭb* (Pole or Axis), according to traditional

Sufi terminology, or, in later North African terminology, the *ghawth* (help). There is much disagreement concerning the titles and numbers of the ranks beneath him. According to a saying attributed to the Prophet's cousin and son-in-law, ʿAli ibn Abī Ṭālib, the total number of saints in the world at any one time is 300, of which 70 are *nujabāʾ* (singular, *najīb*), 40 are *awtād* (singular, *watad*), ten are *nuqabāʾ* (singular, *naqīb*), seven are *ʿurafāʾ* (singular, *ʿārif,* the word for gnostic), three are *mukhtārūn* (singular, *mukhtār*), and one who is the *quṭb*. Yet other traditions use different terms and give different numbers. Ibn ʿArabī, the first to elaborate a detailed, systematic hierarchy of saints, said that the number of saints in the world is always at least equal to the number of prophets that have lived since the world began, which, according to traditional Islamic reports, is 124,000. This is necessary because the saints are the heirs of the prophets, and each prophet must have at least one heir among the saints who are alive in the world. If the saints number more than the number of prophets, it is because the inheritance of some prophets has been divided among several saints (Chodkiewicz 1986, 73).

The *quṭb* (Axis) is called such because he is the center on which the world pivots. According to Ibn ʿArabī, he is both the center and circumference of the circle of the universe (Ibn ʿArabī 1948, 2). Though Sufis agree on the existence of a *quṭb* or *ghawth,* there is no agreement concerning his identity. It is typical for a Sufi to hold his own shaykh in such reverence that he believes him to be the *quṭb.*

The saints are to be found all over the world, even in countries where Islam is poorly represented, and they are the source of blessing on that country. The towns of Ṭanṭā and Dasūq in the Egyptian Delta are thought to be blessed even in their economic transactions because of the presence of the tombs of Aḥmad al-Badawī (d. 1276) and Ibrāhīm al-Dasūqī (d. 1295/6), respectively, in their midst (Sharqāwī 26–27). The saints have a trust to fulfill in this world. In Egypt it is said that they meet in a hidden court, presided over by Sayyida Zaynab, that decides the affairs of the living. It is appropriate, therefore, to seek their intercession. Sainthood increases and decreases, as does faith. Although, theoretically, every Sufi shaykh should be a saint and gnostic, and is likely to be regarded as such by his followers, few Sufis are willing to concede that all who take up the role of Sufi shaykh are true saints. But when a shaykh is a true saint and gnostic of God, he can dispense great blessing to his followers.

A ḥadīth sometimes cited to justify popular belief in the baraka of the saints says, "By means of the righteous Muslim, God repulses affliction from one hundred neighbors" (Māhir 90). The presence of the saints provides an opportunity for ordinary people to come in touch with the baraka, or spiritual power, that came into the world with Muḥammad. The touch of a saint's hand, or any object associated with the saint, conveys blessing to those who love God. Loving the saints is a way of expressing love for God, and the saints provide a means of intercession before God.

After the saints die, they are considered to be alive in their tombs, hearing the greeting of their visitors, returning the greeting, and making intercession for them. The spirits of the righteous are free to roam at will, and are even more powerful to act on behalf of the living after death than they were in life. The dead saints are virtually alive, not only in spirit, but often in body as well. In Egypt and Sudan it is not uncommon at the funeral procession of a Muslim saint to see those carrying the bier running at full speed, with the entire procession of people running behind them. It is said that the saint himself or herself is pulling the bier, and the others are hastening to keep up with it. If there are other saints buried in the vicinity, the saint on the bier may hasten to visit those saints before hastening in joy to its final resting place. A ḥadīth says, "God has forbidden the earth to consume the bodies of the prophets." In popular belief, this privilege also applies to the saints. As one Sufi author wrote, "The saint is alive in his tomb, returning the greeting of his visitors. He knows all those who visit him, and he knows their purpose." He proves his point by the fact that the Prophet's wife 'Ā'isha visited the graves of Muḥammad and her father, the first Caliph Abū Bakr, unveiled, but when the second Caliph, 'Umar ibn al-Khaṭṭāb, was buried with them she visited them veiled, because 'Umar was not related to her, and she understood that the righteous dead were alive (Māhir 91). The sixteenth-century Moroccan Sufi, Aḥmad Zarrūq, said that clinging to the dead indicates a lack of faith in the living, but, say the Sufis of contemporary Egypt, the *madad* (assistance) of the dead is stronger than the *madad* of the living, for the dead are in the presence of God, and clinging to them is without ulterior motive.

Egyptian Sufis say that the bodies of those who are pure do not decompose, but are merely sleeping. Although Goldziher speaks of stories of saints preventing their own exhumation, saying this is regarded as a great desecration (Goldziher 2:286), I heard a number of stories in Egypt of successful exhumations of saints whose bodies were being transferred from one place to another, in which the saint was found, after hundreds of years, not to have suffered any decomposition.

Not only are the bodies of the saints immune from decomposition, but, according to many legends, they actually emit a pleasant fragrance, whereas people who are attached to worldly things emit an unpleasant odor even in life. The blood of people who have bad morals and worldly attachments is itself foul-smelling, according to Sufi belief, whereas the blood of those who attach themselves to God is sweet-smelling. Fragrance or aroma and fragrant breezes are metaphors that are often employed in Sufi literature. The association of the tombs of the saints with pleasant aromas is reinforced by the practice of wearing perfume when visiting saints' shrines and rubbing perfume on the hands of other visitors, or showering them with cologne or perfumed water. Some visitors also rub the grid that surrounds the tomb with perfume or hang blossoms around it.

Shaykh ʿIzz al-ʿArab al-Hawārī, a contemporary Sufi of Egypt, related the purity of the saint whose body defies decomposition to its lack of materiality. Some Sufis, when they are very old, devote themselves solely to a life of prayer and meditation, and restrict their diet to the absolute minimum necessary to remain alive. This makes their excretive processes very limited, and in effect reduces the material aspect of their existence. Such ascetics acquire bodies that are said to be "luminous," and like light, incorruptible. Shaykh Muḥammad al-Ṭayyib of Qurna, on the west bank of the Nile opposite Luxor, was of this type. In the years before his death in December 1988, he limited his daily consumption to a few tablespoons of milk, and his health deteriorated to the point where he was virtually unable to move or to respond to the many visitors who came to receive his blessing. His skin was so delicate that his hand remained wrapped in cloth for all visitors who shook it as he mumbled the *Fātiḥa,* the opening chapter of the Qur'an, on their behalf. He was regarded by many in the region as the *ghawth,* and his lifestyle was seen as appropriate to his position. Shaykh ʿIzz indicated that the *ghawth* typically lives in isolated meditation and fasting, in contrast with Ibn ʿArabī's description of the *quṭb* as never going hungry voluntarily, and giving both the body and spirituality its due (Shaʿrānī 1974, 2:70).[4] Nonetheless, saints engage in many different types of lifestyles, and do not come in a particular personality type. A saint may be cantankerous or serene, intellectual or anti-intellectual, meticulously observant of standard etiquette or deliberately flouting social convention.

The Family of the Prophet (*ahl al-bayt*)

Sayyida Nafīsa, whose life will be discussed in this article as a model of sainthood in Islam, is not merely a saint; she is a member of the family of the Prophet—the *ahl al-bayt*. The *ahl al-bayt* (literally, "people of the house") occupy a special position in Sufism because it is thought that their proximity to the Prophet, who (the Sufis say) was created out of a handful of God's own light, has conferred on them unique moral purity and mystical knowledge. Belief in the special qualities of the *ahl al-bayt* originated in Shīʿī Islam, but Sufism has adopted many features of this belief (Hoffman-Ladd 1992b). While some make a distinction between saints (*awliyāʾ*) and descendants of the Prophet (*sharīf*, plural *ashrāf*), in most cases this distinction is moot because nearly all saints claim descent from the Prophet.[5] The *ahl al-bayt* may be seen as a special type of saint, the ultimate exemplars of holiness and purity.

Sometimes the term *ahl al-bayt* is used to refer exclusively to Muḥammad, his daughter Fāṭima, his cousin and son-in-law ʿAlī ibn Abī Ṭālib, and their sons, Ḥasan and Ḥusayn. More often, the term extends to other close descendants of the Prophet, who are very important in Egyptian Sufism and saint veneration because, like Ḥusayn, their shrines may be found in Cairo—ʿAlī and Fāṭima's daughter Zaynab ("Sayyida Zaynab"), Ḥusayn's son ʿAlī Zayn al-ʿĀbidīn, Ḥusayn's daughters Fāṭima al-Nabawiyya and Sayyida Sukayna, ʿAlī's daughter Ruqayya, Sayyida Nafīsa, a great-granddaughter of the Prophet's grandson al-Ḥasan, and Sayyida ʿĀʾisha, a daughter of the sixth Shīʿī Imām, Jaʿfar al-Ṣādiq (d. 765). A contemporary scholar, Yusuf Ragib, has cast doubt on the authenticity of most of these tombs. The tomb of Sayyida Zaynab, he says, was simply that of an unknown Zaynab until it was identified as that of Ḥusayn's sister in the writings of Shaʿrānī; the real Sayyida Zaynab never came to Egypt at all. He points out that the oldest mention of Sayyida Nafīsa, whom Louis Massignon had called "the true patron saint of Cairo," comes more than 150 years after her death, and that in a Shīʿī document (suspected of distorting history for religious and political purposes). Ragib likewise labels the tombs of Ruqayya, Sukayna, and ʿĀʾisha as spurious. Ruqayya was never in Egypt, he asserts, and the existence of a daughter of Jaʿfar named ʿĀʾisha is entirely unknown (Ragib 1976).

Such academic doubts, however, are unknown and irrelevant to the pious in Egypt, who are certain of the presence of these holy personages in their midst. Egyptians believe that their love for the *ahl al-bayt* is greater than that of other Sunni Muslim countries, without, in their opinion, rising to the idolatrous extremism of Shiʿism. The legends of Zaynab and Nafīsa and the arrival of Ḥusayn's head in Egypt, among others, depict the Egyptians welcoming in great throngs these venerated members of the Prophet's family who had suffered persecution and expulsion in other lands. Egypt is unusually blessed because of the presence of so many tombs of the *ahl al-bayt,* say some Egyptians. The *ahl al-bayt* are extolled for their purity, piety, humility, knowledge, miracles, and ability to guide the wayward back to the true faith. They are, according to one author, "the tree of prophecy, the locus of God's message, a spring of mercy, a mine of knowledge, fountains of wisdom, the treasures of the Merciful. . . . By them we are guided from the shadows. They are the repository of the secret of the Chosen One [Muhammad]" (Abū 'Alam 9).

Love for the *ahl al-bayt* is a holy obligation for all who love God and His Messenger. Whoever loves them may expect God's mercy, and whoever hates them may expect God's wrath (Ibrāhīm 5–6, Abū 'Alam 9). The family of the Prophet are a security for the welfare of the people of the earth. Aḥmad ibn Ḥanbal (d. 855) records this ḥadīth in his collection, the *Musnad:* "The stars are a security for the people of heaven, so that if the stars disappeared, so would the people of heaven. The people of my house are a security for the people of the earth, so that if the people of my house disappeared, so would the people of the earth" ('Alī 19). Love for the *ahl al-bayt* has tremendous spiritual benefits for those who travel the Sufi path, not only because of the high stature of the *ahl al-bayt,* but also because love is the foundation of the Sufi path. Writes one author, "Loving them is the foundation and basis of the way to God. All the spiritual states (*aḥwāl*) and stations (*maqāmāt*) are degrees of love" ('Alī 8). Therefore a song popular among Egyptian Sufis says, "Love for them, my friend, is the best worship."[6]

Women and Sainthood in Islam

Although men have more rights than women in Islamic law, many Muslims today insist that the Qur'an assigns equal spiritual worth to men and women.[7] God created all humanity, male and female, from a single soul (4:1, 7:189). Women are promised the same spiritual rewards as men for the fulfillment of their religious duties, although the depictions of Paradise in the Qur'an, replete with virgins for the sexual pleasure of the believers, are obviously drawn with men in mind. Although much is made in Islamic culture of the importance of modest dress for women, the Qur'an is ambiguous in its definition of modesty norms, and enjoins modesty on men as well as women. However, the fear of sexual temptation often dominates all other concerns pertaining to women in Islamic discourse (Hoffman-Ladd 1987; Ahmed 1992). In Arab society, honor is conceived in a corporate sense in families, and the honor of men resides in the chastity of their women. The very high cultural value given to the chastity of women encouraged Muslims to develop rigorous modesty codes for women, which often result in the frank deprivation of women's spiritual and intellectual lives.

Furthermore, in most Muslim societies, as we can document from both medieval literature and contemporary ethnographic studies, men regard women as more prone to immoral behavior than men, by virtue of their diminished intellectual capacity, and women are seen as a disruptive element in society. This belief is supported by a number of *ḥadīths,* which, while unlikely to be the actual words of the Prophet, do reveal the thinking of Muslims in the eighth through tenth centuries. The frequency with which these sayings are repeated today indicates that they continue to influence the thinking of contemporary Muslims. These sayings include "the majority of the inhabitants of hell are women," and "I leave my community no temptation more harmful to men than women," and "when a man and a woman are alone together, Satan is the third party." One hadith goes so far as to say, "When you see a woman coming toward you, it is Satan approaching." Nonetheless, there have always been some women who have overcome the enormous barriers of their culture, distinguished themselves as religious scholars, and acquired a reputation for holiness on a par with men. Such women are found especially among the Sufis.

The most famous of the female Sufis is undoubtedly the eighth-century celibate mystic and lover of God, Rābiʿa al-ʿAdawiyya (Smith 1928). The majority of early Sufi women were celibates and practiced extreme forms of asceticism. By maintaining a celibate lifestyle, they rejected the guardianship of men and the requirement of obedience to men, as well as the burdens and responsibilities of being a wife and mother. Extreme abstinence from food also inhibits menstruation, which, under Islamic law, prevents women from prayer. Fasting, then, becomes a tool for ensuring their constant access to the presence of God on a par with men (Elias, 210–211). There were married Sufi women as well, such as the ninth-century Fāṭima of Nishapur, wife of Aḥmad ibn al-Khiḍrūyya, who was consulted by such Sufi luminaries as Dhū al-Nūn al-Miṣrī and Abū Yazīd al-Bisṭāmī (Elias 213; Nurbakhsh 144–146; Amri 158–159).[8] The number of women listed in the Sufi biographical dictionaries is fewer than the number of men, and often they are referred to as the wife of so-and-so, or remain utterly nameless, such as "the woman whom Dhū al-Nūn met." One modern Egyptian writer, speculating on the paucity of names of female Sufis and saints in the biographical dictionaries, suggests that this could not be due to a lesser number of women than men, but was probably due to male bias or female seclusion and shyness. Sayyida Nafīsa is the highest model of female piety, he says, but she is by no means alone in living a life of spiritual heroism (Hamza 137–140). Although more is known of Sufi women in the earliest centuries, Sufism continued to produce great women saints in later centuries, as Ibn ʿArabī's account of the miracles of various Sufi women, including one who was his teacher, illustrates (Ibn ʿArabī 1971, 142–146, 154–155).

Yet the archetypal Sufi remains a man. Sufi ethics came to be known as *futuwwa,* "young manliness," based on the word *fatā,* meaning "young man," literally a code of chivalry that demanded courage, self-denial and heroic generosity. This corresponds to the ancient Arab ethic known as *muruwwa,* "manliness," which upheld similar virtues of courage, extravagant hospitality and indulgence toward those who are weak. It is significant that the Sufi biographer, Farīd al-Dīn ʿAṭṭār (d. 1220), listed Rābiʿa al-ʿAdawiyya among the men, rather than among the women. He explains that it is not the outward form that counts, but the intention of the heart, and said, "When a woman becomes a 'man' in the path of God, she is a man and one cannot anymore call her a woman" (ʿAttar, 40). ʿAttar likewise said that the first "man" to enter Paradise will be Mary, mother of Jesus. He explained that "wherever these people, the Sufis, are, they have no separate existence in the Unity of God. In the Unity, what remains of the existence of 'I' or 'thou'? So how can 'man' or 'woman' continue to be?" (Smith, 2). Jamal Elias reports that "biographical dictionaries often have a section entitled 'Women who achieved the status of men' and the Indian saint Farid al-Din Ganj-i Shakar could refer to a pious woman as 'a man sent in the form of a woman'" (Elias, 211). Although this "compliment" paid to Rābiʿa and other Sufi women implies the degradation of the female sex as a whole and that true spirituality is normally found only among men, it also indicates that the sex of the body is not a barrier to the inspiration and grace of God. For this reason Annemarie Schimmel comments, "One should not be misled by the constant use of the word 'man' in the mystical literature of the Islamic languages: it merely points to the ideal human being who has reached proximity to God where there is no distinction of sexes; and Rābiʿa is the prime model of this proximity" (Schimmel 1981, 151).

At times, however, one cannot be so sure that the use of the word "man" is meant in a gender-neutral sense in Sufi sources. Muslim scholars debated whether women in paradise would, like men, enjoy the vision of God, or whether they would be cloistered in the heavenly pavilions, and Sufis discussed whether women were included in the council of saints that gathered around the *quṭb* in the invisible hierarchy of this world. The seventeenth-century Moroccan saint, ʿAbd al-ʿAzīz al-Dabbāgh (d. 1719/20), said that some women would attend, but "their numbers are few" (Chodkiewicz 1993, 9).

Although Sufi literature is directed toward a male audience in a context where the superiority of men over women is assumed to be the natural order, some women nonetheless did participate in the Sufi Orders in medieval Islam. There were Sufi teachers in Mamluk and Ottoman times that catered to women, and some shaykhs admitted women into their Orders, although this and the participation of women in dhikr were denounced by other Sufis (Winter 131; ʿAbd al-Rāziq 28–32). According to the Egyptian ʿAbd al-Wahhāb al-Shaʿrānī (d. 1565), none of the women learned anything from their husbands, so the Sufi shaykhs had to give special attention to teaching them the rules of religion and their obligations in marriage and society (Shaʿrānī n.d. 2:111). Aḥmad al-Ghazālī (d. 1123), the brother of the previously mentioned Abū Ḥāmid al-Ghazālī, deplored the loosening of morals that had occurred over time in the musical gatherings of the Sufis, as evidenced by the fact that women and adolescents were allowed to attend (Meier 218). It appears to have been rare for a woman to become an officially recognized *shaykha,* a most noteworthy exception being Zaynab Fāṭima bint al-ʿAbbās (d. 1394), shaykha of the women's retreat house (*ribāṭ*) in Cairo belonging to the Baghdādiyya Order (ʿAbd al-Rāziq, 28). The *ribāṭ* was founded in 1285 by Princess Tadhkaray for Zaynab bint Abū 'l-Barakāt "al-Baghdādiyya" "and her women" (Ahmed, 110). Some men's Sufi retreat houses may have included women, for Maqrīzī says that one of them had a bathroom for women in addition to the bathroom for men (Ṭawīl, 42).

There were women shaykhas and scholars of the law in medieval times, most of them widows or divorcees, who lived in extreme abstinence and worship in Sufi *ribāṭs* (ʿAbd al-Rāziq 31). It appears that after the tenth century only women who had already completed their duty of marriage were free to devote themselves to the mystical life. *Ribāṭs* also functioned as places of refuge for divorced women who hoped to remarry and wished to keep their reputations unsullied (Goldziher 2:274–277). The Maghribi writer Ibn al-Ḥājj, who opposed popular religion in general, compared the Sufi women to Christian nuns, and criticized them for raising their voices during dhikr, for part of the expected modesty of women was that no one should hear their voices (ʿAbd al-Rāziq, 32). On the other hand, his countryman, the famous Sufi Muḥammad ibn Sulaymān al-Jazūlī (d. 1465), after his experience with a "mysterious but crucial figure of a 'hidden' woman saint," encouraged women to participate in his Order (Cornell, 501). It is difficult to assess the extent to which women participated in the Sufi Orders and assumed spiritual leadership over women or men. The sources are largely silent on this subject, a silence which could easily, but perhaps mistakenly, be construed as a lack of female participation. But in Egypt today, though the Supreme Council of Sufi Orders officially denies women membership in the Sufi Orders, and a woman can never be named head of an Order, unofficially women are very active in the Orders and sometimes assume *de facto* spiritual authority over both women and men (Hoffman 1995, Chapter 8). In Syria and Pakistan, and probably other countries as well, women often have groups that parallel male Sufi groups. Such groups do not necessarily receive official public recognition. The strength of culturally induced shyness in women, considered an essential part of their modesty, may be illustrated by an experience I had in Egypt when I was researching the religious lives of Muslim women there. A man gave me a book on women in Islam, on which he was listed as the author. He told me, "My wife actually wrote the book, but she had me put my name down as the author, out of considerations of modesty."

Sufi tradition represents a constant tension between the broader cultural perspective that women are the source of all evil, and a danger to the spiritual welfare of men, a view espoused by the Sufi writer al-Hujwīrī (d. ca. 1071) in a discussion favoring celibacy over marriage (Hujwīrī, 360–366), and the mystical perspective that the mystic who has entered into the presence of God has gone beyond the distinctions of the flesh. The implications of this latter perspective are vast, allowing for the possibility not only of saintly women, but women exercising spiritual authority over men (a possibility totally denied by non-Sufi Islam), even for a woman to attain the highest spiritual rank, that of *quṭb*. Ibn ʿArabī explicitly says that this is possible, and indeed has occurred. He says concerning the "complete human" (usually translated erroneously as "the perfect man") that it may be a man or a woman. Michel Chodkiewicz writes that, for Ibn ʿArabī "manhood" (*rujūliyya*) "expresses the plenitude of a human perfection that is sexually undifferentiated," and that Ibn ʿArabī believed that the "perfection" Muḥammad attributed to Mary, the mother of Jesus, implied that she had reached the rank of prophethood (Ibn ʿArabī 1966, 1:447, 541, 3:88–89; Chodkiewicz 1993, 12–14). This stands in stark contrast to the writings in standard Qur'anic exegeses that interpret the "rank" men enjoy over women in the Qur'an (2:228) to indicate a vast array of natural, intellectual, and spiritual advantages, including the exclusive enjoyment of the rank of prophet (Ṭabarī 4:535–536; Ibn Kathīr 1:536; Zamakhsharī 1:505; Badawī 1:207). Ibn ʿArabī's attitudes toward women changed, according to his own testimony, from aversion to love, following extended meditation on a ḥadīth in which Muḥammad says, "Three things have been made beloved to me in this world of yours: women, perfume, and prayer." He noted that Muḥammad's love for women did not spring from his own nature, for the hadith specifies that God had "made them beloved to" him. Ibn ʿArabī writes, "I feared God's wrath, for I hated what God had made beloved to His Prophet." He states, "Whoever loves women as Muḥammad did, loves God" (Ibn ʿArabī 1966, 4:84). One of the qualities of the *quṭb,* he writes, is love for women (Ibn ʿArabī 1966, 2:573–574). The *quṭb* loves beauty in all its forms, for they all express the absolute beauty of the divine (Ibn ʿArabī 1966, 2:574). This idea has led some Sufis to seek out the company of that which best reflects the divine beauty, a beautiful girl or a handsome youth. The gnostic's desire for women, according to Ibn ʿArabī, is the desire of the whole for its part as well as the desire and love of the older for the younger, because it has come more recently from God (Ibn ʿArabī 1966, 2:189–190).[9] He concludes, "Whoever knows the value and secret of women does not abstain from loving them. Rather, loving them is part of the perfection of the gnostics; it is a prophetic inheritance and a divine love" (Ibn ʿArabī 1966, 2:190). He says that disciples should follow the rule of their shaykhs concerning keeping the company of women, but if they are true shaykhs they will not be harsh with their disciples (Ibn ʿArabī 1966, 2:190). He adds that one should keep company with beardless youths or women only for the sake of God, and implies that if it is done without this goal, the person suffers (Ibn ʿArabī 1966, 2:191). Setting even more stipulations, he adds:

> The disciple should not take up the company of women until he himself becomes a woman. If he becomes female and attaches to the lower world and sees how the higher world loves it, and sees himself in every spiritual condition and moment in perpetual sexual union as a female (*mankūḥan dāʾiman,* i.e., assuming the passive role in an unceasing act of coition) and does not see himself in his spiritual insight as male first, but purely female, and he becomes pregnant from that marriage and gives birth—then he may keep company with women and incline toward them, and love for them will not harm him. As for the gnostics' keeping company with women, [permission to do so] is absolute, because they see the absolute, holy, divine hand in their giving and taking. Everyone knows his own spiritual condition (Ibn ʿArabī 1966, 2:192).

The Sufi is female in his relation to God, but he is active, like God, in his relation to woman, for man is to woman as God is to man.

The spiritual man and woman may experience a freedom to interact with each other that normal social restrictions do not allow. In Egypt today, men and women who follow the Sufi path occasionally blatantly flout social convention, scandalizing other Muslims but expressing the insignificance of gender once one has entered into the presence of God. Shaykh ʿIzz al-ʿArab al-Hawārī was, in his younger days, a spiritual son of a well-known woman saint and spiritual guide, Ḥāgga Zakiyya ʿAbd al-Muṭṭalib Badawī (1899–1982).[10] He used to sleep with his head on her lap, and she called him her "daughter," not her son (a nice reversal of the "compliment" paid to Rābiʿa), to indicate that labels of the flesh had been overcome and they had returned to the innocence of children. Any lustful thought invalidates this type of free interaction, which is why it is not encouraged for those who have not mastered their fleshly desires. It is said that Fāṭima of Nishapur used to sit regularly, unveiled, with Abū Yazīd al-Bisṭāmī, until one day he complimented her on the henna on her hands. Having noticed the beauty of her body, she deemed him no longer qualified to sit with her face-to-face.

Just as sainthood in general does not presuppose a particular personality type, so is it for women, even women who are members of the *ahl al-bayt.* Sayyida Nafīsa, the great-granddaughter of the Prophet's grandson al-Ḥasan, may be contrasted with Sayyida Zaynab, the Prophet's granddaughter. Both are said to be women of great learning and exemplary piety, enthusiastically welcomed by the people of Egypt. According to popular belief in Egypt, Sayyida Zaynab shares with her brother al-Ḥusayn (d. 680) and the legal scholar Muḥammad ibn Idrīs al-Shāfiʿī (d. 819/20) the honor of sitting on the "hidden court" that decides matters affecting the world of the living. Concerning Sayyida Nafīsa, who is often nicknamed *nafīsat al-ʿilm* ("gem of knowledge"), it is said that many scholars came to learn from her, including the great legal scholars, Aḥmad ibn Ḥanbal and the previously mentioned Shāfiʿī. The latter allegedly became her close friend, and she prayed (fully veiled) at his funeral. Yet as characters, the two women are strikingly different. Zaynab, the "heroine of Karbalāʾ" to quote the title of a popular modern biography (Bint al-Shāṭiʾ 1966), valiantly risked her own life to protect her brother's son, and rebuked the Umayyad Caliph to his face. She represents courage that stands in the face of oppression. She is a militant model of female sainthood that implicitly challenges the dominant cultural model for women—shy, weak, vulnerable. Nafīsa, on the other hand, despite her status as a teacher of the leading male scholars of law, is in many ways a model woman, depicted as shy, modest, weak, weeping, victimized by her husband as well as by rulers. Yet the contemporary popular accounts of her life appear to challenge the dominant notions about the appropriateness of women's invisibility and subordination. The 20th-century Egyptian writer, Aḥmad al-Shihāwī Saʿd Sharaf al-Dīn, portions of whose account of Sayyida Nafīsa's life are translated in the following, criticizes her husband for abandoning his wife, and speaks warmly of her close friendship with al-Shāfiʿī, in whom she found the friendship and mutuality she never had with her husband. Modern Egyptian renditions of the stories of Zaynab and Nafīsa implicitly challenge dominant cultural norms of femininity, though permission to do so is apparently linked to their special status as saints and members of the *ahl al-bayt.*

SAYYIDA NAFĪSA BINT AL-ḤASAN (762–824 A.D.)

What follows is a translation of portions of a short book that is partly an apologetic for devotion to the ahl al-bayt, *and is partly intended as a devotional meditation on the life of Sayyida Nafīsa. It is written by a contemporary Egyptian preacher and prayer leader, Aḥmad al-Shihāwī Saʿd Sharaf al-Dīn, and it is entitled, simply,* Al-Sayyida Nafīsa, daughter of Sīdī Ḥasan al-Anwar. *The book is very repetitive and indulges in emotional excess in describing the spirituality of Nafīsa's family and contemporaries, a trait not uncommon in this type of writing, but one that virtually mandates shortening in translation. The author uses a literary style of successive phrases that repeat the meaning of the first but use different words. Such a style would be difficult and tedious to duplicate in English, and I have preferred to reduce such redundancies, sometimes without inserting elliptical dots, in order to avoid filling the pages entirely with such dots. I have employed such dots only where I omitted entire sentences. In contrast with the extremely brief summaries of saints' lives and their wise sayings and miracles that characterize traditional Sufi biographical dictionaries, this author attempts to make his booklet read like a novel, filling in speculative details about the thoughts and motivations of the actors in the story without allowing, however, the slightest humanizing trait that might diminish the exalted stature of Sayyida Nafīsa or her father, and adding details intended to evoke an atmosphere of intense spirituality. The author explains that Ḥasan al-Anwar had had ten sons and longed for a daughter, despite the usual dislike of daughters, in order to receive the blessings promised by the Prophet for those who raised their daughters with love and care.*

Our lord Ḥasan was sitting in the sacred house [the Kaʿba] in a religious study group, discussing the law with them, and exploring the oceans of the Qur'an in order to extract its previous pearls . . . when someone came to him bringing this good news: "My lord, rejoice!

Tonight a beautiful baby girl has been born to you. I have never seen any face more beautiful than hers, or a more illuminated forehead. . . ." When the shaykh heard this news he could not control himself for joy, but fell to the ground in prostration, thanking God for what He had graciously given him, highly esteeming what He had bestowed upon him, praising Him for the answer to his prayers. . . . He commanded the people, "Call her Nafīsa [which means "precious"], for she will be precious, God willing."

[Ḥasan al-Anwar told the following dream during the first year after Nafīsa's birth, directly after the family moved from Mecca to Medina:] "I saw the Prophet in my sleep tonight. He welcomed me to Medina, and he said to me, 'Ḥasan, I am pleased with your daughter Nafīsa because of your pleasure with her, and God the exalted is pleased with her because of my pleasure.' " . . . From that day, our lord Ḥasan knew that his daughter Nafīsa had a great stature and a bright future filled with glory and miracles. He took care to educate her and give her the best upbringing. He taught her to memorize the Qur'an, and taught her the *Ḥadīth* of the trustworthy Prophet, and taught her the ways of the righteous and the characteristics of the pious. . . . He had her share with him in his devotion and worship, and recite with him all his *aḥzāb* and *awrād.*[11] She often accompanied him to the Prophet's mosque to attend the communal prayer and circles of learning, to hear lessons on law, and to join them in the recitation of the Qur'an. . . . She never left her father's side, but learned from his example of piety and high morals. Prayer was made beloved to her, and worship was made beautiful in her heart; her breast was opened to the light of faith, and her soul was mixed with the sweetness of obedience. While she was still young she prayed: "My God, prevent anything from diverting my heart's attention away from you. Make beloved to me all that brings me close to you, and make the way of obedience to You easy for me. Place me among the people of your friendship [saints]. You alone are the one who is sought in hard times, and You alone are the goal in adversity and calamity."

The greatest and most pious of the religious scholars Nafīsa knew was Mālik ibn Anas, may God be pleased with him, about whose knowledge everybody spoke, especially those in Medina who admired his unique book, *Al-Muwaṭṭa'*.[12] It was the first book of Ḥadīth ever written, and it became very famous and much admired. . . . Sayyida Nafīsa, may God be pleased with her, was in the first row of those who sat with the Imam and listened to him. She was among the vanguard of those who read his book and understood it. . . . The lady had a great intellect, and high spiritual ambition, true determination, sound thought, a pure spirit, and serious effort. . . .

Sayyida Nafīsa did not cease from her earliest youth to devote herself to worship and obedience, and to strive to please God in learning and good deeds. Her femininity matured and she became known for her beauty. . . . The righteous desired her, and serious youths desired to marry her, especially those who belonged to the *ahl al-bayt*. . . . The one who loved her and desired her most was Isḥāq, son of Jaʿfar al-Ṣādiq [great-grandson of Muḥammad's grandson, Ḥusayn], who was known among the people as "Ishaq the Trustworthy." . . . This youth was no stranger to the ʿAlid family, but came from the best genealogy, the purest and most noble, the most knowledgeable and pious, with the best morals and religion. He was the son of Jaʿfar al-Ṣādiq, son of Muḥammad al-Bāqir, son of ʿAlī Zayn al-ʿĀbidīn, son of our lord Ḥusayn, son of our lord ʿAlī ibn Abī Ṭālib, may God be pleased with all of them. . . . [Ḥasan al-Anwar has a dream in which the Prophet commands him to marry Nafīsa to Isḥāq.] The ʿAlids rejoiced greatly in this marriage, which united the branches of Ḥasan and Ḥusayn [the two sons of ʿAlī and grandsons of the Prophet]—a good sign, a symbol of the unity of the whole and a joining of ranks. Sayyida Nafīsa was foremost among the *ahl al-bayt* in rejoicing over this marriage. . . . Isḥāq took her with him to Mecca, but she did not neglect, before leaving Medina, to enter the mosque of the Prophet and pray at his grave, to sit in his room, and bid farewell to her grandfather,[13] the Apostle. . . .

Her new house did not divert her from the burdens of obedience and worship she had placed on herself, fasting, rising in prayer during the night, remembering [God], asking His forgiveness, reciting *aḥzāb* and *awrād*, reciting the Qur'an at dusk and in the darkness of night. The duties of marriage did not keep her from fasting and attending religious lessons, studying the law and religion, and circumambulating the house of God at all times. All this was not enough, . . . but her soul longed to visit our lord Abraham.[14] She would often say to her husband Isḥāq, "I long to visit the Friend of God (*khalīl Allāh*), Abraham." He would promise her that they would do so as soon as they had the opportunity and circumstances permitted, when God prepared the way for them. But her longing to visit our lord Abraham stirred her, and yearning to see his tomb seized her. . . . She wept bitterly, and asked God night and day, silently and audibly pleading with Him to prepare the way for her. . . . Her longing increased until Isḥāq found that her gaunt body bore the marks of her intense longing and love. . . . Finally she went to visit him.

Her eyes were adorned with his lights, she roamed in the kingdom of his secrets, and in her body and heart she circumambulated his tomb. There in his pure courtyard, at his gate where throngs of pilgrims passed, in his blessed place of visitation, in his vast court where he received his guests, she shed tears and poured forth words, asking God to immerse her heart in the blessings and fragrances of the Friend, and to cause her to be complete with his divine effusions and graces [*karāmāt,* which can also mean miracles]. Then she sat in the shrine and began to read in God's book the description of His Friend, Abraham. When her heart and emotions calmed down, she dozed in the hospitality of the father of the prophets. . . . She had barely begun to sleep when she saw the Friend of God in her sleep welcoming her and greeting her, speaking to her spirit, counseling her, and telling her of her high standing with God. . . .

She returned to Mecca after visiting Abraham, but she did not remain there because of political circumstances that forced her to return to Medina. There she remained for three years, during which she performed the pilgrimage thirty times, walking the whole way.[15] If a caravan offered her a ride, she refused, saying, "My grandfather Ḥasan used to perform the pilgrimage on foot, though he had beautiful horses and fine camels, out of desire for a spiritual reward and the pleasure of God."

In the next section, the author gives his interpretation of a very touchy subject: the persecution of the Prophet's family by the leaders of the Sunni Islamic state. As a Sunni who loves the family of the Prophet, the author is at pains to uphold what he sees as their right to honor and preference, but as a Sunni he wishes to avoid inserting Shīʿi implications by making this persecution a brief and unfortunate phase in ʿAbbāsid rule, not a permanent feature of their policy. The ʿAbbāsid Caliph al-Manṣūr (754–775), says the author, had appointed Ḥasan al-Anwar governor of Medina, but the great love of the people for Ḥasan aroused the Caliph's jealousy. He dismissed Ḥasan and arrested him, confiscated his property, and launched a full-scale persecution of the ahl al-bayt.[16] *When he died, his successor al-Mahdī (775–785) released Ḥasan from prison and sought to rectify the injustices committed by his father.*

Sayyida Nafīsa was held in high esteem by the Muslims in general, and in the souls of the Egyptians in particular. They often met with her during the pilgrimage seasons, and out of their love and admiration for her and their respect for her knowledge and virtue, they asked her to visit their country. . . . When the Caliph oppressed the *ahl al-bayt* . . . they inevitably began to think of choosing a place other than Medina as their home. . . . It was the good fortune of Egypt and the Egyptians that the *ahl al-bayt* chose their country to be their second home and their safe residence. . . . They were helped in their decision by the fact that a portion of their family that had been cut off from them was there, and needed to be reconnected. There [in Egypt] was the visiting place of the heroic fighter, the eternal lady, the patient believer, the pious saint, the pure lady, Sayyida Zaynab, daughter of ʿAlī, sister of Ḥasan and Ḥusayn, daughter of Fāṭima al-Zahrā', and granddaughter of the Prophet Muḥammad. She was the first fruit of the *ahl al-bayt* and she was the first to honor the land of Egypt [with her presence]. There was Sayyida Sukayna, daughter of Ḥusayn and sister of our lord ʿAlī Zayn al-ʿĀbidīn. And there were others. . . .

The Egyptians welcomed the arrival of the *ahl al-bayt* with great joy, considering their coming to Egypt a source of pride and honor for their country for days and years to come. For this reason they competed in efforts to give them honor and receive them as guests in their homes. . . . Jamāl ibn al-Jaṣṣāṣ obtained what no one else did, for he alone had the honor of being their host. They settled in his house, where he gave them every honor and the best reception. His home became a Kaʿba for those coming from every quarter, seeking the baraka of the pure ones who stayed there, and to see the grandchildren of the Apostle. They did not cease to come until the house was filled with them. [The crowds impinged on the lives of the *ahl al-bayt* to the point that they were prevented even from praying and performing their devotional exercises.] Sayyida Nafīsa was among those who were most concerned over this situation, . . . and she could see no other solution than to return to the Ḥijāz whence they had come. . . . [Her family agreed, but when they announced this to the Egyptians, they protested vehemently, and begged them tearfully not to leave, but to no avail. It was only with the intervention of the governor of Egypt, al-Sarī ibn al-Ḥakam, who appealed personally to Sayyida Nafīsa, that the *ahl al-bayt* were persuaded to remain in Egypt. When the governor heard Sayyida Nafīsa's complaints about the cramped conditions under which she was living and the crowds that interfered with her devotional life, he offered her a spacious home in Darb al-Sabāʿ, and proposed allowing visitors only two days a week, Wednesday and Saturday. She agreed to these terms.]

In this way God blessed [the governor's] intercession and by it Egypt received honor and glory, blessings and gifts. The virtuous, blessed, and fortunate lady lived in Egypt with her family, and the land of Kināna[17] gained another portion of the *ahl al-bayt* to add to the portion it already had. . . .

After al-Sarī ibn al-Ḥakam, a tyrannical governor named al-Khaṣīb ibn ʿAmr ruled Egypt. He oppressed the people, . . . filling them with fear and anxiety. . . . No one among them could confront him. . . . A number of the scholars of the law and religion and the leading merchants went to Sayyida Nafīsa's gate and spoke to her of the governor's injustice, and requested that she look into the matter for them or think of a way out of their dilemma. She acceded to their request, and was not too haughty to do so, but promised them good. Then they left her, thanking her for her graciousness. She took a parchment and wrote:

> In the name of God, the Compassionate, the Merciful.
> From the servant of God, Nafīsa daughter of al-Ḥasan, to al-Khaṣīb ibn ʿAmr, governor of Egypt:
> Peace be upon you. It is the ruler's right that his subjects correct him if he deviates from the truth, and guide him if he strays from the right path. You have possessed and imprisoned, you have taken mastery and coercively exerted control. You have plundered and committed immoral acts. Great provision has come to you, and you have been blessed. Do you not know that the arrow of the night operates,[18] especially from hearts you have hurt and livers you have made hungry, and bodies you have stripped bare? It is doubtful that the oppressed will die and the oppressors remain. Do what you like—we are patient! Oppress us, for we take refuge with God! Do us injustice, and we complain to God, and He will know those who oppress, and will turn the tables against you!

These are words of great elegance, prophetic expressions, having a magical effect on hearts and spirits. Al-Khaṣīb had barely read these radiant words . . . when he righted his government, and ruled justly, and treated his subjects fairly. Justice and peace spread, and the regulations of the religion were enforced. The injustices were lifted, and the rights of the subjects were honored. May God have mercy on Sayyida Nafīsa and be pleased with her, and grant her the greatest reward for her struggle in the path of Muḥammad's community!

After she had confronted the governor and counseled their ruler, and the governor heeded her words, Sayyida Nafīsa occupied a position of great esteem in the hearts of the Egyptians. From that time, they came to her with all their great problems, seeking her assistance with them. In the following days, relations between the ʿAbbāsids and the ʿAlids became better. The ʿAbbāsids wanted to prove their good will to them, and they offered the governorship of Medina to Isḥāq, Sayyida Nafīsa's husband. He accepted. He asked the lady to travel with him to Medina, but she declined, because her father al-Ḥasan was ill and bedridden since he came out of the ʿAbbāsid prison and since he had suffered so much calamity at their hands. The lady decided to remain with him until God issued a decision regarding him according to His will. Her husband did not oppose her in that. But he decided to travel alone. [Al-Ḥasan blessed Isḥāq and counseled him to rule Medina with justice.] Isḥāq promised to do as al-Ḥasan advised, and to work according to his counsel. Then the tender-hearted father went to his children, al-Qāsim and Umm Kulthūm, and embraced them warmly, . . . not knowing that this was the last time he would see any of the members of this beloved family until they were buried in the grave. . . . When departure was inevitable, Isḥāq gave his hand to his weeping wife to bid her farewell. She saw a tear glistening in his eye like the one in hers that was trying to flow, but the two of them tried to control their tears out of consideration for their dear children. The pious lady tried to help her husband in his affairs. She bravely bade him farewell, and held back her tears. [Isḥāq bids farewell with an appropriate line of poetry, which Nafīsa completes, counseling him to remember their weakness and need for him, and the youthfulness of his children.][19]

Sayyida Nafīsa looked after her sick father until God's will overtook him, and God's decree afflicted him. She prepared his body and prayed over him, then bid him a final farewell. Then she consoled herself over her separation from her husband and the death of her father by attending to her children and raising them with care. . . .

Fate had prepared for her a bitter cup and a painful circumstance. She had to submit to God's decree. That circumstance, that cup, and that distressing affliction was the illness of her dear daughter, Umm Kulthūm. She remained by her bedside and patiently nursed her and devoted herself to her care until God's command was fulfilled. . . . From time to time she asked God to restore her health and heal her, but her prayers and hopes were not heeded. God's decree descended on Umm Kulthūm, and this was the greatest trial Sayyida Nafīsa had ever suffered. Her grief was doubled because her beloved daughter never ceased to mention her absent father. This was even more grievous than her death. . . . The lady had barely buried her and recovered from burying her when her son al-Qāsim was stricken. He slept in her bed, and took to repeating the name of his father in great longing, just as Umm Kulthūm had done. . . . But he left this world without seeing [his father], and his death shook the lady's heart violently. . . . All her devotees and disciples grieved with her. [Just before her son was buried, Nafīsa requested to see his corpse one last time. She fainted. When she regained consciousness, she visited his grave on foot, declining to ride the animal prepared for her. There she prayed the following prayer:]

> God, you promised your reward, mercy, and forgiveness for those who are patient in calamity. I have been patient with all that You have made me suffer. I welcome the reward You have promised to me. I give the gift You have set apart for me to al-Qāsim and Umm Kulthūm, as a bond from me to them. Do not deny them that, and do not let them know any bad thing. Be merciful to me and to them until we meet You.

Then she recited what was easy for her of the Qur'an, until she had calmed herself, and she was healed [of her grief]. She returned to her home, [singing a verse about the calamities that had struck her.]

Since Sayyida Nafīsa came to Egypt, her blessed house was like a school that received visitors and pupils. It was visited by the scholars of religion and leading authorities on the law and the ascetic shaykhs and worshippers and the purest gnostics among the great Sufis. These included our lord Bishr ibn al-Ḥārith, known as Bishr al-Ḥāfī ["the Barefoot"], and the pious imām, our lord Aḥmad ibn Ḥanbal. . . . Bishr became ill. He had frequently attended her assembly, receiving from her the principles of asceticism, and hearing from her the rules of etiquette. He learned at her hands the principles of the transcendent truth (*al-ḥaqīqa*) and the law (*al-sharīʿa*) together.[20] He used to benefit from her valuable counsels and her superior wisdom. Then suddenly he stopped visiting her. She asked his brethren about him, and they told her he was ill. She felt it incumbent upon her to go minister to him and inquire about his condition. [The people of his house were overjoyed at her coming, seeing it as a tremendous blessing and benefit to them. When Aḥmad ibn Ḥanbal visited his friend Bishr, he was glad to meet her.] Undoubtedly the sight of the virtuous lady is better than all treasures and wealth. . . . The illness departed from him, and his health and happiness were restored. The cups of purity and the drink of devotees circulated in Bishr's assembly. . . .

Our lord Bishr said to the pure saint of God [Nafīsa], "Aḥmad ibn Ḥanbal wants you to pray for him." She extended the palms of supplication to God and raised her face to heaven, and said, "My God, Bishr ibn al-Ḥārith and Aḥmad ibn Ḥanbal ask you to save them from hellfire, so do so." Then she excused herself and bade them farewell. . . .

She did not cease to visit the religious scholars and be visited by them, and to meet with them, until God prepared for al-Shāfiʿī a visit to

Egypt. She rejoiced at his coming, and hastened to meet him. His coming moved her soul and her heart with sorrow and anxiety, for he was accused of loving the *ahl al-bayt* and was known for his partisanship [*tashayyuʿ*, that is, an inclination toward Shiʿism] to them, and he was characterized by loyalty to ʿAlī and the sons of ʿAlī. He was a true member of Quraysh [the Prophet's tribe]. . . . Shāfiʿī shared her feelings of longing and love. Above all that, they shared sorrow, and sorrow binds people together more than kinship. The lady grew in love for al-Shāfiʿī and attachment to him for his knowledge and piety. She strove to be in his assembly, to listen to and witness his opinion in matters of the law, and his efforts in understanding the texts of the religion, because of her great love for him and her trust in him. She asked him to lead her in the obligatory prayers, and he agreed to that. When the month of Ramaḍān came, which she used to love and honor, and in which she would increase her acts of obedience and worship and be exceedingly devoted to fasting and praying, she asked him to lead her in the special nightly prayers of Ramaḍān, and he agreed. Her mosque was full of worshippers night and day, emptying itself of worshippers only at the hours of teaching. When opposition arose against al-Shāfiʿī, and the followers of Imām Mālik asked the ruler of Egypt to banish him, . . . the governor acceded to their request, and warned al-Shāfiʿi to leave Egypt after three days. Sayyida Nafīsa stood by his side and insisted that he be allowed to remain. Only God knows what would have happened to Egypt if the fates had not intervened to solve this problem, for three days did not pass before the governor died, and Shāfiʿī remained Imam of the country. We do not know whether this was a miracle of the lady or a miracle of the Imam.

However, fate did not leave Shāfiʿī long in Egypt, for he was taken by illness. It was his habit when he was sick to send for Sayyida Nafīsa and ask her to pray for him. The messenger would scarcely have returned when he would be healed. When his final illness descended upon him, he sent for her and she said to the messenger, "Tell him: 'May God bless you with the vision of His noble face,'" and he knew that he would die. He requested that Sayyida Nafīsa pray for him at his funeral, and she did, led in prayer by his first disciple, al-Buwayṭī. When his coffin was being carried to the grave, she looked at him, weeping, and said, "May God have mercy on you, Shāfiʿī. You performed a proper ablution."[21]

With his death, sorrows returned to her. She lived only a short while before she joined him. Her death was in the year 208 of the Hijra.

May God bless al-Shāfiʿī in particular, and the *ahl al-bayt* in general, and bless the righteous and pure and the chosen ones, both the living and the dead.

Her Miracles

An old woman had four daughters who worked spinning wool. They lived off the profits from this, selling the spun wool every week and buying more wool with some of its price, spending the rest on food and other necessities. Their mother used to take it to the market and sell it and buy what they needed. One day the old woman took the spun wool and placed it in a red cloak and took it to the market. While she was on her way, with the wool on her head, a bird fell on the wool and carried it away. The woman didn't know what to do, and was overwhelmed. She began to weep and wail. The people gathered around her and asked what was the matter. She told them that a huge bird had carried off her wool from the top of her head. She wept and said, "Now what shall I do?" . . . The people sent her to Sayyida Nafīsa, saying, "Remain at her gate and ask her to pray to God for you for a way out of your problem. Perhaps God will release you from your difficulty." The old woman went and told her the story and asked her to pray for her. The heart of the lady was tender toward her, and she began to pray and ask God to release this old woman from her difficulty. . . . Then she told the old woman, "Sit down. God is able to do anything." She sat at her gate full of sorrow.

As she was sitting there, a group of people came to the lady's house and asked leave to enter. They were given leave, and they greeted her and told her, "A strange thing has happened to us. We are a group of merchants who have traveled long in the sea in our boats wherever we like. We came to trade in Egypt, but when we came near to land, a plank of our boat broke and the water came into the boat, and we were about to sink. We began to plug up the place where the plank had been, but the water continued to come in. We called on God for help, for fear of drowning, and we sought the intercession of your stature with God. We had barely finished when a bird approached us and threw us a red cloak in which there was some spun wool. We placed it in the hole, and it was plugged up, and the water ceased to flow in, by God's permission. We knew that this was by your baraka. We have brought you five hundred dirhams of silver as an offering of thanks to God for our safety."

The people had barely finished their story when the lady wept and said, raising her eyes to heaven, "My God, what kindness and mercy You have for Your servants!" Then she called the old woman, and told her, "For how much did you sell your daughters' spun wool every week?" She said, "For twenty dirhams." The lady said to her, "Rejoice, for God has compensated you for each dirham with twenty-five dirhams." Then she told her the story and gave her the entire sum of money. . . .

A Muslim man married a Christian woman, and she gave birth to a boy. This boy grew up until he became a handsome youth. He reached the age of military conscription, and he went to fight in the way of God. The enemy captured him. When his mother knew this, she nearly went mad with grief. She went to the synagogues of the Jews and the churches of the Christians and the mosques of the Muslims to beseech God to return him to her. Days and years went by, and her son did not come. The people counseled her to go to Sayyida Nafīsa. She was too shy to go to her, since she was not of her religion, but she said to her husband, "I have heard that a woman named Sayyida Nafīsa lives among us nearby, and it is said that she has a link with God. Go to her so she will pray for us and ask God to release our prisoner and return him to us. I testify that if my boy returns to me, I will enter her religion." Her husband went to the lady and told her the story. Sayyida Nafīsa rose to pray and remained knocking on her Lord's door and asking God to return the boy safely to his parents. Not a single night went by before the boy came to his house and knocked on the door. His mother went out to him and found him standing at the door. She could not believe her eyes and was amazed. She began to embrace him and weep and asked him, "My son, tell me what happened!" He told her, "Mother, I was standing inside the prison of the enemy at such-and-such a time—and it was the time went the lady called on her Lord to save him—and I was busy with my own affairs and not paying attention to the weight of my shackles, when suddenly my shackles fell off me. I heard someone say out loud, 'Free the prisoner, for Sayyida Nafīsa daughter of al-Ḥasan has prayed for him.' So they released me and I left the prison, and somehow I came to be standing at your door." His mother rejoiced greatly and thanked God for His great kindness to her. News of the miracle spread among the people, until seventy households embraced Islam out of joy at the baraka of the lady, just as the mother of the youth converted to Islam, keeping her promise. She and her husband came to serve Sayyida Nafīsa.

Her Death

Isḥāq, the husband of Sayyida Nafīsa, never returned to Egypt after the ʿAbbāsids appointed him governor of Medina. He married there and children were born to him. He never saw the death of his uncle or the death of his beloved children, Qāsim and Umm Kulthūm, although the Egyptians called on him to do so. When he did not come, the lady knew that Isḥāq had become a different person, unlike the man she had married, and he had left her life forever. She saw his image in the face of her dear children, and consoled herself for his loss by attending to them and to her father, al-Ḥasan. God desired to give her a replacement for her children, an intimate companion who could console her for the loss of those she loved. After her family and closest relatives, this companion was Imām al-Shāfiʿī, may God be pleased with him, who used to write and recite verses of poetry, and whose liver was eaten by fate until it destroyed him, and pierced his heart until it killed him. When he met Sayyida Nafīsa, may God be pleased with her, he rejoiced in her and was at ease with her, and she found in him solace and comfort, for he would often recite verses of bereavement and the sayings of those who are grieved. . . . The lady used to listen to him and find in his words the coolness of comfort and the calm of patience, and the pleasure of contentment with the decree of God.

But death did not spare him, for it hastens to meet every living thing. Sayyida Nafīsa wept the day of his death more than she had wept for her departed father and her two lost children and her distant husband. The people that day did not know whether all these tears were for the Imām alone, or whether they were for all the loved ones taken from her who would never return. Sayyida Nafīsa's life was empty of all loved ones and relations after the death of the Imām. She was visited only by strangers who loved the Prophet's family, and all that had happened affected her, especially the shock, and her heart and body bore the traces of all the calamities that had struck her. Finally her heart could bear no more, and her delicate body could no longer bear the strain.

What grieved her soul most was that her departed children had died without seeing the face of their father Isḥāq since he had had left for Medina. The last word repeated by their tongues the day of their death was his beloved name. How she wished, and the people wished with her, that Isḥāq would come to bid his dear children farewell, as every tender-hearted father would do if his children's life term was over and the hour of departure had drawn near. The lady's heart was made more bitter because the Egyptians wrote to him pleading with him to come visit, living in urgent expectation and long hope. But he did not come. They continued to write to him a second and third time, but he still did not come. Their efforts were wasted, and Qāsim and Umm Kulthūm died without this hope coming to fruition. It hurt the lady yet more when she heard that Isḥāq had married and had children in Medina, and had become proud, in need of no one, and having no desire to see any one, not even his wife and children.

What a grievous trial, what an agony, what a painful situation! Marriage in and of itself is neither prohibited nor reprehensible in religion, but what the religion finds reprehensible and has prohibited is that a Muslim abandon his children and family through no fault of their own. In any case, the lady was content with all that God had decreed for her, patient in her trials, enduring all that the days brought. Although they added to her portion of grief and her share of affliction the maltreatment of her husband Isḥāq, she nonetheless received it in contentment in her soul, with a smile on her lips, and with gentleness of spirit. . . . Her most outstanding trait in the midst of these events was her silence and stillness, except for recollecting the names of God or reciting His noble Book, or for the purposes of studying or teaching or giving a legal opinion.

The lady continued to raise the banner of knowledge and carry the banner of struggle on behalf of God, performing all the deeds required of her toward God and toward the servants of God. She slept little at night and ate little in the day. She did not neglect her daily devotions (*wird*) in hard times or in ease.

In the month of Rajab, in the year 208 [in the Islamic calendar, equivalent to November–December 823 A.D.] she was struck by a severe illness. That day she was fasting and did not break her fast. The illness grew worse until the month of Ramaḍān came [January–February 824 A.D.], when her illness reached its end and wasted her body, stilling all movement, even that of prayer. A doctor was inevitably called to see her. He had barely seen her when he ordered her to eat. She shouted in his face:

> Turn away my doctor from me, and call to me my Beloved
> My desire has increased for Him, and my love burns brightly
> I care not whether I pass away, since it has become my fate.

So they turned him away from her. When he had left her, she ordered them to remove a curtain that was near her. When they did so, they found that behind the curtain was a covered grave. She gestured toward it and said, "This is my grave. Here I will be buried, God willing. I have recited the entire Qur'an in it one thousand times, and I have prayed in it 100,000 cycles of prayer (*rakʿas*), and I have recollected the name of God in it twice that many times. I ask God that it be sufficient for me. When I am dead, bury me in it." Then she became too weak to speak, and she refrained from it. They brought her a little water, but she was fasting and gently refused to let it pass her lips. They urged her to drink it, for God had permitted her to break her fast, but she told them, "I am amazed at you! For thirty years I have asked God to take me while I am fasting. He has answered my prayer and fulfilled my desire—shall I reject His gift? I will break my fast on the nectar of the eternal and blessed abode, God willing." Then she began to recite the Qur'an, repeating its verses and words in love and ardent zeal, captivated in delight by its expressions. The Qur'an had been her friend and companion, as she recited it in all humility. Not a word of it was absent from her tongue. She never tired of reciting it night and day, until the 26th of Ramaḍān, in the same year. On that day she began her daily devotions (*wird*) after the dawn prayer. Her tongue moved in recitation of the Qur'an, and when she reached the chapter of *Al-Anʿām* [Cattle, Chapter 6 of the Qur'an], her voice became weak, and her reading was stilled, and she ceased reading or reciting. . . . Her tongue ceased to say anything except the name of the Absolute Reality and the confession of faith. She recited it, while the callers to prayer called it from the minarets as they summoned people to the noon prayer. Then her pure spirit and her blameless soul returned to their maker, rising to the heavenly council.

When the news of her death spread, the Muslims were shaken. They came from every place in delegations from every region, insisting on praying over her body. They prayed for her as individuals and in groups, the tears pouring down their cheeks like a torrential flood. That was a noteworthy day, a day when all the people—men, women, and even children—went out to bid a final farewell to Sayyida Nafīsa.

It is a great honor and pride for Egypt that it contained her pure body and her blessed mortal remains, and was happy with her in her life and in her death.

When her husband heard of her death, he came to Egypt after a number of days and tried to transport her body to Medina to bury her in the Al-Baqīʿ cemetery with her [great-great-grand]mother, [Fāṭima] "al-Zahrā'" ["the Radiant," daughter of the Prophet], her [great-grand]father Ḥasan, and her [great-great] uncle [Ḥusayn], the prince of martyrs. But the Egyptians stood up to him and intervened between him and what he wished to do. They gathered money for him brought on a she-camel, but he refused to take it. They sought the intercession of the governor, but Isḥāq rejected his intercession. The Egyptians wept then as they had wept the day of her death. They left no ruse or means untried with Isḥāq, but he remained firm in his resolve. Some of the lady's devotees even thought of affronting him and forcing him to leave her, but then they remembered that he is a son of the Messenger of God. When they saw their was no way to avoid letting her take the body, they yielded their affair to God. The people spent that night at her grave calling on God, asking forgiveness for Sayyida Nafīsa, and supplicating

God humbly by the baraka of the lady, that they would not see the hour of her departure twice, and that they not see her carried on the shoulders of pallbearers another time. God had regard for their cries and was merciful toward their hearts and answered their prayer, rescuing them from the frightening prospect of this catastrophe. He removed from them the ghost of remote departure and decreed that Sayyida Nafīsa should remain as a blessing for Egypt and the Egyptians, and the beloved of all Muslims. He decreed that she remain in her grave that she dug with her own hand, and when she illuminated by her recitation, prayers, recollection of God, and supplications for forgiveness. At whose command did Sayyida Nafīsa remain the treasure of the Egyptians? By the command of her grandfather the Apostle. Her husband Isḥāq, who was broad-minded and good-hearted, came with an illuminated face to the assembled throng, whose hearts were heavy and whose eyes were weeping, in fear of the hour of departure. He approached them and said:

> Egyptians, greetings! The blessing of Sayyida Nafīsa is among you. By God, the only God, I saw the Apostle of God—may God bless him and grant him peace—in my sleep tonight, and he said: "Leave Nafīsa daughter of al-Ḥasan to the Egyptians where she is, for God—splendid and mighty is He—will cause mercies to descend on them by her baraka."

He had barely finished speaking when the mosque was filled with praise to God, and the entire throng offered a prayer of thanksgiving. Somebody said, "God would not deprive the land of Kināna of the baraka of Sayyida Nafīsa after her pure breaths perfumed its air, and her noble feet tread on its soil."

May the peace of God be on the lady among those who dwell eternally, and may God's peace be upon her among those who have renounced self-indulgence, and among those who are patient and content. May God's peace be upon her in the heavenly council until the Day of Judgment, and may we benefit from her fragrances and her blessings. Amen. Peace be on the apostles, and praise be God, Lord of all being.

Notes

1. Tirmidhī's tenth-century collection of Ḥadīth is one of the six "canonical" collections recognized by Sunni Muslims. Tirmidhī is also the author of an important work, *Khātam al-Awliyā'* ("Seal of the Saints").

2. A *ḥadīth qudsī* is a special type of saying of the Prophet, which contains a divine saying not included in the Qur'an. Sufis are particularly fond of this genre.

3. Annemarie Schimmel quotes a ḥadīth to the same effect: "Miracles are the menstruation of men." *Mystical Dimensions of Islam* (Chapel Hill: University of

North Carolina Press, 1975), p. 212. Schimmel's book has an excellent section on the miracles of saints and attitudes toward them, pp. 205–213. Shaykh Abū 'l-Wafā al-Sharqāwī was a well-known Sufi intellectual who lived in Najʿ Ḥammādī in the Qinā province of Egypt. This saying is a pun on the homonym *ẓuhūr,* which means both "appearance" and "backs."

4. Shaʿrānī's *Al-Yawāqīt wa 'l-jawāhir* is a popular summary of Ibn ʿArabī's major writings and doctrines. Ibn ʿArabī (1165–1240) is known as *al-shaykh al-akbar*—the greatest shaykh—but his writings are notorious for their length and difficulty. The enormous influence and popularity of Ibn ʿArabī's ideas owe a great deal to their popularization in the writings of Shaʿrānī (d. 1565), ʿAbd al-Karīm al-Jīlī (d. 1408), and other writers.

5. Clifford Geertz believed this to be a particularity of the *marabout* form of sainthood in Morocco, where the importance of descent from the Prophet is emphasized in the efforts of the legendary saint, Sidi Lahsen Lyusi, to obtain recognition as a *sharīf*—a claim that might appear doubtful, given the man's Berber origins. (*Islam Observed: Religious Development in Morocco and Indonesia,* 2nd ed. [Chicago and London: University of Chicago Press, 1971], pp. 8–9, 29–35, 43–54.) However, I have not come across any claimant to sainthood in Egypt who did not also claim descent from the Prophet.

6. The text of this song and a longer discussion of this topic may be found in Chapter III of my book, *Sufism, Mystics, and Saints in Modern Egypt.*

7. This statement is so pervasive, that it appears almost arbitrary to cite one source to the exclusion of another. I choose a recent feminist interpretation of the Qur'an written by an African-American Muslim woman: Amina Wadud-Muhsin, *Qur'an and Woman* (Kuala Lumpur: Penerbit Fajar Bakti Sdn. Bhd., 1992), especially Chapter 1. Fatima Mernissi, a Moroccan feminist and sociologist, examines the early history of Islam to find an explanation for Muslim misogyny despite what she sees as the essential egalitarianism of Islam. She believes that social pressures led Muḥammad, near the end of his life, to abandon his original project of merging public and private space and of social egalitarianism, allowing the "veil" (*ḥijab*) to separate men from women, distinguish the free woman from the slave, and conceal private life from the public. *The Veil and the Male Elite: A Feminist Interpretation of Women's Rights in Islam,* trans. Mary Jo Lakeland (New York et al: Addison-Wesley Publishing Co., 1991).

8. Nurbakhsh's *Sufi Women* contains brief biographies of 124 Sufi women. Nelly and Laroussi Amri's *Les femmes soufies ou la passion de Dieu* is a similar project in French, based primarily on Al-Kawākib al-durriyya fī tarājim al-sāda 'l-ṣūfiyya, by al-Munāwī (d. 1621). It includes a biography of Sayyida Nafīsa (Nafīsa bint al-Ḥasan), pp. 160–162.

9. This is reminiscent of a ḥadīth in which Muhammad honored early fruits for the same reason.

10. Ḥāgga Zakiyya is one of the four saints whose lives are discussed and

analyzed in Chapter 9, "Models of Sainthood," of my book, *Sufism, Mystics, and Saints in Modern Egypt.*

11. These are the special prayers of the Sufis, recited several times a day and especially at night. They often involve repeated invocations of God's name and repeated recitations of formulas of praise of God and of blessing on the Prophet. While the highly stylized form of the Sufi *awrād* undoubtedly took centuries to develop—and it varies from one Sufi Order to another—they are nonetheless patterned after the earliest Muslim forms of worship, for the Qur'an speaks of those who stay up during the night reciting praise and portions of the Qur'an.

12. Mālik ibn Anas (d. 795) was a legal scholar of great reknown and importance. One of the four recognized schools of law in Sunni Islam is named after him, the Mālikī school, which predominates in most of Muslim Africa, with the exception of northern Egypt. He was the teacher of the famous Shāfiʿī (d. 819/20), who articulated the principles of Islamic jurisprudence and also figures in the story of Sayyida Nafīsa.

13. The Prophet was in fact her great-great-great-grandfather, but the term "grandfather" is also used for "ancestor." I preferred "grandfather" because it conveys the sense of closeness implied in the original.

14. Abraham of the Hebrew Bible, father of Ishmael and Isaac, who figures in the Qur'an as a model of Muslim piety and monotheism. The Qur'an says he and Ishmael built the Kaʿba in Mecca at God's command as a place of pilgrimage and worship, and they announce that they are in submission to God; that is, that they are Muslims. The longing expressed by this narrative to visit a tomb is entirely typical of Egyptian Sufi devotion to God, which often expresses itself in terms of a longing to visit and honor a particular deceased saint or prophet. Sufis in Egypt often sing of their longing to be in Medina, the burial place of the Prophet, and of the light of Medina that is in their heart, an expression of the light of the Prophet himself, whose love illumines their hearts. Because the holy personages are thought to be virtually alive in their tombs—their bodies sleeping, but their spirits alive and in full communication with their visitors—a visit to a tomb is tantamount to a visit to the person him or herself, and indeed often no distinction is made in everyday speech between visiting a person and visiting his or her tomb. When I asked one woman why she attended the celebrations of the saints' days (*al-mawālid*), she replied with fervor: "I am driven to do so! If I did not, my heart would burn within me!"

15. Medina is nearly 300 miles north of Mecca. The true pilgrimage (the hajj) can only be performed at a particular time of year. Although the author uses the word *ḥajj* here, he must mean the "lesser pilgrimage," the *ʿumra,* which may be performed at any time.

16. On al-Manṣūr's attempts to consolidate his power through suppression of ʿAlid enthusiasm, see Marshall G. S. Hodgson, *The Venture of Islam: Conscience and History in a World Civilization* (Chicago and London: The University of Chicago

Press, 1974), 1:284–285. Moojan Momen describes the impact of al-Manṣūr's persecution of the ʿAlids on the life of Jaʿfar al-Sadiq and Musa al-Kazim, the sixth and seventh Imams of the Twelver Shīʿa. *An Introduction to Shīʿi Islam* (New Haven and London: Yale University Press, 1985), pp. 38–40. Momen does not depict al-Mahdi as making any amends for the policies of his father, and says the persecution of the ʿAlids culminated under the Caliphate of Harun al-Rashid (786–809).

17. A nickname for Egypt.

18. A reference to the nightly prayers of the faithful.

19. The recitation of lines of poetry is a highly valued and very common way of demonstrating intelligence and wit in Arab society. Nearly all traditional Arabic biographies end with lines of poetry composed by the person in question, regardless of whether or not that person was known as a poet. The ability to complete a poetic line begun by another demonstrates Nafīsa's quick wit and, in this case, the harmony of her relationship with Isḥāq. In other circumstances, of course, the completion of a line of poetry could just as easily thwart the original intent of the one who began the line of poetry, and be a way of turning the tables back on an opponent. The depiction of the entire scene, with its emphasis on mutual love and restrained emotion, clearly lets us know what traits are valued and which are not. The author does not name his sources. Entries in biographical dictionaries on Sayyida Nafīsa are typically very brief, and I can only surmise that the author is filling in the gaps found in accumulated traditions with details that appear plausible.

20. In Sufi discourse, the Sharīʿa—Islamic Law—is sometimes contrasted with the *ḥaqīqa*—the Truth that the Sufis perceive in their mystical experiences and which is thought to transcend the letter of the law. In contemporary Egypt, under pressure from Islamic reformist tendencies that tend toward legalism, many Sufis say there is no distinction between the Sharīʿa and the *ḥaqīqa*. This author is emphasizing that the mysticism of Sayyida Nafīsa and Bishr al-Ḥāfī in no way contradicted a scrupulous adherence to the law.

21. This saying undoubtedly appears odd to the person outside the tradition. The ablutions performed before ritual prayer in Islam are intended not only to purify the outer body, but to ready the heart and mind for prayer. It is often said of saints that they performed their ablution well.

Works Cited

ʿAbd al-Rāziq, Aḥmad. *Al-marʾa fī miṣr al-mamālīk.* Cairo: Al-Sharīf wa Saʿīd Raʾfat, 1975.

Abū ʿAlam, Tawfīq. *Ahl al-bayt, 1: Fāṭima al-Zahrāʾ*. Cairo: Dār al-maʿārif, 1972.

Ahmed, Leila. *Women and Gender in Islam: The Historical Roots of a Modern Debate.* New Haven: Yale University Press, 1992.

ʿAlī Mūsā Muḥammad. *ʿAqīlat al-ṭuhr wa ʾl-karam al-Sayyida Zaynab.* Cairo: Dār al-turāth al-ʿarabī, 1984.

Amri, Nelly and Laroussi. *Les femmes soufies ou la passion de Dieu.* St-Jean-de-Braye, France: Editions Dangles, 1992.

ʿAttār, Farīd al-Dīn. *Muslim Saints and Mystics,* trans. A. J. Arberry. Oxford: Oxford University Press, 1966.

Bayḍāwī, ʿAbd Allāh ibn ʿUmar al-. *Beidhawii Commentarius in Coranum,* ed. H. O. Fleischer. Leiden: F. C. W. Vogel, 1846–1848.

Bint al-Shāṭi' [ʿĀ'isha ʿAbd al-Raḥmān]. *Al-Sayyida Zaynab: Batalat Karbalā'*. Cairo: Dār al-Hilāl, 1966.

Chodkiewicz, Michel. *Le Sceau des saints: Prophétie et sainteté dans la doctrine d'Ibn Arabi.* Paris: Editions Gallimard, 1986.

———. "La sainteté féminine en Islam." Unpublished paper delivered at "Table ronde sur l'hagiographie islamique," Paris, 1993.

Cornell, Vincent. "Mirrors of Prophethood: The Evolving Image of the Spiritual Master in the Western Maghrib from the Origins of Sufism to the End of the Sixteenth Century." Unpublished Ph.D. dissertation, Department of History, University of California at Los Angeles, 1989.

Elias, Jamal. "Female and Feminine in Islamic Mysticism." *Muslim World* 78: 209–224, 1988.

Goldziher, Ignaz. *Muslim Studies,* trans. C. R. Barber and S. M. Stern. 2 vols. London: George Allen & Unwin Ltd, 1971.

Ḥamza, Muḥammad Shāhīn. *Al-Sayyida Nafīsa.* Cairo: Dār al-fikr al-ʿarabī, n.d.

Hoffman, Valerie J. *Sufism, Mystics, and Saints in Modern Egypt.* Columbia, South Carolina: University of South Carolina Press, 1995.

Hoffman-Ladd, Valerie J. "Polemics on the Modesty and Segregation of Women in Contemporary Egypt." *International Journal of Middle East Studies* 19, no. 1: 23–50.

———. 1992a. "Mysticism and Sexuality in Sufi Thought and Life." *Mystics Quarterly* 18, no. 3: 82–93, 1987.

———. "Devotion to the Prophet and His Family in Egyptian Sufism." *International Journal of Middle East Studies* 24, no. 4: 615–637, 1992b.

Hujwīrī, ʿAlī ibn ʿUthmān al-Jullābī al-. *Kashf al-Maḥjūb of Al Hujwīrī,* trans. Reynold A. Nicholson. E. J. W. Gibb Memorial Series vol. XVII. London: Luzac & Co., 1911.

Ibn ʿArabī, Muḥyī al-Dīn. *Kitāb manzil al-quṭb wa maqāmuhu wa ḥāluhu.* Hyderabad: Maṭbaʿat jamʿiyyat dā'irat al-maʿārif al-ʿuthmāniyya. Included in *Rasā'il Ibn al-ʿArabi.* Beirut: Dār iḥyā' al-turāth al-ʿarabī, 1948.

———. *Al-Futūḥāt al-makkiyya.* 4 vols. Beirut: Dār Ṣādir, 1966.

———. *The Sufis of Andalusia: The Rūḥ al-quds and Al-Durrat al-fākhira,* trans. R. W. J. Austin. London: George Allen & Unwin, 1971.

Ibn Kathīr, ʿImād al-Dīn Abū 'l-Fadā' Ismāʿīl. *Tafsīr al-Ḥāfiẓ Ibn Kathīr,* ed. Muḥammad Rashīd Riḍā. 9 vols. Cairo: Maṭbaʿat al-Manār, 1924/5–28/9.

Ibrahim, Ezzeddin and Denys Johnson-Davies, trans. *Forty Ḥadīth Qudsī.* Beirut and Damascus: Dār al-Qur'ān al-Karīm, 1980.

Ibrāhīm, Muḥammad Zakī. *Al-tabṣīr bi mushāhid shahīrāt āl al-bayt bi 'l-qāhira,* 2nd ed. Cairo: Al-ʿAshīra 'l-muḥammadiyya, 1980.

Māhir, Farīd. *Karāmāt al-awliyā'*. Cairo: Al-maṭbaʿa 'l-ʿālamiyya, 1971.

Meier, Fritz. "Soufisme et déclin culturel." In *Classicisme et déclin culturel dans l'histoire de l'islam,* eds. R. Brunschvig and G. E. von Grunebaum. Paris: Editions Besson-Chantemerle, 1957.

Nurbakhsh, Javad. *Sufi Women.* New York: Khaniqahi-Nimatullahi Publications, 1983.

Qushayrī, Abū 'l-Qāsim al-. *Al-Risāla 'l-qushayriyya.* Cairo: Muḥammad ʿAlī Ṣubayḥ and Sons, n.d.

Raḍwān, Aḥmad. *Al-Nafaḥāt al-rabbāniyya,* 3rd ed. Kom Ombo, Egypt: Yūsuf Jaʿlūs, 1986.

Ragib, Yusuf. "Al-Sayyida Nafīsa: sa légende, sa culte, et son cimetière." *Studia Islamica* 44: 61–81, 1976.

Schimmel, Annemarie. "Women in Mystical Islam." *Women's Studies International Forum* 5:145–151, 1981.

Sharaf al-Dīn, Aḥmad al-Shihāwī Saʿd. *Al-Sayyida Nafīsa bint Sīdī Ḥasan al-Anwar.* Cairo: Maṭbaʿat Dār al-Ta'līf, 1972.

Shaʿrānī, ʿAbd al-Wahhāb al-. *Al-Ṭabaqāt al-kubrā.* 2 vols. Cairo: Muḥammad ʿAli Ṣubayḥ and Sons, n.d.

———. *Al-Yawāqīt wa 'l-jawāhir fī bayān ʿaqā'id al-akābir,* 2nd ed. Beirut: Dār al-maʿrifa, 1974.

Sharqāwī, Ḥasan al-. *Al-Ḥukūma 'l-bāṭiniyya.* Cairo: Dār al-maʿārif, 1982.

Smith, Margaret. *Rābiʿa the Mystic and Her Fellow-Saints in Islam.* Cambridge: Cambridge University Press, 1928.

Ṭabarī, Abū Jaʿfar Muḥammad ibn Jarīr. *Jāmiʿ al-bayāyn ʿan ta'wīl āyy al-Qur'ān,* ed. Maḥmūd Muḥammad Shākir. 16 vols. Cairo: Dār al-maʿārif, 1954.

Ṭawīl, Tawfīq al-. *Al-taṣawwuf fī miṣr ibbāna 'l-ʿasr al-ʿuthmānī.* Al-Jamāmīz: Maktabat al-adab, 1962.

von Grunebaum, G. E. "The Place of Parapsychological Phenomena in Islam." In *Malik Ram Felicitation Volume,* ed. S. A. J. Zaidi. New Delhi: The Printsman, 1972.

Winter, Michael. *Society and Religion in Early Ottoman Egypt: Studies in the Writings of ʿAbd al-Wahhāb al-Shaʿrānī.* New Brunswick: Transaction Books, 1982.

Zamakhsharī, Abū 'l-Qāsim Jār Allāh Maḥmūd ibn ʿUmar al-. *Al-Kashshāf an ḥaqā'iq al-tanzīl wa ʿuyūn al-aqāwīl fī wujūh al-ta'wīl.* 4 vols. Beirut: Dār al-kitāb al-ʿarabī, 1947.

V

Janābāī: A Woman Saint of India

Rajeshwari V. Pandharipande

Water and cloud,
Cloud and water
Is there a difference
between the two?
eye and the pupil
pupil and eye
can we separate the two?
santa is God
and God is *santa*'
Janī says,
"The difference is
only in the name."

—*Nāmdeva Gāthā.*[1] *abhanga* 250

The above *abhanga*[2] (*a verse couplet*) is eloquent of Janābāī's view of *Santa* 'saint' Janābāī, a thirteenth-century woman saint of India has contributed significantly to the lives of women in rural Maharashtra in India. Her devotional songs are sung in the morning by women while grinding the grain in the villages. Although the rhythm and the melody of her songs has continued to be part of the ambience of village Maharashtra for the last seven centuries, Janābāī has not received much attention from scholars who have worked on the spirituality of the saints in India. This lack of recognition could be because Janābāī has always been known as the maid and disciple of Nāmadeva, a well-known male saint of her time. Janābāī's poetry is always seen as a reflection of Nāmadeva's spirituality. However, even a cursory look at her devotional poetry shows that Janābāī was different from Nāmadeva and that her contribution to the tradition of saints of India is unique. No other saint (male or female) of India besides Janābāī, has grasped and described such diverse dimensions of the secular and spiritual life of a socially downtrodden woman. The most significant contribution of Janābāī is that she projects a very powerful image of woman. Janābāī depicts the power of woman in her enormous tolerance for pain and suffering in the secular world, her ability to transcend social barriers to relate to the divine, and finally, her power to liberate the divine from its male form of Viṭṭhal and transform him into Janī—the woman, the downtrodden maid! Janābāī's poetry is a unique celebration of womanhood. The following discussion is aimed at examining various aspects of Janābāī's sainthood in the context of: a) the notion of "saint" in Hinduism in general, and b) the thirteenth-century socioreligious situation in Maharashtra. It is hoped that the following discussion will provide a better understanding of Janābāī's position among the saints in India. The major themes of discussion are the following: a) The concept of sainthood in Hinduism; b) The biographical sketch of Janābāī; and the *Vārkarī Pantha* in thirteenth-century Maharashtra; c) Various images of Janābāī: from a maid to a saint; d) Janābāī's position as a woman saint; and e) Translation of selected *abhangas* of Janābāī.

The Concepts of Sainthood in Hinduism

As Cohn (1987:3) correctly points out, "Saint is a designation that Christianity has used to recognize individuals deemed to have lived lives of heroic virtue and who, as a result, dwell eternally with God." However, the category of saint is also commonly used in various other religious traditions to designate those who epitomize the highest religious ideal. There is a great deal of variation within the interpretations of the term "saint" across traditions since the concept of "religious ideal" varies considerably from one tradition to another. However, all religious traditions seem to venerate as saints those who possess "holy" or "divine" qualities. Gold (1987:7) calls the saint "a holy man . . . a man because he is alive in a body; holy because he is looked to for salvation." Saints represent a point at which the separation between the divine and the human diminishes. Thus, religious traditions have defined saints either as the human beings who have "divine qualities" or as the divine which has become incarnated as holy human beings.

The Hindu tradition recognizes both—the incarnations of the divine (*avatāra*) and human beings who are endowed with divine qualities as saints. However, it is important to note here that there is no single unified definition of sainthood in Hinduism. During different periods, from the Vedic to the modern, the descriptions of saints have been so diverse that it is impossible to present a definition that would incorporate all of the various facets of sainthood. The major reason for this diversity is that "divinity" was recognized by the people in different forms and qualities at various points in time. In the Vedic period (2000 B.C.), the composers of hymns, *ṛṣiṣ*, were viewed as those who had *apauruṣeya* "divine" (beyond human) vision of the ultimate truths. They were visionaries who imparted their knowledge to the people. In the Brāhmaṇa period immediately following the Vedic period, saints were priests who performed sacrifices on behalf of the people and who were supposed to have had divine powers to guarantee the efficacy of the sacrificial rituals. In the epics (the Rāmāyaṇa and the Mahābhārata 400 B.C. to 400 A.D. and Purāṇas (700 B.C.), the saints were considered to be those who had rescued the world from various disasters and who were viewed as the incarnations of Viṣṇu, the god of sustenance. Another group of the philosopher-saints were *ācāryās* "the learned teachers" such as Śaṅkarācārya (eighth-century A.D.), Rāmānujācārya (eleventh-century A.D.), Madhvācārya (thirteenth-century A.D.), and Vallabhācārya (fifteenth-century A.D.), who provided various possible and logically verifiable definitions and explanations for the nature of phenomenal reality and its relationship to the underlying divine phenomenon. Moreover, the *ācāryās* presented the role of various paths (*jñāna* "knowledge," *karma* "action," and *Bhakti* "devotion") toward enlightenment.

Additionally, a large group of saints and mystics in the south as well as in the north of India over a period of about 2,000 years were recognized as *santa* "saints," and this term continues to be used for saints in the modern period as well. The term *santa* etymologically means "one who expresses/bears truth or the divine (*sat*) or, inferentially, one who has the divine qualities of compassion, love, and selflessness." The saints often identified themselves as *bhakta* "devotees" of either personal gods (*saguṇa*) such as *Viṣṇu* and/or *Śiva* or impersonal gods (*nirguṇa*). However, most commonly, they were recognized by their followers as the *guru* "the guides" or "teachers" as well as the incarnations of the divine. The prominent branches of this group were first, the *Vaiṣṇava* saints: *Aḷwars* in the South (sixth to ninth century A.D.), Rāmānanda (fourteenth-century A.D.), Mīrābāī (sixteenth-century A.D.), Tulsīdās (sixteenth-century A.D.),

Narsī Mehta (fifteenth-century A.D.), *Vārkarī Pantha* (twelfth-century A.D. to eighteenth-century A.D.), Caitanya (fifteenth-century A.D.) and Kabīr (fourteenth-century A.D.). There were also the *Śaiva saints:* the *Vīraśaiva sampradāya* (group) in the South Karnātaka (twelfth-century A.D.), Kāśmīr śaīva sampradāya (group) (eighth to tenth century A.D.), and *Nāth Sampradāya* (thirteenth century). Additionally, mystics in the nineteenth and twentieth centuries, such as Ramakrishṇa Paramahamsa, Śāradādevī, and Sāi Bābā, are also recognized as saints because they epitomize the divine through their personal qualities of selflessness, compassion, as well as their vision of the essential divinity of all. What is interesting about these various groups of saints is that they each interpreted the religious beliefs for the people according to their needs at various points in time. Therefore, the saints, by their very nature are innovators since they interpret the religious beliefs to make them relevant within the context of a particular time and the sociocultural reality. People perceive this ability of saints to contextualize the divine at various points in time as the expression of their experience of the divine.

However, the saints (*santa*) of the north and south of India, from the period of the fourth-century A.D. until today, were identified as such primarily because of their ability to integrate diverse religious beliefs and castes (social groups) by lifting the barriers of language (Sanskrit) and rituals from the common people. They shifted the emphasis of religion away from doctrinal conformity and towards experience. They used the language of the common people, metaphors from their daily lives, and promoted the religious practices of *japa* "repetition of god's name," *kīrtan/bhajan* "singing the praise of God," and religious pilgrimage as substitutes for the orthodox Brahmanical rituals. Moreover, they made religion accessible to the common people and lower classes by promoting the oral tradition. While in the north they integrated the Hindu-Muslim faith, in central and south India, they primarily integrated various sects and castes of Hinduism. The period fourth-century A.D. until sixteenth-century A.D. is particularly significant in the tradition of saints in India because it marks the emergence of women saints whose poetry depicts: a) the conflicts faced by women in their social and spiritual life, and b) their vision of the divine. Thus, women saints such as Mīrābāī from the north (sixteenth-century A.D.) and Āṇṭāl from the south (ninth-century A.D.) and a group of women saints such as Mahadambā, Muktābāī and Janābāī (thirteenth-century A.D.), and Bahiṇābāī from central India (seventeenth-century A.D.), contributed to the role of saints in the socioreligious climate of their time.

A Biographical Sketch of Janābāī

Janābāī belonged to the *santa* tradition of the *Vārkarī Pantha* which has contributed immensely to the religious, social, and literary traditions of Mahārāshtra from the twelfth through the sixteenth centuries. Jnāneśwar and Nāmadeva (thirteen-century A.D., Eknath (sixteenth-century A.D.), and Rāmdās and Tukārām (seventeenth-century) were the major male saints and Muktābāī, Janābāī, and Bahiṇābāī were the major female saints of this tradition. Janābāī is known to be a maid as well as a disciple of the saint Nāmadeva. Nāmadeva's date of birth is 1270 A.D. Janābāī's reference to Nāmadeva's birth and his naming ceremony (for which she was present) indicates that Janābāī must have been at least six or seven years older than Nāmadeva. Therefore, Janābāī's approximate date of birth can be assumed to be 1263 A.D. This assumption is further supported by the fact that (according to the historical sources) Janābāī passed away in the state of *samādhi*[3] "the state of enlightenment" at the same time as Nāmadeva. Since the date of Nāmadeva's *samādhi* is believed to be July 3, 1350 A.D., the same date is assumed to be the date when Janābāī passed away. However, it is extremely difficult to assess the exact dates of birth and death of the saints in India. In many respects, a saint is like a river that is constrained by its context and yet it always finds a way to transcend contextual barriers (including those of time and space) and get to its goal—union with the ocean! There is a belief in India which says, "What difference does it make what the origin of a saint is? A saint is a *Jīvanmukta* "one who is liberated from *saṃsāra*—the cycle of time"! Why should we bind a saint to this world by recording the dates of birth and death?"

It is also not surprising that there are no separate historical records of Janābāī's compositions or her life-history. Information about her is available through historical records about Nāmadeva in the various editions of his *gāthā* (a collection of Nāmadeva's religious poetry (*abhanga*) put together by various editors). Janābāī's *abhangas* are also included in these editions. These are the only records of Janābāī's compositions. The following are the major editions of Nāmadeva's *gāthā,* which include Janābāī's *abhanga:*

a) *Santa Nāmadevācī āṇi tyānce kutumbātīl va samakālīn sādhūcyā abhangācī Gāthā:* T. T. Gharat (ed.) Bombay: Tattvavivecak Chapkhana, 1894.
b) *Nāmadevācī Gāthā:* R. S. Gondhalekar (ed.) Pune: Jagadhitecchu Chapkhana, 1896.

c) *Śri Nāmadeva Mahārāj yā̃cyā abhangā̃cī Gāthā:* T. H. Avte Pune; Indira Prakashan, 1953.
d) *Śri Santa Nāmadeva Mahārāj yā̃cyā abhangā̃cī Gāthā:* V. N. Jog (ed.) Pune: Citrashala Prakashan, 1957.
e) *Śri Nāmadeva Gāthā,* S. Babar (ed.) Shasakiya mudran va lekhan samgri, (edited and published by the Government of Maharashtra), Bombay, 1970.
f) *Śri Nāmadeva Gāthā.* Shri Nanamaharaj Sakhre (ed.) Pune: Smita Printers, 1990.

Mahipatibuwa Taharabadkar, in his work *Bhakta vijay* includes Nāmadeva's biography in which he gives a brief sketch of Janābāī's life.[4] Additionally, Bhingarkar (1989:100) mentions two other sources of Janābāī's poetry—one entitled *Santa Janābāī: caritra va kāya* published in Janābāī's birthplace and the other called *Gāthāpancak.* Although the number of Janābāī's *abhanga* ranges between 340 to 348 couplets in the previously mentioned sources, it is beyond doubt that there are at least 340 couplets that are commonly shared in all of these aforementioned sources. There are very few works dedicated entirely to Janābāī's biography, analysis of her poetry, or her contributions. Some of these are:

a) *Santa Janābāī: Caritra āṇi kāvya.* Ajgaonkar, J. R. Pune: Anmol Prakashan, 1976.
b) *Santa Kavayitrī Janābāī: Caritra, kāvya āṇi Kamgirī* by D. B. Bhingarkar. Bombay: Majestic Prakashan, 1989.
c) *Janābāīce Nivaḍak Abhanga:* ek cintan. By S. Irlekar, Aurangabad: Hoshi Brothers, 1981.
d) *Nāmāyācī Janī.* By R. C. Dherea, Pune: Shri Vidya Prakashan, 1960.

All of these works are in Marathi. It should be noted here that Bhingarkar (1989) in his treatise on Janābāī, includes forty-two additional *abhanga/ ovī* which he has collected from various libraries in Maharashtra and Tanjavur. The themes in these *abhangas/ovīs* are similar to those in the other editions (See translation III:1). There is no English translation of Janābāī's work available at this time; neither is there any systematic analysis of her work or her biography available in English. There are, however, two references in English to Janābāī. Tulpule (1970) in his work entitled, *Classical Marathi Literature,* while discussing Nāmadeva's work, briefly refers to Janābāī as Nāmadeva's maid, the "mystic poetess," whose place was "next to that of Muktā, the sister of Jñānadeva." Ranade (1933:190) devotes a paragraph to Janābāī in his treatise on *Mysticism in Maharashtra* and places her among the highly respected saints of Maharashtra. Based on the aforementioned sources, the following biographical sketch of Janābāī is provided as follows (for further description see Bhingarkar (1988) and Inamdar (1987).

In Maharashtra, in the district of Parbhani, on the banks of the river Godavari, there is a small village called Ganagakhed. A tailor by profession (*śūdra* by caste), called Dāmā, lived there with his wife named Kuruṇḍ. They were a happy couple, deeply devoted to Viṭṭhal (Viṣṇu's incarnation as a male god. See the following section for details). The only discontent in their life was that they did not have any progeny. The legend has it that the couple went to Pandharpur and prayed to Viṭṭhal. Viṭṭhal appeared in Dāmā's dream and told him, "You will get a daughter, not a son but she will uplift your family. Name her Janābāī and give her to Dāmāśeṭh; she is destined to be associated with Nāmadeva." At the destined time, Kuruṇḍ gave birth to Janābāī and died soon thereafter. Dāmā, her father, gave her to Dāmāśeṭh when she was five or six years old, and soon after that he too died.

Janābāī spent her entire life in Dāmāśeṭh's home. Nāmadeva, Janābāī's *guru,* was Dāmāśeṭh's son and a great devotee of Viṭṭhal. Janābāī adopted Nāmadeva's family as her own and remained in the family as a maid until her death. She repeatedly called herself *Nāmayācī dāsī Janī* "Nāmadeva's maid, Janī."

The *Vārkarī Panthā* in Maharashtra in the Thirteenth Century

In order to understand Janābāī's spirituality, it is necessary to understand the religious principles of the devotional sect of *Vārkarī Pantha.* The major ingredients of Janābāī's spirituality—her vision of the divine, her devotion toward Viṭṭhal, and the expression of her religious experience in her poetry—were influenced and shaped by the *Vārkarī Panthā,* "the path of the saints" of her time. This sect was originally constituted in Karnataka state in south India in the twelfth-century A.D. under the political rule of the Yadava kings. After Karnataka was included in Maharashtra under the Yadava rule, the *Vārkarī* sect was introduced to Maharashtra. Pandharpur, which was the place of origin of *Vārkarī Panthā* thus became one of the holiest cities of pilgrimage in Maharashtra.

The "path" is known as *Vārkarī Panthā* because of its emphasis on *vārī,* a pilgrimage to Pandharpur twice a year in the months of Āṣāḍha and Kārtika (August through September). The word *karī* means the one who undertakes the practice of visiting Pandharpur twice a year on a regular basis. A *vārkarī* is a devotee of Viṭṭhal (an incarnation of Viṣṇu/Kṛṣṇa), wears *tulsī* beads around his neck, constantly repeats God's name (*nāmasaṃkīrtana*), and is a strict vegetarian. Legend has it that Kṛṣṇa took the form of Viṭṭhal and came to Pandharpur for the sake of his devotee Puṇḍalika, who had dedicated his entire life to the service of his parents. The *vārkarīs* commemorate Puṇḍalika and his devotion to his parents and Kṛṣṇa when they observe the ritual of letting out a cry, "*Puṇḍalika-varada-Hari-Viṭṭhala.*" "*Oh, Hari-Viṭṭhala,* the granter of wishes to Puṇḍalika," when they walk to Pandharpur twice a year on *ekādaśī* (the eleventh day of the bright half of the lunar month). Under the patronage of Rāmdeva Yadav, the temple of Viṭṭhal at Pandharpur became an established place of pilgrimage in 1273 A.D.

The *Vārkarī Pantha* contributed immensely toward the spiritual, religious, social, and literary life of Maharashtra. By breaking social barriers, the *Vārkarī Pantha* firmly established and reiterated the belief in *ekatā,* "equality"—spiritual equality of all. The *Vārkarī Pantha,* which was open to all regardless of their caste and their affiliations to various deities, thus functioned as a great integrator of all castes as well as various religious sects. The most important and valuable contribution made by the saints and mystics of this *Pantha* in particular, and the saints in India in general, is that of opening the door of spirituality to the *bahujansamāj,* the "common people."

The saints revived the confidence of the people in their own religion, culture and language when India was ruled by foreigners and morale of the people was low. The thirteenth century was the time of Mughal rule that had demoralized the entire nation (Bhingarkar 1989:9–14). The saints had to fight against the foreign rule, which did not support the pursuit of the native Indian religion (Hinduism), and also against the orthodox and conservative priestly caste of the Brāhmaṇas, who wanted to hold power for themselves by excluding the lower castes from participation in religious activities. The common people's lack of knowledge of traditional scriptures such as the *Vedas,* the *Bhagavadgītā,* and so on, had forced them to depend entirely on the teachings of the Brāhmaṇas for their religious needs. Through their emphasis on rituals and caste, the Brāhmaṇas had gained more power in the secular and spiritual dimensions of life; however, the *Vārkarī Pantha* convinced the people that rituals and caste were irrelevant in accomplishing the spiritual goal. Discrimination based on gender, caste, and religious sect is man-made; in God's eyes, there is no discrimination. God is mother (*māulī*) and God's place is the mother's place (*māher*). What is the need for a particular ritual, or language, or caste to experience and to express one's love for one's mother? All that is needed is devotion. Thus the *Vārkarī Pantha* advocated the path of devotion (*bhaktimārga*).

The *Pantha* de-emphasized the importance of the rituals and methods and focused on the goal. It brought about this universalization of the faith by advocating equality of all—low caste and high caste, men and women, and various paths to God. The holy pilgrimage to Pandharpur, the holy place of Viṭṭhal, included people from all castes and sects, both men and women. The mystics and saints removed from the minds of the people the amnesia that made them forget their own religious heritage. The saints did not require people to renounce their families in order to achieve *mukti* "liberation"; rather, they asked people to follow the path of desireless action. While performing their duty to their families and society, they could still achieve the goal of life. The qualities of a holy man, they claimed, could be inculcated by anyone. Purity of action and thought, compassion for all—these were some of the qualities the saints adored and epitomized. They did not advocate liberation from *saṃsāra,* family; they proposed liberation in *saṃsāra.*

Jñāneśwar (also known as Jñānadeva) and Nāmadeva, two of the most important saints of this *Pantha,* revitalized the Hindu religious faith among the common people of Maharashtra and also influenced Janābāī. Through his Marathi commentary on the Bhagavadgītā (which is in Sanskrit) Jñāneśwar brought the knowledge of the Bhagavadgītā to the common people. Nāmadeva freed religion from the traditional rituals by substituting for them *kīrtan,* "singing the glory of God and repeating God's name." Janābāī lived within this religious context of thirteenth-century Maharashtra. Under the spiritual patronage of Nāmadeva, Janābāī reached her spiritual goal of union with Viṭṭhal. Janābāī's contribution to the *Vārkarī Pantha* was that she demonstrated with her own example that womanhood and the low social status of a maid could not be barriers in accomplishing the spiritual goal.

Janābāī: From a Maid to a Saint: Diverse Images, Single Source

In this section, I will take a look at various images of Janābāī's personality (from a maid to a saint) reflected in her own compositions. We may ask why we should delve into the worldly life of a saint who has transcended the world and has "touched" the divine? The answer is that often, it is in the worldly life that the reflections of sainthood are revealed. It is generally the saints' worldly lives that (though not necessarily the primary motivation), become the reference point of their spiritual instinct, their relationship to the divine and "this world," and finally, the expression of their religious experience. For example, it was Ravidas'[5] life as a *camār,* a shoemaker, a low-caste Hindu, which became the major reference point of his spirituality. His revolt against social inequalities is expressed in devotional poetry when he exclaims "O well-born of Banares, I too am born well known: my labor is with leather. But my heart can boast the Lord." Ravidās' devotion is inspired mostly by the need to transcend worldly social inequalities and not so much by the need to terminate the cycle of rebirth. In contrast to this, Mīrābāī,[6] the woman saint who was a princess and was endowed with every possible pleasure of worldly life, had to struggle against those pleasures to reach her ever-cherished divinity, Kṛṣṇa. The pleasures had become barriers in her path to Kṛṣṇa which she "transcends" in her union with Kṛṣṇa. It was this worldly life that she called the "poison cup" sent to her by the king (her husband), which she had to first drink (that is, experience) in order to "transcend" the bonds of worldly life. Thus the worldly life of "deprivation" or "abundance" has always been a point in a saint's life from which he/she departs or in the context of which he/she finds freedom. To put it differently, it is the worldly lives of the saints that contextualize their spiritual lives.

Therefore, in order to understand Janābāī's spirituality and her devotional poetry, it is necessary to look at her worldly life as *Nāmayācī dāsī Janī,* "Nāmadeva's maid Janābāī" and also her spiritual life as a *bhakta* "devotee" of Viṭṭhal. We encounter various images of Janābāī in her own poetry. In the following sections, we will take a look at these images. It also will be shown that these diverse and (at least apparently) mutually exclusive images begin to relate to each other once we understand their common source, Janābāī's womanhood, which encompasses her secular as well as spiritual life.

The following *abhanga* succinctly portrays the major dimensions of Janābāī's character—her desperate need to "catch" Viṭṭhal (the divine), her devotion to and final identity with him, and her unwavering resolve to "hold on to him!"

That trickster of Paṇḍharī, that Viṭṭhal,
I have caught him,
holding him with a rope
around his neck,
I locked him up
in my heart.

I lashed him repeatedly
with these words,
"*So'ham so'ham* (I am He)."
Viṭṭhal implored, "Let me go!"
Janī said, "O Viṭṭhalā!
I will not let you go
till the end of your life!"

—*NG: abhanga* 316

In her own poetry, we find three images of Janābāī. The first is of Janābāī as an orphan-maid, deprived of parents and family. She is lonely and overburdened with the daily chores she is expected to perform for Nāmadeva's family. Here is Janābāī, a woman suffocated by the pain of her worldly existence as a maid, who is desperately struggling for release from this suffering. In her second image as *Nāmayācī dāsī* Nāmadeva's maid, Janābāī does not appear as a helpless, lost, low-caste woman, but rather, as a disciple of the saint Nāmadeva in whom she has found her *guru*. Here she considers herself to be blessed in her role as maid to Nāmadeva, whom she calls *parīs* (a stone which is believed to have the magical power to transform iron into gold). In Nāmadeva, she finds her goal, as well as the way to achieve it. For Janābāī, reaching the divine Viṭṭhal is the goal and Nāmadeva is the path to reach it. The third image of Janābāī is of *Santa Janābāī*, "Janābāī the saint," who has attained the spiritual goal (*śreyas*) of union with the divine and thereby has transcended the suffering of her worldly existence as a maid. She is *Nāmayācī dāsī*, "Nāmadeva's maid," no more. She is Viṭṭhal himself. It is Viṭṭhal who performs all of the chores (of the maid) of grinding grain, washing clothes, and so on. All three images of Janābāī are real. Since these images portray almost mutually exclusive characteristics of Janābāī's personality (that is, a helpless woman versus a contented saint), it is possible to assume that these were various phases through which she passed in her life. However, a close look at Janābāī's poetry shows that these images need not be treated as sequentially occurring phases in Janābāī's life. Moreover, they are not necessarily various phases of her spiritual development (from the maid to the saint); rather, they are various expressions of her spirituality which does not negate or exclude any of these images through which Janābāī passes at will at various times. This is the vision of Janābāī's *mukti*, the ultimate freedom. It is not the freedom **from** but freedom **in** living in this world of names and forms (*nāmarūpa*). Janābāī's spiritual experience not only involves the transformation of Janābāī into Viṭṭhal but also Viṭṭhal's transformation into Janābāī. For her, who had experienced *advaita* (nonduality or union with the divine), *dvaita bhāva* (duality—separation from the divine) was merely an excuse to relate to Viṭṭhal. *Dāsī Janī* provided her a way to relate to Viṭṭhal. Janābāī was simultaneously a *bhakta,* "devotee" as well as Viṭṭhal—the divine itself. Added to this, Janābāī's image as a poet who composed devotional poetry in the form of *abhanga* and *ovī* (two very popular forms of poetry of her time) is well-known in Maharashtra.

Nāmayācī Dāsī Janī, 'Janī, Nāmadeva's Maid'

Janābāī celebrated her role as Nāmadeva's maid. She acknowledged that Nāmadeva's family was her family. Her spiritual life was also very much guided and influenced by Nāmadeva. Calling herself *Nāmayācī Janī,* she is very proud of being part of his life. She says that just as iron is transformed into gold by the touch of *Parīs,* so was she transformed into Viṭṭhal because of her spiritual association with Nāmadeva. She claims that she could associated with Viṭhobā (a term of endearment for Viṭṭhal) only because of Nāmadeva:

> "Only by being
> Nāma's *dāsī*"
> says Janī,
> "I could see Viṭṭhal."
> Blessed (indeed) is my birth,
> Blessed is my line (of ancestors)
> and Blessed is my *swāmī* (Nāmadeva),
> the devotee of Viṣṇu.
>
> —*NG: abhanga* 341

> Nāmā,
> the devotee of
> four *yugas*
> is singing
> the praise (of God)
> And with her eyes closed
> in meditation
> Janī is standing
> behind him.
>
> —*NG: abhanga* 484

According to Janābāī, her association with Nāmadeva had continued through several births. "Nāma was Prahlād and I was Padminī, his *dāsī* in his second birth; he was Angad, the devotee of Rāma and I was Mantharā.

In the Dvāparayuga, he was Uddhav, who served Kṛṣṇa, and I was Kubjā, who was uplifted by the god Kṛṣṇa. In Kaliyuga, he is born as Nāmadeva who is lost in the meditation of Viṭṭhal, and Janī is born to serve him." (*NG: abhanga* 431).

In all her earlier births, Nāmadeva, she claims, was a devotee, while she was his *dāsī,* the maid. In her *tīrthāvaḷī* "pilgrimages" Janābāī reveals the depth of her affection for Nāmadeva in the following episode of which she is the narrator. The context of the narrative is as follows (*NG: abhanga* 334–337).[7]

> Jñāneśwar wants to take Nāmadeva along with him on a pilgrimage. Janābāī describes the intimate conversation between Jñāneśwar and Viṭṭhal. Viṭṭhal says, "Do not take Nāmadeva with you. I cannot live without Nāmadeva!" But then he calls Nāmadeva and says to him, "Nāmyā, you have to go with Jñāndeva. I cannot help but let you go. I cannot go against Jñāndeva's insistence." As Nāmadeva is leaving, Viṭṭhal says to all saints, "All of you are wise and knowledgeable. My Nāmadeva is innocent and naive. Take care of him, make sure that the thorns do not bother him. Walk slowly. Nāmadeva is not used to walking such a long distance. Make sure that he eats well." And with these words, Viṭṭhal starts crying!
>
> Unable to bear separation from Nāmadeva, Viṭṭhal stopped going to the temple. Rukmiṇī said to him "*Swāmī, puruṣottamā,* go to the temple." Viṭṭhal said, "When my Nāmadeva returns from the pilgrimage, I will come to the temple. All four directions seem empty to me without Nāmadeva. My mind does not settle on anything." Janābāī says, "It is because Viṭṭhal is so much attached to Nāmadeva, that I have become his maid."

In another *abhanga,* Janābāī asks Viṭṭhal to allow her to be reborn over and over again to serve Nāmadeva. She says:

> God,
> grant me a birth again!
> then alone
> my mind will
> rest in peace.
> But make sure
> O lord of Paṇḍharī!
> that in each birth
> I am blessed
> to serve Nāmadeva
> may it be a birth of

a bird, a pig, an animal,
a baest, or a cat!
This is my wish, says Janī.

—*NG: abhanga* 296

Through this narrative Janābāī not only glorifies Nāmadeva's bond with the divine, but she also indicates that she was *naturally* attracted to Nāmadeva because of his divine connection.

Janābāī: A Helpless Cry

Another equally powerful image of Janābāī is that of a socially downtrodden woman who is deprived of the relationships that are normally cherished by a woman in her worldly life. Janābāī, though adopted by Nāmadeva's family, was always acutely aware of her loneliness and her position as an orphan. She does not say much about her personal relationship with the other members of Nāmadeva's family. In fact, her *abhangas* are distinctly expressive of her deprivation of worldly relationships. She finds her mother, father, and friend in Viṭṭhal. Like a child, she approaches Viṭṭhal, takes her complaints to him, and, like a friend, she gets angry with him. Finally, when depressed, she finds solace in him.

My father and mother passed away
now you take care of me Viṭṭhalā!
my mind is distressed,
O *Hari*,[8] truly, I have no one of my own!

—*NG: abhanga* 266

What should I do,
O lord of Paṇḍharī!
even time is not on my side.
I am left in the alien land
Viṭhā![9]
I can bring this outcry only to you.
I am really tired, Keśavā![10]
you are my only refuge.
who else besides you, my friend
can console me?
a lowly and helpless woman as I am,

Janī says,
"Bring me under your refuge."

—*NG: abhanga* 208

In the following *abhangas,* Janābāī expresses her intense desperation and her plea to Viṭṭhal to accept her as his own. Janābāī's spirituality is inseparable from her human need to relate to and to belong to someone, depend on someone naturally, without having to justify this dependence.

In this desperation she reminds Viṭṭhal that his rejection will be the declaration of her ultimate abandonment by him, and that she will feel betrayed and hopeless.

If Gangā (the Ganges)
goes to the sea
and is rejected by him
Tell me, Viṭṭhal, who should she turn to?

If the water abandons
the water-creatures
and mother rejects her own child
who should they turn to?
Viṭṭhalā! I have to seek
refuge in you, says Janī
"If you reject me,
It will be a breach of promise!"

—*NG: abhanga* 182

Janābāī's helplessness and total dependence on Viṭṭhal is expressed in the metaphors she employs for Viṭṭhal. She calls him *āndhaḷyācī kāṭhī,* "the blindman's stick" (*abhanga* 183). She repeatedly asserts that one gets everything—money, wife, mother by relating to Viṭṭhal. She calls him mother (*āī*).

Come, Viṭhābāī!
Come, my mother of Paṇḍharpūr!
Come with your two daughters—Bhīmā[11] and
Chandrabhāgā[12] and dance
in my courtyard.

—*NG: abhanga* 211

When her daily chores tire her out, Janābāī runs to Viṭṭhal as a child runs to its mother. What underlies this is Janābāī's deep conviction about the mother-child relationship between her and Viṭṭhal. The metaphors she uses for this relationship are poignant.

> The bird flies to the end of
> the horizon
> and brings food for its young.
> The mother-eagle wanders in the sky
> but hastens back to her young
> Mother is busy with her work
> and yet her mind never leaves her child.
> Mother monkey jumps over a tree
> with her child holding onto her stomach.
> Similarly, mother Viṭṭhal watches over Janī
> over and over again!
>
> —*NG: abhanga* 228

> Mother Doe!
> Where in this forest are you lost?
> speechless calf as I am,
> I am lost in the maze,
> searching for home.
>
> —*NG: abhanga* 306

> Life is departing from me, mother! come soon
> Janī requests the saints,
> "Please, take me to my mother!"
>
> —*NG: abhanga* 6

Janābāī's *Devapise* "Divine Frenzy"

Another equally powerful dimension of Janābāī is her complete identification with Viṭṭhal. Janābāī has two identities—one Janābāī and the other Viṭṭhal himself. As Janābāī, she sees herself as Nāmadeva's maid or Viṭṭhal's *lek* "daughter." However, her body awareness vanishes when she meets Viṭṭhal. She merges into Viṭṭhal as salt dissolves into water. This experience of dissolving her separate identity into that of Viṭṭhal is beautifully described by her in the following *abhanga:*

> The divine flood of self-knowledge came over me
> I tried to resist it and directed it

to my heart.
That flood of divine light
blinded my eyes
Janābāī says,
the one who watched the
flood was Raghuvīr[13] himself!

—*NG: abhanga* 332

This was a complete transformation of Janābāī into Viṭṭhal. This experience is described by her in the following *abhanga:*

What I eat is divine
What I drink is divine
My bed is also divine
The divine is here, and it is there
There is nothing empty of divine
Janī says—Viṭhābāī has filled
everything from the inside out.

—*NG: abhanga* 328

Janābāī describes the various phases of this experience of identity with Viṭṭhal as the gradual emptying out of various levels of consciousness until one reaches the point when the knower and known merge into each other. She uses the metaphor of *śūnya* "emptiness" for these levels. Janī says, "The one who experiences that divine joy loses oneself completely. *Yogī,* he remains no more. Nāmadeva's Janī has merged into the ocean, never to return again!"

One is established
in the utmost joy.
The consciousness
of body has
completely vanished.

Having experienced
this divine slumber
one does not ever
wake up to the *bhāva* (worldly happenings) again!
Such is the divine peace
permeated with radiant joy.
When the entire being is

blessed,
even the memory of
linga-deha[14] vanishes
in the oblivion
Having attained that oneness
dāsī Janī is no more!

—*NG: abhanga* 322

Janābāī describes that state of complete freedom from the body, where all body consciousness is gone. Those who awaken to this joy never again return to consciousness of this world! When she becomes one with the Divine,

Janī is *dāsī* no more!
The experience was of joy
The experiencer was joy itself
And the object of experience
was also joy!
When this oneness is experienced
the illusion of separation vanished!

—*NG: abhanga* 228

In the following *abhanga,* Janābāī describes Viṭṭhal's transformation into maid.

(Once) Janī, hungry and fatigued, took
the wash (clothes)
to the nearby (river)
Viṭṭhal ran
behind her
and implored her,
"Why did you not take me
with you?"
"God, why did you come
running like this?" asked Janī.
Viṭṭhal,
the very life-force
of the world,
looked down in bashfulness

and kept following her
silently, without uttering a word!

—*NG: abhanga* 262

Womanhood as the "Core" of Janābāī's Existence

Although all of the images discussed in the previous sections are real, they are all rooted in Janābāī's existence as a woman. The apparent discrepancy in the images (that is, desperate Janābāī versus peaceful Janābāī) are resolved if we look at their source—her womanhood. Janābāī's suffering and deprivation is the suffering and deprivation of a *dāsī*, a woman who perpetually yearns for a family, mother, father, husband, and children. She is a woman desperately trying to relate to someone. It is in Viṭṭhal that she realizes all of these relationships. Viṭṭhal becomes her mother, father, friend, husband and child. Viṭṭhal becomes her *māher* "mother's home." The following episode in Janābāī's life (as reported by her as well as Nāmadeva) clearly shows Janābāī's true identity as a woman, that is, it reveals her identity as a lover of Viṭṭhal. The event is interpreted differently by Janābāī and the people around her; it provides a clear documentation of both Janābāī's faith and other people's disbelief in her conviction. The event is vividly described by Janābāī as follows (*NG: abhanga* 285–287):

> Once *dev* (God) came and lay down by Janī on her comfortable bed and whispering the secrets of love, *dev* dozed off (and the whole night passed). In the morning, Janī said to Viṭṭhal, "Wake up, O bearer of *cakra!* The light of dawn has filled the world!" Viṭṭhal woke up and rushed back to his temple. In that moment of haste, Viṭṭhal left his garment and his necklace with a pendant set with precious jewels (*Vaijayantī mālā*) at Janābāī's, covered himself with Janābāī's *vākaḷ* (a light shawl), and hastened back to the temple. Viṭṭhal stood in his place in the temple wrapped in Janī's shawl. What a miracle it was! The devotees visit the *mahādvār* (the entrance to the temple) (to redeem themselves from their sins) and the real thief (*Viṭṭhal*) is standing still inside the chamber of the temple!" Early in the morning, the priests noticed that Viṭṭhal was stripped of his garments and necklace, and they announced the "big robbery" that had occurred in the temple. Janī's *vākaḷ* on Viṭṭhal convinced them that Janī was the thief! "O tailor's maid! return the precious pendant which you've stolen!" they said to Janī, and lo and behold! the pendant fell down from the shawl. They were even

more confident now that it *was* indeed Janī who had stolen the pendant. Janī implored them, "Be kind to me, I swear in the name of my friend Viṭṭhal, I have not stolen it. Don't beat me, the real thief is the lord of Paṇḍharī." (NG: *abhanga* 287) But no one listened to her. She was taken to the place of execution. Janī prayed to Viṭṭhal to come and rescue her from disaster, but she did not see Viṭṭhal anywhere around. Finally, she agreed to be executed. She bathed in the river *Candrabhāgā,* prayed to Viṭṭhal, and prepared herself for execution. A large group of people were following her, clapping and repeating Viṭṭhal's name. As the procession reached the place of execution, Janī said in desperation, "Janī publicly announces today that Viṭṭhal is dead indeed." (that is, he is not there to save his own devotee!). However, just as she was about to be executed, a miracle happened! She did not see the gallows standing in front of her; instead, she saw a tree. And soon that tree melted into water. People were astonished by this *camatkār,* "miracle." They clapped and proclaimed, "Janī is indeed blessed!" This event established Janī as a saint among the people and liberated her from her status as a maid. Additionally, this event vividly expresses Janābāī's yearning for passionate love (which she directs toward Viṭṭhal) as well as people's distrust toward a lower caste maid. For Janābāī, however, it was a public recognition of Viṭṭhal's love for her! Nāmdeva also has narrated this event in his *gāthā.* What Janābāī wanted was not so much to be recognized as a saint as much as to be recognized as Viṭṭhal's lover Janī!

Janābāī's suffering as a woman and a maid is expressed in many *abhangas.* She complains that she was never really accepted as a member of the family by Nāmadeva's relatives (*NG: abhanga* 207). She was never allowed to enter the temple because she was a maid. Janābāī's revolt is a revolt against social customs that did not allow her to participate in the secular (family) and spiritual (temple) domains of society. However, she does not want to renounce her status as a woman. In fact, she celebrates her womanhood and expresses her emotions in the most powerful language. When she is angry with Viṭṭhal (for not lifting the social barriers between them) she threatens him with a public declaration of her relationship with him. She is not worried about being called a *vesavā* "immoral woman" (or a prostitute). She is willing to place a *veenā* "a musical instrument" on her shoulder, unveil her face, and proceed toward Viṭṭhal's temple, singing his praise in the marketplace (*NG: abhanga* 362). Again, Janābāī does not want to be "stripped of" her status of a woman or maid; rather, she wants the acceptance of the "divination" of both.

If we examine Janābāī's selection of themes in her narrative poetry (*ākhyāna*), it becomes clear that these themes are excuses or opportunities for her to reinforce her relationship with Viṭṭhal. Although Janābāī follows the *vārkarī* tradition of narrative devotional poetry, the selection of themes is her own. They are taken from popular stories originally found in the epics (the *Rāmāyaṇa* and the *Mahābhārata* and the *purāṇas*). The major characters in these stories are those who transcend worldly calamities because of the grace (*kṛpā*) of the god. Draupadī, in the narrative entitled *Thālīpāk* "the dish-in-the-pan," and *Draupadīvastraharaṇ* "disrobing of Draupadī," is a woman who is about to be disgraced and humiliated, but is saved by Kṛṣṇa. These two narratives occur in the *Mahābhārata.* The third narrative, *Hariścandrākhyān* "story of Hariścandra," occurs in the *Mārkaṇḍeya Purāṇa* and is a tale of a chain of disasters faced by the virtuous mythical King Hariścandra and his wife Tārāmatī, and their deliverance from suffering by the grace of Kṛṣṇa. It seems that Janābāī identifies with these characters and relives her own suffering as a downtrodden woman, and, finally, assures herself that Kṛṣṇa (in the form of Viṭṭhal) is certain to liberate her (as he did those characters) from the worldly suffering. Again, Janābāī is not seeking liberation from womanhood, but rather liberation in womanhood.

A very delicate texture of her woman's heart is revealed in her role as mother, which she assumes toward baby Kṛṣṇa in *pāḷṇā* "lullaby." She calls him *māze acaḍe bacaḍe* "my tiny little baby," with jingling anklets, who attracts the attention of the "three worlds" through his playful tricks (*NG: abhanga* 475). Janābāī wants to enjoy and realize her motherly instinct through this mother-child relationship. She pays the ultimate tribute to Viṭṭhal's greatness when she calls him Viṭṭhal, "the mother of many children." For Janābāī, the most attractive form of the divine is its form as mother. Janābāī's ultimate wish is to experience the essential divinity of all forms and actions. Her spiritual vision divinizes all. She does not see anything separate from the divine. Therefore, she wants to continue to be Janī, who pounds and grinds the grain; but, she wants to do this with the vision that the pounder, the grinder, and the grain are all Viṭṭhal himself (*NG: abhanga* 317). In general, Janābāī's identity as a woman underlies her experiences—the experience of suffering in her secular life and the one of divine frenzy in her spiritual life.

Janābāī: Merely a Reflection of Tradition?

As mentioned earlier, Janābāī was greatly influenced by the philosophy, theology, and socioreligious mission of the *Vārkarī Panthā.* Her devotion to Viṭṭhal shows a remarkable blend of the worship of the *saguṇa* (personal) and the *nirguṇa* (impersonal) divine, which was typical of the *Vārkarī Panthā*. Her Viṭṭhal is both *saguṇa* (personal god) and *nirguṇa* (impersonal god). *Saguṇa Viṭṭhal* leaves *Vaikuṇtha*, "the divine abode," and comes to be with Janī (*abhanga* 230). He sweeps floors along with her (*abhanga* 224), bathes her (*abhanga* 224), grinds the grain (*abhanga* 226), and Janābāī relates to him in many different ways. At times Janābāī is Viṭṭhal's (Kṛṣṇa's) mother singing a lullaby, and at other times she is his daughter, friend, or his beloved! However, her complete identification with Viṭṭhal as *nirguṇa* (impersonal God) is equally real. She calls him Viṭṭhāi, mother Viṭṭhal, as well as *agocar*, "beyond the grasp of senses."

Janābāī shares her vision of the divine with other saints of the *Vārkarī Panthā* such as Nāmadeva, Jñāndeva, and Tukārām. Janābāī's Viṭṭhal is similar to Tulsidas' Rām, Mirābāi's Kṛṣṇa, and Nāmadeva's Viṭhobā in that all of these are various forms of the *nirguṇa* (impersonal divine). However, Janābāī's vision differs significantly from theirs in other respects. The ultimate experience/vision of the divine for the saints was transcendence from body awareness, and, thereby, release from *saṃsāra* (the cycle of rebirth) and suffering. It is, for most of the saints, a unidirectional journey of the devotee toward the divine. The divine remains the divine through his various incarnations of Kṛṣṇa, Rāma, or Viṭhobā; it is the devotee who, through his/her intense devotion, reaches out to the divine. The saints also assume various roles and relationship vis-à-vis their divine. For Mīrā, Kṛṣṇa was her lover and she was Rādhā; for Tulsīdās, Rām was his god and he was his devotee; for Nāmadeva, Viṭṭhal was his *sakhā*, friend.

Janābāī was different. Her relationship with Viṭṭhal took many forms and embraced every relationship that can exist between two people. Viṭṭhal was her *māy-bāp* "parent (mother-father)," her child (she calls him *māze acaḍe*, "my baby, my child"), her lover Viṭhobā, her *dās* "servant" and *Viṭhyā* (a derogatory address-term) and Janī herself. Janābāī related to Viṭṭhal as a child, mother, lover, friend, and devotee. Janābāī's vision is also unique in another sense. When Janābāī says *dāsī Janī nāhī ātā*, "Now Janābāī is not a maid anymore," She is not simply describing her transcendence from her body as Janī, rather, she is describing her transformation into Viṭṭhal, as well as Viṭṭha's transformation into Janābāī. Her vision of *advaita*, a total identification with Viṭṭhal, is expressed in the following *abhanga:*

"*dev* (the divine Viṭṭhal) is here,
dev is there
there is nothing

empty of the divine"
Janī says
"Vithabai! (a term of endearment for Viṭṭhal)
you have
embraced me
within and without"

—*NG: abhanga* 328

And the following *abhanga* illustrates her vision of the transformation of Viṭṭhal into Janābāī:

Janābāī decides to
pound *sālī* (a kind of grain)
And Viṭṭhal cleans the grind-stone!
By continuously pounding the grain
The lord of Panḍhari (Viṭṭhal)
is fatigued and worn out!

—*NG: abhanga* 226

Scope of Janābāī's *Abhanga*

Janābāī's devotional poetry covers a large number of themes. Some of the themes such as *nāmasaṃkīrtan,* 'the repetition of (God's) name," biographies of saints such as Jñāneśwar, Senā nhāvi, Nāmadeva, *Daśāvatāra,* narratives based on the ten incarnations of Viṣṇu), and birth and life of Kṛṣṇa are typical of *Vārkarī Panthā.* Other themes focus on her relationship to Viṭṭhal (that is, *Viṭṭhal mahātmya* "the glory of Viṭṭhal," *karuṇā* "cry for help," *bheṭ* "meeting with Viṭṭhal," *bhaktavatsalatā* "the divine love for the devotee," *māgṇe* "wish"). Additionally, some themes relate to her spiritual experience—*ātma svarūpasthiti,* "the state of spiritual experience," *Janābāīcā niścay* "Janābāī's resolve." Finally, there are themes of advice—*upadeś* "advice," *santastuti* "praise of saints," and *bhāruḍ* (simple religious feelings expressed in simple metaphors for the common people).

Janābāī's poetry is a unique mixture of tradition and innovation. The traditional religious themes of *daśāvatāra,* "the ten incarnations," and *thālīpāk* "the dish-in-the-pan" depict her knowledge of Purāṇa literature. The selection of these traditional themes clearly indicates the compassionate nature of the divine who, time and again, takes various forms and saves the devotees. Janābāī's compositions, including biographies and praise of the saints, the importance of the name of God, and the significance of pilgrimage all conform to the tradition of *Vārkarī Panthā.* They locate her in the *Pantha* and show her identification with its mission of propagating devotion to Viṭṭhal, transcendence from caste barriers, and repetition of God's name as a legitimate path. In the other themes, we find Janābāī's expression of her independence and her personal spiritual experience. All through these themes, Janābāī is searching for her own identity, the identity of one who is helpless at the worldly level—like the world itself in the stories of ten incarnations, like Draupadī in *thālīpāk,* and like several others whom the divine released from their suffering in various forms. Additionally, Janābāī uses *bhāruḍ,*[17] a folk genre, to express her religious sentiment. A *bhāruḍ* is a song that is meant to be "acted out" with dramatic facial expressions and gestures. It serves as a counterpart of the elite Hindu religious practices of temple worship, and recitation of the traditional scriptures. It is composed in the language of the common people, with the powerful metaphors from their daily life. The goal of the *bhāruḍ* is the most personal expression of the religious sentiments. A *bhāruḍ* has a janus-like character; "It can be interpreted as an allegory of casting off various sins and attachments" (Zelliot 1987:98). However, it can also be interpreted as a statement of social restrictions on women imposed through the social/family system that would not allow them the freedom to pursue their religious goals. In the following *bhāruḍ,* Janābāī assumes the role of a woman who is struggling to break away from the worldly/family ties or restrictions and as a result, prays to God to liberate her from them by letting them die. Once again, we witness Janābāī's empathy with women suppressed by the society and their desperate struggle to transcend the social barriers to reach the divine!

> God, *Khaṇḍerāyā!*
> I offer *navas,*
> my special prayers, to you!
> let my mother-in-law die.
> Then, O lord of Paṇḍharī,
> my support, my connection
> will be broken!
> Let my father-in-law die too!
> And I will truly rejoice!
> O *Khaṇḍerāyā!*
> let my sister-in-law die!

Once she dies,
I will be liberated
once and forever!
Then I will wear
the bag of your *bhaṇḍār,*[18]
around my neck!
Janī says, "Viṭṭhalā!
let every one pass away,
let me be alone, and free
to be at your feet
forever!

—*NG abhanga* 478

Janābāī's Position among Women Saints

One may ask at this point if Janābāī is similar to other women saints in India in general and to women saints who belonged to the *Vārkarī Pantha* in particular. The answer is "yes" and "no." Yes, because Janābāī shares some of the features of her personality and poetry with other women saints. For example, similar to the other two women saints of the *Vārkarī Pantha,* Muktābāī (Jñāneśwar's sister) and Bahiṇābāī (Tukāram's disciple), Janābāī was associated with a male saint (Nāmadeva) and was very much influenced by his beliefs as a devotee regarding Viṭṭhal as personal god, repetition and singing of God's name as the path toward union with the divine, and the composition of devotional poetry in the language of the common people. However, Janābāī distinctly differs from them in social status and expression of spiritual experience. Muktābāī was never married; nor did she ever express the need for any worldly relationships, including marriage. She belonged to the Brāhmaṇa caste and a very spiritually oriented family of saints such as Sopān, Nivṛtī, and Jñāneśwar. She saw her role as a guide for those who suffer in *saṃsāra.* In her poetry, we do not see any struggle to go beyond "this world." She appears as one who has reached the "other shore." Muktābāī is "born free." Janābāī, though unmarried like Muktābāī, is socially downtrodden and is struggling to transcend the suffering of this worldly life. She has a feeling of acute deprivation.

Bahiṇābāī is married and remains so until the end of her life; she seeks and finds liberation from worldly suffering in the family. For

Bahiṇābāī, the life of a woman is difficult. It is difficult for a woman to renounce her family and turn to God. She says, "A woman is not independent. Denouncement of worldly life is not the solution for her suffering. I despise sensual pleasures. But who cares about me?" (Bahiṇābāī: *abhanga* 67). Bahiṇābāī does not revolt against social traditions; rather, she compromises her spirituality with her duty toward her husband. Her devotional poetry is the poetry of compromise between the *pativratā,* "a devoted wife," and *virakta,* "detached" Bahiṇābāī. Thus these three women saints, though devoted to Viṭṭhal, differ from each other in their experience of worldly life.

Janābāī differs from Muktābāī and Bahiṇābāī in her expression of spirituality as well. For Muktābāī, worldly existence was nominal (*nimittamātra*); she had no conflict with worldly life. She had transcended it. Therefore, her devotional poetry is the expression of her state of union with the divine. "Muktābāī is indeed one with the divine. She lives in this world of duality, but she has gone beyond it. She sees that eternity in herself." (Muktābāī: *abhanga* 11). Muktābāī is aloof, unattached, and, therefore, beyond struggle. Her devotional poetry is for *sādhaka,* "seekers of truth," and not for *prāpañcika,* "householders." Her sainthood is in her "other worldliness." Unlike Muktābāī, Janābāī's spirituality is rooted in "this world" and her experience of it as a downtrodden woman; her sainthood lies not in her withdrawal from worldly life but rather in her extraordinary capacity to transform it into life with or in the divine. Janābāī's message is simple but strong. Social inequities cannot prevent one from reaching the divine. The solution to worldly suffering is devotion to Viṭṭhal. Once one is united with Viṭṭhal, one sees the whole world permeated with him. The one who has this "vision" is liberated from all suffering. It is Janābāī's rootedness in this world, her revolt against social traditions, and, finally, her faith in the divinity of all, that have made her one of the most influential women saints of Mahārashtra. She never had any direct mission to uplift the downtrodden; neither does she claim to have any desire to be a spiritual guide to the "oppressed" ones.

Though her poetry does not explicitly advocate any such mission, Janābāī has been a source of powerful spiritual inspiration for women in rural and urban Mahārashtra who find their spiritual ideal realized in her. Her devotional poetry, though an expression of self, has become an enigmatic symbol of feminine power. Her simple words "Do not be depressed because you are a woman; saints and mystics are born in this form (of a woman) among the people!" speak of her confidence in the spiritual power of women. Janābāī differs sharply from Bahiṇābāī in that she is not for any compromise between the secular and the spiritual dimensions of life; rather, she believes in the transformation of the secular into the divine. In her *ekāgra* "unwavering" devotion to Viṭṭhal and her disregard for social traditions, Janābāī is similar to Mīrābāī, who boldly expressed her love for Kṛṣṇa in the wake of her marriage with a king. However, Mīrā's relationship to Kṛṣṇa was well-defined; it was a relationship between two lovers. Mīrā's *Kānhā* always remained the "lifter of the mountain." Janābāī's Viṭṭhal had to become her lover, father, mother—even her child! Janābāī not only transformed herself into Viṭṭhal but transformed Viṭṭhal into Janābāī.

Finally, it is interesting to consider whether Janābāī's spirituality differed from Nāmadeva's. Janābāī herself claims that her spiritual union with Viṭṭhal was entirely due to Nāmadeva. She celebrates her role as *nāmayācī dāsī Janī* (Nāmadeva's maid, Janī). The form (*abhanga*), and the devotional content of Janābāī's poetry certainly show the direct influence of Nāmadeva (as well as Jñāneśwar). Similar to Nāmadeva, she incorporated into her poetry narrative (*ākhyāna*) selected from earlier scriptures. She also included biographies of saints and followed the Vārkarī tradition of promoting the *nāmasaṃkīrtana,* "repeating and singing God's name," as well as *tīrtha,* "pilgrimage," as legitimate paths of devotion (*bhakti*). Finally, she, like Nāmadeva, strongly argued for social equality. However, unlike Nāmadeva (and Jñāneśwar), she did not base her views on any philosophy; nor was her primary concern to establish or promote a path. Her devotional poetry remains the genuine expression of her personal experiences of secular and spiritual life. Her poetry narrates a saga of her worldly suffering, her quest for release from that suffering through union with Viṭṭhal, and, finally, her experience of the divine in everything—including her suffering! It would not be an exaggeration to say that this self-expression became a guiding force for the downtrodden women in the following centuries. However, that was not the intention behind Janābāī's devotional songs. Nāmadeva provided her with the framework of the *Vārkarī Pantha* to express her spirituality. Janābāī extended the spiritual vision of the *Vārkarī Pantha* by strongly emphasizing and elevating her womanhood into a medium through which to connect to or identify with the divine. In this sense, Janābāī differed from most of the saints. For her, the form of a woman was not a barrier to be crossed in order to relate to the divine; rather, she perceived her womanhood as the power to embrace the divine through multiple relationships, as well as the power to humanize the divine. We do not see subversion of womanhood in Janābāī's poetry. What we see is the elevation of womanhood to the divine. In this sense, Janābāī was a woman saint in her secular as well as her spiritual life.

Translations of Janābāī's (Selected) *Abhangas*

"Efficacy of God's Name": Nāmasamkīrtan Māhātmya

1. Sing the glory of Viṭṭhal,
and the greatest of the sins
will be burnt away.
Remember him,
the source of joy
and you will fear nothing!
says Janī, "Let your actions, speech
and mind sing the glory of God."

—*NG: abhanga* 145

2. While pounding and grinding
(the grain), O Infinite Viṭṭhalā!
I will sing your name.

—*NG abhanga* 342

Janābāī and Viṭṭhal: A Dynamic Relationship

1. This lord of Paṇḍharī
is divine inheritance
He rescued me from
my suffering!

—*NG: abhanga* 360

2. "Come, give me a hand, Viṭṭhalā!
I am exhausted.
O Viṭṭhalā! you are my *māher*'
Why this delay?
Why are you trying my patience?
O lord of Paṇḍharī!
Haven't I offered my whole self
at your feet?
Thus says the daughter Janī
to her divine father.

—*NG: abhanga* 197

3. Salt touches water
so I touched Viṭṭhal,

and soon I was dissolved into him!
Blessed is my *māybāp* Nāmā
who took me to Paṇḍharī,
and led me to Viṭṭhal.
Day and night,
I could think of nothing but Viṭṭhal.
My mind,
scattered in multifold directions,
finally merged into Viṭṭhal.
Paṇḍuranga himself
came to see Janī.
How can I possibly describe
the joy of that meeting?

—*NG: abhanga* 217

4. Janī sweeps the floor,
and Viṭṭhal—the bearer of the *cakra*[15]
collects the dust,
and carries it in a basket,
and throws it away for her!
Viṭṭhal lost himself
in Janī's devotion,
and started doing
such lowly jobs!
Janī said, "Viṭṭhalā!
how will I ever repay
this debt?"

—*NG: abhanga* 287

5. *dev*[16] was trapped
in Janī's intense devotion!
and left Vaikuṇṭha,
his own heavenly abode
and descended
down to Pandharī.

—*NG: abhanga* 431

6. Viṭṭhal writes down Janābāī's poetry:

"I wrote down Janī's words
as she uttered them

Jñānadevā! let it be
known to you,
This has not made me
any less divine!
"The absolute truth
is the paper, and
with ink of eternity
Viṭṭhal writes on it
Incessantly
with Janī."
Jñānadeva smiled
at these words
and clapped.
Janī's victory was
proclaimed in the
entire world!

—*NG: abhanga* 281

7. Viṭṭhal comes to meet Janābāī:

Once, in the middle of the night
Viṭṭhal came (to meet Janī)
Nāmā said, "Janī! look,
who is at the door!"
The whole house
was overflowing with divine light

Everyone was awakened!
(Nāmā watched)
Viṭṭhal and Janī embraced each other
Nāmā said, "Janī is blessed!"

—*NG: abhanga* 267

8. Angry Janī scolds Viṭṭhal:

I have no fascination for you, God!
I am not going to serve you anymore!
You are not magnanimous
Why do you carry this false pride
of greatness?

What will you gain by getting angry with me?
We the devotees are the source of your strength.
You have no power of your own.
Harī, haven't I understood your secret?

—*NG: abhanga* 345

9. Janābāī abuses Viṭṭhal when he does not come to rescue her:

"Oh, you Viṭhyā! Viṭhyā!
you are dead indeed!
you—the irresponsible child,
born of mother's lust!
your wife has become
a widow today!
who once wore the
bracelet of *janma-sāvitrī*—
a promise of
your eternal life!
Today was your funeral!
Even Time cried to see you die!"

Thus, standing in her courtyard,
Janī abused Viṭṭhal.

—*NG: abhanga* 163

Janābāī's Mystical Experience:

1. I received everything I had wished.
The *ananta* blessed me
with everything I had aspired for.
He led me to the state
beyond the consciousness of body,
my ego is vanished,
he has blessed me with eternal peace!
He crushed the very
source of anger,
and established knowledge
(in me).
Viṭṭhal granted me refuge in him.

Janī says, "God is indeed gracious!"

—*NG: abhanga* 340

2. Janī's dialogue with herself:
You are singing alone,
but another voice always seems to accompany you.
Janī, who sings with you?

Pāṇḍuranga is my father,
Rakhumāī is my mother,
Janī says, "I entered their home,
and was blessed with joy!"

—*NG: abhanga* 221

3. Transformation of Janābāī's vision:
Janābāī sees Viṭṭhal everywhere:

I see Kṛṣṇa everywhere,
I look to my left—and see Kṛṣṇa
I look to my right—and see Kṛṣṇa
If I look down,
Kṛṣṇa is there too!
everything I see,
moving and non-moving
is radiating Kṛṣṇa
where am I?
I don't recall anymore!

Janābāī's Wish: (Translation of an Unpublished Abhanga*)*

"I will be a dāsī of Pandharpur!"
this is my ardent prayer to Viṭṭhal!

I will be the earth of Pandharpur!
and,
Viṭṭhal will walk on it
with Rakhumāī!

I will be the sand of Pandharpur!
and,
my *māybāp* Gopal
will play with it!

I will be the cow dung of Pandharpur!
and,
annoint the courtyard
of Viṭṭhal!

I will be the step at the (temple) of Pandharpur!
and,
will be blessed
with the touch of Hari's feet
on their way in
and out (of the temple)!

I will be the way to Pandharpur!
and,
countless great saints
will come from everywhere
to meet Viṭṭhal!
and,
Janī, the humble dāsī
will be famous!

abhanga 36 (from the handwritten manuscript of Janābāī's abhangas at Saraswati Mahal library, Tanjavur. Bhingarkar 1989:267)

Notes

1. *Nāmadeva Gāthā* (abbreviated as *NG* in the rest of the text) is the treatise in Marathi composed by Nāmadeva and edited by S. Baber and published by the Government Press, Bombay (1970). (See reference in the text, page 000: Shasakiya mudran a lekhan samagri, Bombay 1970). The English translations of Janābāī's *abhanga* (in Marathi) in the paper are based on those that appear in *Nāmdeva Gāthā* unless noted otherwise.

2. *abhanga* and *ovī:* The word, *abhanga,* means "unbroken" or "straight." In the context of the meter, it means the meter in which there is a consistent (unbroken) pattern. Each *abhanga* has couplets ranging from four to twenty-two. The couplet is called *kaḍva.* Each couplet has four parts (*caraṇ*) of eight letters each. Thus one couplet has thirty-two letters. In *ovī* there are four *caraṇs.* The first three have eight or six letters each while the fourth is invariably shorter than the first three. It generally has four letters. It is called a couplet of 3½ *caraṇs.* Although this is a general pattern of *abhanga* and *ovī,* there is some flexibility in the number of letters in every *caraṇ.*

3. *Samādhi* is a Sanskrit word which means the state of mind in which the saint has transcended the awareness of his/her worldly existence and is in union with the divine. It is believed that when a saint reaches this state, he or she may withdraw from his/her worldly existence. Thus, to take *samādhi* means to voluntarily withdraw from the world (that is, pass away).

4. This reference is taken from (Bhingarkar 1989:2).

5. Ravidās was a saint of the low *camār* (shoemaker) caste. The approximate period of Ravidās was fifteenth- to sixteenth-century A.D. The poems (*padas*) are originally composed in Punjabi. The English translation of Ravidās' poem is taken from the text entitled *Songs of the Saints of India.* Hawley and M. Juergensmeyer (translators) 1988: Oxford University Press, p. 9.

6. Mīrābāī was a woman saint of the sixteenth century who is well-known from her devotional poetry/songs (for Krishna) in Rajasthānī.

7. This narrative is based on the *abhangas* 334 to 337 from *Shri Nāmdeva Gāthā,* (ed.) Shri Nānāmaharaj Sakhre. 1990. Puṇe: Smita Printers.

8. Harī, Vithā, Keśavā are various terms of address which Janābāī uses for Viṭṭhal. While Harī and Keśav are names of Viṣṇu, Vithā (bāī) is a (feminine) term of endearment for Viṭṭhal. Additionally, Viṭhobā and Viṭhābāī are also used by Janābāī for Viṭṭhal.

9. Ibid.

10. Ibid.

11. Bhīmā and Chandrabhāgā are the names of rivers near Pandharpur.

12. Ibid.

13. Raghuvīr is another name of Rāma. Janābāī uses it for Viṭṭhal whose identity with Rāma (the seventh incarnation of Viṣṇu) and thereby with Viṣṇu is implied.

14. *Linga-deha,* "the subtle body." The term refers to the material base of the body made of five elements *ākāśa* (space), *agni* (fire), *āp* (water), *vāyu* (wind), and *pṛthivī* (earth).

15. *Cakra* is a sanskrit word which literally means "disk." In the Purāṇas, it refers to the disk that Viṣṇu holds on his finger. The disk indicates Viṣṇu's power of sustenance of the universe which goes through the cycle of creation, sustenance, destruction, and recreation. Here the metaphor "the bearer of *cakra*" indicates Viṭṭhal's true identity as a powerful god.

16. *dev* is a Marathi/Sanskrit word for God/divine.

17. There is no particular etymological meaning of the word *bhāruḍ* in Marathi. This form of poetry has been used by other saints such as Nāmadeva, Eknāth, etc. For an elaborate discussion on Eknāth's *bhāruḍs,* see Zelliot (1989:91–110), and Dhereb (1978).

18. The word *bhaṇḍār* refers to the yellow powder the devotees of Viṭṭhal place on their foreheads as a marker of Vārkarīs. In the ritual of singing (and dancing)

the praise of Viṭṭhal, the devotees sprinkle the powder in the air to create the ambience of a religious congregation. The devotees generally carry the bag of *bhaṇḍār* around their neck. Therefore, the phrase "to be free to carry the bag of *bhaṇḍār*" symbolizes freedom (of the woman) to become Viṭṭhal's devotee.

References

Bhingarkar, Damodar, Balkrishna. *Santa Kavayitrī Janābaī: Charitra, Kāvya, āni Kāmgirī.* Bombay: Majestic Prakashan, 1989.

Cohn, Robert. In *The Encyclopedia of Religion,* ed. Mircea Eliade, vol. 13, p. 1. New York: Macmillan Publishing Company, 1987.

Dherea, Ramchandra, Chintaman. Nāmayācī Janī, Puṇe: Shri Vidya Prakashan, 1960.

Dhereb, Ramchandra, Chintaman. *Santa Sāhitya āṇi lokasāhitya: kāhī anubandha.* Puṇe: Shri Vidy Prakashan, 1978.

Gold, Daniel. *The Lord as Guru: Hindi Saints in North Indian Tradition.* New York: Oxford University Press, 1987.

Hawley, John Straton, and Mark Juergensmeyer (English Translations). *Songs of the Saints of India.* New York: Oxford University Press, 1988.

Inamdar, Hemant, Vishnu. *Santa Nāmadeva: Kāvya Sambhār āni Santa Parivār.* Puṇe: Sanjay Prakashan, 1987.

Irlekar, Suhasini. *Prācīn Marāthī Santa Kavayitrice vāngmayīn kārya.* Aurangabad: Parimal Prakashan, 1980.

Ranade, Ramchandra, D. *Mysticism in Maharashtra: Indian Mysticism.* (2nd ed.) Delhi: Motilal Banarsidass, 1933, 1982.

Tulpule, Shankar Gopal. *Classical Marathi Literature: From the Beginning to* A.D. 1818. In *A History of Indian Literature,* vol. IX, Edited by Jan Gonda. Weisbaden: Otto Harrassowitz, 1979.

Zelliot, Elinor. *Eknāth's Bhārud: The Saint as a Link between Cultures.* In *The Saints.* Edited by Karine Schomer. Delhi: Motilal Banarsidass, 1989.

VI
Women Ch'an Masters: The Teacher Miao-tsung as Saint

Miriam Levering

Reflections on the Category "Saint" and Its Usefulness in Understanding Ch'an Buddhism

It is safe to say that it would be widely accepted among scholars of religion in the world whose religious categories tend to come from Christianity that Ch'an Buddhism in China and Zen Buddhism in Japan have produced extraordinary human beings worthy of being called "saints." It is not difficult to find in the hagiographies of those traditions, and among living masters, men regarded within their own communities in ways that Christians have regarded saints. But few Western readers and scholars, indeed, few Asian participants, have realized or paid much attention to the fact that the Ch'an and Zen Buddhist traditions in China and Japan have produced saintly women as well.

When we think of "saint," we think of a number of different characteristic qualities and activities. The category of "saint" as members of European and American culture understand it has its root in Western Christianity, particularly in Roman Catholicism. In the West the Roman Catholic Church, before approving of the public veneration of someone as a saint, first determines that the person is one the church is sure is in Heaven. Roman Catholics think of a saint as one who can intercede with God and Christ to perform miracles. And the Roman Catholic Church has always held that one worthy to be venerated as a saint in a public cult must be doctrinally sound, and known to have lived a life of heroic virtue.[1]

Beginning with van der Leeuw, Kristensen, and Joachim Wach, and continuing with a recent multiyear, comparative study of social values that culminated in two books on sainthood, there have been attempts to develop the category of "saint" into one useful to the cross-cultural comparative study of religion.[2]

Scholars in comparative religion have suggested that an important feature of the saint is her or his exemplariness, or imitability. A saint is to be emulated by others. Joachim Wach distinguished "saint" as a social type from "prophet," for example, by saying that what distinguishes the saint is that the individual's personal character is exemplary. J. S. Hawley points out that there are two kinds of exemplariness. The first is the capacity to exemplify virtues that have already been identified as ideals in the culture, while the second is to create a new ideal by exemplifying a virtue that the community for the first time recognizes as a virtue by observing the life of the saint.[3]

But on the other hand, as a type of religious person, the saint displays also an otherness or inimitability. A number of authors in the recent multiyear project point out that saints are often portrayed as displaying gifts that cannot be acquired by an easy or common emulation, or that are not within the experience or reach of most ordinary followers. They also point out that saints sometimes transgress ordinary morality, and thus in another sense are not in a straightforward way exemplary, for their conduct, as opposed to their dedication, cannot be safely emulated. Miracles, signs, and extraordinary powers are expressions not only of the potency but also of the otherness of the power operating through a saint, and it is often the perception of this power that results in the veneration associated with the individual's memory or relics.

In what follows, I will argue that in Mahayana Buddhism the category that is closest to that of "saint" is "bodhisattva," and that in the Ch'an and Zen tradition it is the bodhisattva teacher's ability to express sacred gnosis in words, and to teach skillfully, that makes him or her a saintly person.

Mahayanists have widely held that one becomes a bodhisattva by giving rise to the aspiration to awaken others and rescue them from suffering. A bodhisattva seeks to perfect the power to do these things. She does this through the cultivation of giving, morality, patience, effort, unification of consciousness, and transcendent wisdom. The fruits of this cultivation of these virtues, powers, and character traits are a mind and heart characterized by profound insight into the way things really are, and deep active compassion for the sufferings of all. Bodhisattvas practice and demonstrate heroic virtues, and bodhisattvas become persons whose virtuous conduct, compassion, insight, and freedom from self-concern are qualities that others want to emulate. Along the way bodhisattvas acquire certain supernormal powers. But perhaps the single most defining characteristic of bodhisattvas is that they teach others the Dharma. They rescue others from suffering primarily through effective teaching. If we look at the characteristics of the various stages of spiritual heroism attained by the bodhisattva as detailed in numerous Mahayana scriptures and commentaries, we find that the ability to teach accurately and effectively is one of the chief goals of the bodhisattva, and becomes an attribute of the bodhisattva only at the very highest stages (*bhumi*) of the path.

Let us take a closer look at the way in which saints and other types of holy people have been defined and discussed in the West. This will help us see whether the category as developed in the West should include the Ch'an/Zen teacher bodhisattva, and whether the category is helpful in understanding the sacredness of such people.

Joachim Wach sees bodhisattvas in Mahayana Buddhism, the branch of Buddhism to which Ch'an and Zen belong, as saints. He says that in Mahayana Buddhism "elaborate theological systems have been outlined with a detailed classification of the various stages of sainthood," referring to the many Mahayana scriptures and commentaries that detail the stages of progress toward Buddhahood traversed by the bodhisattva.[4] Although not every aspect of Joachim Wach's way of distinguishing the figure of the saint from other types of religious figures fits well with the Mahayana Buddhist tradition's concept of the bodhisattva, some do. According to Mahayana Buddhists, the bodhisattva teaches others by skillful words and by the influence of her or his own personal charisma as one who has attained higher stages of the path and has been transformed in the process. Correspondingly, for Wach what distinguishes the charisma of the saint from that of other religious figures is that it is personal, not institutional.[5] Further, what characterizes a saint for Wach is that his or her prestige "depends not so much on achievement as on his personal nature and character. . . . The saint influences others more by the indirect effect of example than by precept. The life of the saint is wholly determined by his basic religious experience, which sometimes comes early in life. The biographies of many saints tell of a decisive 'conversion.' He enjoys communion with the deity in a particularly intensive way."[6] Wach suggests that it is characteristic of the saint to guide and direct the lives of others; his or her guidance is eagerly sought. While Buddhists would not want to make the distinction that Wach makes when he says that saints influence others more by example than by precept, other aspects of this description could well fit the Mahayana depiction of the Bodhisattva.

Interestingly, Wach does not draw a firm line between the saint and the religious teacher, as some other comparativists and phenomenologists do. Wach sees guidance of others as a fundamental characteristic of the saint.

Another phenomenologist of religion to attempt to shape and define a category called "saint" is Gerardus van der Leeuw, one of the geniuses of the Dutch phenomenological school of comparative religion. Van der Leeuw divides holy persons into two large categories: those who bear and distribute Power as God's representatives, and those who manifest Power as objects of veneration. The bodhisattva teacher in Ch'an and Zen combines characteristics of both. As a representative, the bodhisattva teacher corresponds to van der Leeuw's subtype of the Speaker, but can also be an object of veneration.

The speaker, preacher, and teacher for van der Leeuw belong to a category of religious figures appointed by God whose offices are to bear Power as God's representative and to complete the apportioning of it to the totality, the community. These representatives include 1) the king; 2) the medicine man or priest; 3) the speaker of divine Word, who utters against his will and with no intention of his own. In this category van der Leeuw includes the Hebrew prophet, the soothsayer, and poet; 4) the preacher and teacher; and 5) the consecrated; for example, the vestal virgins of Rome.[7]

It is the van der Leeuw's speaker, not his saint, nor indeed his teacher, who most nearly fits the Mahayana and particularly the Ch'an/Zen conception of the teacher as bodhisattva and the bodhisattva as teacher. Van der Leeuw writes that prophets and poets, as speakers, utter the word of Power with no intention of their own; their words are saving deeds. "[The teacher] is generally less important personally; for he neither imparts salvation nor announces it, but merely speaks *about* it. . . ."[8] According to Buddhists, bodhisattvas in the Mahayana and masters in Ch'an and Zen do not merely speak *about* liberation from suffering; rather, like van der Leeuw's speaker, they utter the word of Power that occasions and triggers liberation with no distorting intention of their own; their words are saving deeds.

But van der Leeuw's concept of the speaker becomes useful only if we recognize that the assumption that the real power is outside the speaker does not fit straightforwardly with the Buddhist model. A Buddhist would doubtless rather say that the power is outside the speaker's ego, and would agree that the words that transform people come from a source beyond the speaker's own intelligence or will.

For van der Leeuw, the saint, on the other hand, is chiefly an object of veneration, not primarily one who distributes divine power to a community as a representative of the divine. Van der Leeuw says that "saints are no longer wholly representative; to a markedly high degree they are objects of veneration. Certainly, *orare pro nobis*—they are potent helpers of mankind as over against the great powers. But the principal feature is Power revealing itself in them."[9]

This Power is first of all revealed in the bodies of the saints, in van der Leeuw's view. If living, those bodies produce concrete and palpable miracles and physical signs. But "the saint is primarily a sacred, that is powerful, object—a relic."[10] "The desire to possess a portion of the powerful individual, a part of his body or even something that he has touched, begins even during his lifetime."[11] But "the grave, which contains relics in the most literal sense, is . . . the guarantee of sacred power."[12] Van der Leeuw writes, "The world has no use for living saints; they are dead persons, or still better: the potency of the dead."[13]

This kind of sainthood, the sainthood of the relic and the miracle-producing body, the sainthood of the one who is primarily a vehicle for the display of the miraculous power of the sacred, is not completely unknown to the Mahayana Buddhist tradition in general and the Ch'an/Zen tradition in particular. Among Mahayana Buddhists, the conviction was widespread that a person who practiced the bodhisattva path toward Buddhahood naturally developed certain supernormal powers and might occasion the manifestation of miraculous phenomena. These powers were regarded as the fruits of the yogic practice of concentration that, along with the practice of morality and giving and the cultivation of wisdom, was an important part of the path. Yet supernormal powers and miracles, while useful, not least in winning the support of lay patrons, were never greatly valued by the tradition. As one writing of the lesser importance of miracles in demonstrating sanctity in the Buddhist as compared to the Christian case, Donald Lopez states that in Pali Buddhism, forms of thaumaturgy "are not signs of snactity, but are merely the results of yogic practice. They imply no particular level of insight, and are obtainable by Buddhist and non-Buddhist alike."[14] Mahayana hagiographies record miracles, but they are clearly secondary to insight and teaching.

Similarly, the display of sacred power and spiritual attainment in the body and the relic is far from being the only or even the principal form of display of holy person and holy power venerated in the Mahayana tradition. The Mahayana tradition is interested in the living bodhisattva who rescues and teaches, and only secondarily in the potency of the dead.

In the case of Ch'an, as in the Mahayana as a whole, miracles were reported and supernormal powers were manifested by some bodhisattva teachers. As Bernard Faure, Robert Sharf and others have recently shown, the early Ch'an tradition included practices and hagiographies that reflect the notion of the Ch'an teacher as one whose body and relics are themselves sacred.[15] The bodies of the Sixth Patriarch Hui-neng and other figures who were the founders of lineages and sublineages were venerated after their death, having been preserved and displayed as "flesh bodies" that miraculously do not decay. *Śarīra,* crystalline relics, were collected from the ashes after the cremation of certain Ch'an masters. Pagodas were built over relics, ashes or bodies, and long hagiographical epitaphs were written for them. Portraits and statues of masters, "true images," were produced and venerated in ancestral rituals.[16] The veneration of the body of the founder or the exemplary master was more prominent prior to 900 C.E., but continued throughout Ch'an history in China.

Women teachers in Ch'an in China prior to 1278 also received postmortem veneration. Pagodas were built for them, and hagiographical epitaphs written for placement at their pagodas.

But the bodies, graves, and relics of none of the women teachers recorded in mainstream Ch'an texts prior to 1276 and of extremely few of the men in the Ch'an tradition in the same period became the objects of active veneration outside their own lineages, so far as we know. The full-blown cult of the miracle-working human saint and the saint's tomb as in Christianity did not develop in Ch'an. In so far as it was present in Mahayana Buddhism, Ch'an and Zen, it was largely centered around relics of Śakyamuni Buddha himself and around images of the so-called celestial bodhisattvas like Avalokiteśvara (Guanyin). Bernard Faure suggests that after 900 C.E., Ch'an eschewed the working of magic and miracles, saying that any good meditator should ignore such powers, not seek them.[17] Faure notes that stories of magic and miracles play a very small role in Ch'an in the Sung period (960–1276), the period in which the biographies of women Ch'an bodhisattva teachers first appear. The Sung dynasty was a period when "Ch'an was not a marginal religion but an elite, establishment religion, highly regulated by its codes of rules. Both the magician and the trickster do not serve—rather, the ideal holy man becomes the Bodhisattva ideal of morality, wisdom and compassion." We could add in this conception of the holy woman or man Ch'an was in the mainstream of international Buddhist "high tradition" orthodoxy.

Ch'an' and Zen's principal forms of sacred text are two. The first is the genre of geneological histories of the transmission of awakened mind from teacher to student over generations, known as "records of the transmission of the flame, *ch'üan-teng lu*." The second is the genre called "recorded sayings (*yü-lu*)" compilations of the words and doings of individual teachers that chiefly contain liberating dialogues known as encounter-dialogues. Miraculous events of the kind familiar from hagiographies of Western saints play a very small role in these texts. As the popularity of these forms indicates, the Ch'an/Zen tradition, like the Mahayana tradition as a whole, is interested primarily in the effective moments in which the awakened mind is displayed by a living teacher, and a student awakens.

A more recent Western writer whose views on charisma, sacred biography, and by extension, sainthood, provide a broader framework within which to understand variations around the world is the anthropologist Charles F. Keyes.[18] The notion of charisma, Keyes writes, and by extension the notion of the saint in a given group reflects that group's notion of how the sacred or contact with the sacred "is made manifest in the lives of actual human beings." Since the sacred is always ineffable, it is apprehended by means of signs that are taken as pointing to it. "It is through traffic with such 'outward and visible' signs" that humans attain and recognize in themselves or others an appearance of the sacred or a state of communion with the sacred.[19]

Certain individuals are charismatic, because they are deemed by those in their culture or group to have an especially close relationship with the sacred "because they have assimilated some of their actions—either on particular occasions or on a regular basis—to models that are recognized as sacred signs. . . ."[20] They have a quality that others interpret as being itself sacred or as being a gift of the sacred.

Keyes, still speaking of the charismatic person, says that a charismatic "is one who has realized in her or his own actions (or nonaction) direct contact or union with some being, force or state that is believed to transcend chaos."[21] Charismatics have domesticated chaos. "The signs that people take to indicate that a person is charismatic will be shaped by ideas of how chaos has been domesticated by this person."[22]

Keyes suggests some signs of having domesticated chaos widely recognized around the world are: 1) acts that entail a conquest of death—through resurrection, martyrdom, or symbolic death; 2) acts that end suffering that yields to no normal remedies, restore health: that is, curing; 3) gnosis, or a union, of greater or lesser degrees of permanence, with the ultimate, as through a vision quest, the ordeals of initiation rites, or the spiritual disciplines in the historic religions, carried out in the main by world renouncers; and 4) any miracle: "any act believed to be impossible given what for any people is known about the normal processes of life and nature, may be deemed a sign of charisma."[23]

Interestingly, Keyes does not give pride of place to miracles. He writes:

> Yet, while the lives of saints, holy men, and other charismatics are rife with references to miracles, it is doubtful that miracles, other than those associated with curing and the conquest of death, serve as the primary signs of charisma. Rather, it is more likely that once a person has been deemed to be charismatic then evidence of miraculous powers will subsequently be discovered in their acts.[24]

Keyes reflects usefully on a problem that arises in respect to saints and other charismatic persons. He writes:

> [F]or most people, charismatic acts are but memories or stories told by others. This distancing from the actual events that are interpreted as having a charismatic quality generates another problem associated with charisma, namely, how it can be recorded in such a way that it continues to carry authority when it is not manifest in actual events.[25]

Keyes suggests two strategies that can turn charismatic acts into discourse. The first is the discourse between teacher and disciple. He writes:

> It is [a teacher-disciple relationship], whether formalized or not, that makes possible the ordering of the memory of charisma into a discourse, a structured way of talking about experience. The disciple in turn translates this discourse into a model for his or her own action, action that may entail charismatic experiences of his or her own.[26]

The second is the discourse of sacred biography. Keyes' ideas are very helpful in recognizing and understanding the particular forms of the manifestation of the sacred recognized in the lives of women in Ch'an Buddhism from 900 C.E. to 1276 C.E., the first period when women in Ch'an were publicly visible and had their sacred biographies composed and recorded. In the sacred biographies of Ch'an women, signs of exemplary life include: choosing celibacy, not marriage; firmly setting her will on the practice of the Dharma; having no interest in ordinary pleasures, rather preferring or opting for restraint. In Keyes' terms, these are ways that they have assimilated some of their actions to models that are recognized as sacred signs. Through their unusual preferences and acts of will, celibacy and restraint, they manifest qualities that others interpret as being sacred or as being a gift of the sacred. Through their leaving household life, their ordination, their willingness to sacrifice all for enlightenment, they undergo a symbolic death and arrive at a conquest of death (*samsara*). They experience gnosis, or a union with the ultimate through a spiritual discipline. They experience a sudden enlightenment or awakening which is interpreted in the tradition as a very significant sign of their knowledge of the sacred, and gives them great charisma. As Keyes writes, "The force with which an experience of 'sudden deliverance'—of any charismatic experience—impresses itself has often led people to credit the experience with a true knowledge of the sacred that can be gained no other way."[27]

But there is an aspect to the sanctity that is recognized by other Sung Buddhists in these Ch'an women's lives and actions that Keyes's ideas do not help us to elucidate. As Ch'an students and as Ch'an teachers, the words of the Ch'an women teachers themselves and their ability to preach and teach are recognized and hailed as signs of their sainthood. They speak strongly when challenged by men, and they also challenge men boldly. More than that, they manifest their attainment of high stages of bodhisattvahood in the way they teach. Recognizing certain kinds of words and teaching abilities as signs of sainthood is important in Mahayana Buddhism, where it is seen particularly as a sign of advanced bodhisattvahood; of this more will follow. And it has been definitely a sign of sanctity and charisma in men and women in Ch'an throughout Ch'an's history in China as Ch'an students study by means of the contemplation of words and through verbal "Dharma combat," and Ch'an teachers display their sanctity as they perform their principal office, teaching, explaining, challenging through impenetrable koans and enigmatic words.

The recognition of speech and words as the most miraculous things, as the definitive sign of sanctification, also has a long tradition in Buddhism. There is precedent for this in the Pali canon, in the *Kevaddha Sutta* (D.1.211ff.); George D. Bond provides a summary: "A young layman tells the Buddha that he should command one of his monks to perform a miracle in order that the Buddhists might get more attention from the townspeople. The Buddha, however, explains that he can perform three kinds of miracles. The first kind includes physical miracles, such as walking on water, and the second kind includes telepathic powers, such as discerning the mind of another. The Buddha states that although he can do these two kinds of miracles, he disapproves of them and clearly has no desire to gain attention by them. He approves only of the third kind of miracle, the miracle of instructing others in the Dharma. Whereupon he proceeds to outline the way to arahantship in the path suttas. Donald Lopez, summarizing this passage, says that the Buddha says that he abhors the first two types of miracles "because the power to perform them can be obtained with charms and thus cannot be judged as infallible signs of spiritual attainment. The marvel of teaching is not open to such suspicion."[28]

In the Mahayana, the entrance onto the path of sanctification, or bodhisattvahood, begins with giving rise to "the aspiration to enlightenment (*bodhicitta*)." This arises from the cultivation of compassion. The aspiration is as follows: "May I become a Buddha in order to benefit all sentient beings." It includes a strong aspiration to attain the wisdom and skill-in-means necessary to teach. Lopez writes: "The nature of that benefit is specified by Haribhadra, an Indian Buddhist commentator, in his version of the wishful aspiration: 'Having become a complete and perfect Buddha, may I strive to teach the doctrine of the three vehicles for the welfare of others in accordance with [their] abilities.'"[29] Haribhadra thus emphasizes that the greatest benefit that a Bodhisattva seeks is that of being able to teach the path to freedom.

Classic scholastic models of the bodhisattva path also emphasize power to teach as a rather late, and high, and essential, attainment. The bodhisattva progresses to Buddhahood through five paths and ten stages (grounds, *bhūmis*). In the Indian Mahayana scholar Candrakirti's version of the ten stages in a text called *Madhyamakāvatāra,* the bodhisattva is held at the eighth stage as long as he is unable to teach the doctrine in all its aspects. On the ninth stage, the bodhisattva has a special understanding of the doctrine, which allows him to teach unerringly. This understanding is based on four knowledges. The tenth stage of bodhisattvahood is called the Cloud of Doctrine (*Dharmameghā*). Just as rain falls from a cloud, the excellent doctrine falls spontaneously from the bodhisattva for the sake of increasing the harvest of virtue of transmigrators. Here he practices the perfection of exalted wisdom, whereby he is possessed of a special skill to ripen the minds of sentient beings. He gains omniscience, an unimpeded understanding of all objects of knowledge. Simultaneously he attains Buddhahood.[30]

In the Mahayana, the Buddha's words are a very important symbol of his truth and his realization. In a famous article on the cult of the book in the Mahayana, Gregory Schopen discusses the early Mahayana phenomenon that the sutra, the book containing the Buddha's own words as remembered by his disciples, is treated ritually and in worship as the very Dharma body of the Buddha, and is enshrined and worshipped in stupas the way that the Buddha's relics are worshipped. In Ch'an/Zen perhaps the most important form of the veneration of the saint is the preservation of the saint's words. Faure notes in reference to Ch'an that *The Platform Sutra of the Sixth Patriarch* is claimed as especially holy and enshrined as a sacred object not only by the sect that does not have the sacred place associated with the Sixth Patriarch Hui-neng and his "flesh body," but also by the sect that does.[31] In Ch'an and Zen uniquely among East Asian Buddhist schools the words of teachers, male and female, were collected, edited, and published by their students as verbal expressions that were important occasions in which the Dharma body of the Buddha manifested itself directly, and students were brought to enlightenment.

In sum, if we look at the ways that the Ch'an and Zen master of either sex was thought to have transcended the ordinary human plane, to have manifested the sacred as experienced in person through signs that others can recognize, and in ways that are not easy to emulate, one feature is consistently emphasized: the miracle of speech, of receiving the student and knowing how to teach her or him; of teaching; of words.

The Nun and Ch'an Teacher Miao-tsung's Sacred Biography

I have chosen the sacred biography of a woman whose Dharma-name was Miao-tsung who in the Southern Sung dynasty (1126–1279) became a Ch'an master to illustrate how power of insight and its expression in words was the chief sign of sanctity in Sung Ch'an. Her full Dharma name was Wu-cho Tao-jen Miao-tsung.

The basic text that I am translating here is a biography of Miao-tsung preserved in a compilation called the *Jen-t'ien pao-chien*, the *Precious Mirror of Humans and Gods*, compiled in 1230, some sixty years after the likely date of Miao-tsung's death.[32] The lengthy inscription carved on Miao-tsung's grave, her pagoda, would have been her most official biography; unfortunately it is now lost. This text in the *Precious Mirror of Humans and Gods* is the longest and most detailed biographical essay on Miao-tsung that we now have. The *Precious Mirror of Humans and Gods* cites its source as a now lost text called the *T'ou-chi chuan; chuan* is the term often translated "biography." Since Miao-tsung's enlightenment poem is called *T'ou-chi sung*, it may be that the *T'ou-chi chuan* was either specifically a biography of Miao-tsung focusing on the story of her awakening, or a larger compilation containing such biographies.

Other sources give us additional biographical information. In sermons and letters Miao-tsung's teacher and dharma-father Ta-hui gives biographical information about Miao-tsung centering on the story of her awakening. Entries for her in the transmission of the flame genealogical histories contain a biographical frame narrative preceding and following examples of her sermons and dialogues. These are all early and reliable sources. Yet another Sung dynasty Ch'an text contributes an episode that added to Miao-tsung's fame particularly in Japan. I have added translations from these sources into my basic narrative taken from the *Precious Mirror* biography.

> Tse-shou [Miao-]tsung Ch'an Master, lay surnamed Su, was the granddaughter of a Grand Councilor named Su Sung (1020–1101).[33] When she was 15 years old she was ignorant of Ch'an. She only wondered about how human beings are born into the world—we are born and we do not know where we come from, we die and do not know where we go. From collecting her thoughts and focusing on this [problem] she had an insight. But she did not think [her new awareness] was different from that of others. She thought that [human beings], as the most numinous of sentient beings, must all be like this. And so she never mentioned it to others.
>
> Later she was forced to obey her father's and mother's order, and married Hsü Shou-yuan of Hsi-hsü.[34] But before long she began to dislike deeply the forms of this world, and performed abstinences and purified her mind as before. She wanted to transcend the mundane world and leave it behind, to discipline her will and emulate the ancients. So she went to visit the Ch'an master Chien-yen Yüan.[35]
>
> [Master] Yüan said: "A well-brought-up lady from a wealthy family [protected from any knowledge of the world], how can you be prepared for the business of a great (male) hero?"
>
> [Miao-]tsung replied: "Does the Buddha Dharma distinguish between male and female forms?"
>
> [Master] Yüan questioned her further. He said: "'What is the Buddha? This mind is the Buddha.' What about you?" [—is your mind also the Buddha?]
>
> [Miao-]tsung replied: "I've heard of you for a long time, [I'm disappointed to find that] you still say that kind of thing."
>
> [Master] Yüan said: "[What about the story that] when someone came in the door, Te-shan immediately hit him."
>
> [Miao-]tsung replied: "If you would carry out that mandate, you would not receive the offerings of humans and gods [that are given to Buddhas and their sons, the monks] in vain."

[Master] Yüan said: "You are not there yet [i.e., Your answer is not good enough yet]."

[Miao-]tsung hit the incense stand with her hand.

Yüan said: "There is an incense stand for you to hit. What if there were no incense stand?"

[Miao-]tsung immediately left, [thereby displaying non-being as opposed to being, the empty as opposed to the "real."]

Yüan called after her: "What truth have you seen that has made you like this?"

[Miao-]tsung turned her head around and said, "Everywhere there is not a single thing."

Yüan said: "That is what Yung-chia said—[let's have *your* insight]."

[Miao-]tsung said: "Why shouldn't I take [my feelings] out on him?"

Yüan said: "A real lion cub!"

At the time Ch'an master Chen-hsieh was living in a small cloister at I-hsing. [Miao-tsung] went directly to see him there. Chen-hsieh was sitting upright on a rope mat. The instant that [Miao-]tsung was inside the door, Chen-hsieh said: "Are you ordinary or a sage?"

[Miao-]tsung said: "Where is the third eye?"[36]

Chen-hsieh said: "The real thing appears right in front of your face—what is that like?"

[Miao-]tsung held up her kneeling and bowing cloth.

Chen-hsieh said: "I did not ask about that."

[Miao-]tsung said: "Too late—it's gone!"[37]

[Chen-]hsieh shouted: "Ho!"

[Miao-]tsung also shouted: "Ho!"

[Miao-]tsung had visited various famous masters in Kiangsi and Chekiang when she went with her husband to Chia-ho where he was to take up an official post.[38] Her only remaining thought was that she had not yet met Ta-hui (Ta-hui Tsung-kao [1089–1163]).[39] Just then it happened that Ta-hui and Feng Chi-ch'üan arrived by boat at the city wall.[40] Miao-tsung heard about it and went [to where they were]. [When she saw Ta-hui] she only bowed silently in respect.

Ta-hui said to [Feng] Chi-ch'üan, "That woman who just came, she has seen something.[41] But she has not yet encountered the hammer and tongs, forge and bellows [of a real master]. She is just like a ten thousand *hu* (thousand ton) ship in a closed-off harbor—she still cannot move." Feng said: "How can you say that so easily?" Ta-hui said: "If she turns her head back this way, I will have to make a finer discrimination."

The next day Miao-tsung's husband [Hsü] Shou-yüan commanded Ta-hui to preach the Dharma. Ta-hui looked at the assembly and said:

"Today among you there is a person here who has seen something. I inspect people like a customs officer—as soon as they arrive, I know whether or not they have dutiable goods." When he stepped down from the (preaching) seat, Miao-tsung asked him for a name in the Way. He gave her the name "No Attachments (Wu-cho)." The following year she heard that the Dharma-seat at Ching-shan (where Ta-hui was then teaching) was flourishing, and went there to spend the summer retreat.[42] In a formal instruction to the whole assembly by Ta-hui[43] she heard raised the *kung-an* (an already ancient story of the dialogue or action that served as the karmic cause of someone's awakening) of when Yao-shan Wei-yen (774–827) first went to study with Shih-t'ou Hsi-chien (700–790), and then later saw Ma-tsu Tao-i.[44] It included the line:

"Shih-t'ou said: 'This way won't do; not this way won't do. This way and not this way both won't do.' "

As Miao-tsung listened she suddenly awakened.[45] But after the sermon was over she did not immediately go to Ta-hui's chamber to describe her awakening.[46] At the time during the sermon the Vice Director Feng Chi, who was below the [high] seat [on which Ta-hui was preaching] suddenly had an insight.[47] He hastened to the abbot's quarters to report to Ta-hui, saying: "A moment ago you brought up [before the assembly of monks] Shih-t'ou's saying. I understand it."

Ta-hui said: "How do you understand it?"

Feng Chi said: "This way won't do, *soro shabaho.* Not this way won't do, *hsi-li shabaho.* Both this way and not this way won't do, *soro hsi-li shabaho.*"[48]

At this moment Miao-tsung arrived. Without telling him whether it was good or bad,[49] Ta-hui brought up the Vice-Director's answer to Miao-tsung. Miao-tsung laughed and said: "Kuo-hsiang commented on Chuang-tzu. Those who know say that Chuang-tzu commented on Kuo-hsiang."[50]

Ta-hui saw that her words were different [from the ordinary]. So he raised another *kung-an* for her, asking her about the story of Yen-t'ou and the woman.[51] The story goes as follows: "Yen-t'ou became a ferryman by the shores of Lake Ou-chu in Hupei. On each side of the lake hung a board; when someone wanted to cross he or she would knock on the board. Yen-t'ou would call out, 'Which side are you crossing to?' Then he would wave his oar, come out from the reeds and go to meet the traveller. One day a woman carrying a child in her arms appeared. Eventually he asked her, 'Where did the child you are holding in your arms come from?' She said 'I have given birth to seven children; six of them didn't meet anyone who understood them. If this remaining one does not prove to be of any use, I will throw it in the river right away.' "

Miao-tsung replied with a four-line *gatha:*

"One tiny boat drifts across a vast stretch of water
He makes his oars dance, chanting his tunes wonderfully;
The clouds, mountains, sea, and moon are all thrown in;
Alone I doze off into Chuang Chou's butterfly dream."[52]

Ta-hui remained silent and departed.

The next day Ta-hui hung up the sign [for individual interviews in his chamber], so she entered his chamber. Ta-hui asked: "Since the ancient virtuous ones did not go out of their gates, how were they able to eat oil-fried rice cakes in the village?"[53]

Miao-tsung said: "Only if you promise to let me off easily will I say [what is on my mind]."

Ta-hui said: "I will let you off easily, try giving your reply."

Miao-tsung said: "I will also let you off easily."

Ta-hui said: "But what about the oil-fried rice cakes?"

Miao-tsung then shouted "Ho," and went out.

Miao-tsung composed a verse on the occasion of her awakening.[54]

"Suddenly I came across my nose.
My cleverness was like ice melting and tiles crumbling.
Why did Bodhidharma need to come from India?
The second patriarch did not need to give three bows.
If you still want to ask 'what's it like?'
The whole troup of bandits are defeated utterly."[55]

Ta-hui repeated the verse, [and composed one of his own], saying:

"You have awakened to the living intention of the patriarchs,
Cutting all in two with one stroke, directly finishing the job.
As you meet karmic occasions one by one, trust to naturalness.
Whether in this world or outside of it [in the realm of Buddhist matters] there is no excess or lack.
I compose this *gatha* as testimony [to your enlightenment].
The four ranks of sages and six types of ordinary beings are in shock.
Stop being in shock.
Even the blue-eyed barbarian [Bodhidharma] still does not know [what you know]."

Once when [Miao-]tsung entered [Ta-hui's] chamber for personal instruction, [Ta-hui] asked her: "The monk who was just here answered you—tell me, why didn't I agree with him?"

She replied: "How can you suspect me?"

Ta-hui raised his bamboo stick and said, "What do you call this?"

She said: "Blue sky, blue sky!"[56]

Ta-hui then hit her. She said: "Someday you will hit someone mistakenly."

Ta-hui said: "When the blow lands, I'll stop. Why worry about whether it is a mistake or not?"

[Miao-]tsung said: "Only for the sake of circulation."[57]

[According to one account,] when Miao-tsung, who was not yet a nun, studied with Ta-hui at Ching-shan, Ta-hui lodged her in his abbot's quarters.[58] The Head Monk Wan-an always made disapproving noises.[59] Ta-hui said to him, "Even though she is a woman, she has strengths." Wan-an still did not approve. Ta-hui then insisted that he should interview her. Wan-an reluctantly sent a message that he would go.

[When Wan-an came,] Miao-tsung said, "Will you make it a Dharma interview or a worldly interview?"

The Head Monk replied: "A Dharma interview."

Miao-tsung said: "Then let your attendants depart." [She went in first, then called to him,] "Please come in."

When he came past the curtain he saw Miao-tsung lying face upwards on the bed without anything on at all. He pointed at her and said, "What kind of place is this?"

Miao-tsung replied: "All the Buddhas of the three worlds and the six patriarchs and all the great monks everywhere—they all come out from within this."

Wan-an said: "And would you let me enter, or not?"

Miao-tsung replied: "It allows horses to cross; it does not allow asses to cross."[60]

Wan-an said nothing, and Miao-tsung declared: "The interview with the Senior Monk is ended." She then turned over and faced the inside.

Wan-an became embarrassed and left.

Ta-hui said, "It is certainly not the case that the old beast does not have any insight." Wan-an was ashamed.[61]

(The phrase "old beast" is used to revile or scold people, particularly for lacking all human manners. Here it might refer to Miao-tsung, because like an animal she violated etiquette by presenting herself naked to Wan-an. It also might refer to Ta-hui, because in lodging her in his quarters he violated monastic rules. The Japanese commentarial tradition read it as referring to Miao-tsung.[62])

One day Miao-tsung bowed and took her leave to return to her home.[63] Ta-hui asked: "When you leave this mountain, if someone asks about the teaching here, how will you answer?"

She said: "Before I arrived at Ching-shan, I could not help doubting."

Ta-hui said: "And after you arrived?"

[Miao-]tsung said: "As of old, the early spring is still cold."

Ta-hui said: "Does not such an answer make me out to be a fool?"

[Miao-]tsung covered her ears and left.

The Layman Feng [Chi] doubted that her awakening had any real roots.[64] Later he specially invited Miao-tsung to come from P'ing-chiang fu to meet him. When he went to her boat, he asked her the following:[65]

"'A woman gave birth to seven sons . . . Six had never found anyone who really understood them. If this last one is also not any use, I will immediately abandon him in the water.' My teacher (Ta-hui) says that you have understood this. What is it that you understand?"

[Miao-tsung] said: "What you have testified to is the truth."[66]

Feng was greatly startled.

Thereafter she was greatly admired by the monastic assembly and became famous throughout the world. After a long time in concealment, she put on the robe [of a female monastic]. Even though she was advanced in years, she kept the precepts with great strictness, and polished herself with austerity and frugality, having models from older generations. Because of her fame in the Buddhist Way, the governor [of P'ing-chiang-fu (Kiangsu province)] Chang An-kuo ordered her to come out from her reclusive life and become the abbess and Ch'an teacher of Tse-shou [Nunnery].[67] Before long she asked leave to retire, and returned to her old home.

We can see that Miao-tsung's life was shaped by the power of an early religious experience, as Joachim Wach suggests is common with saints. This early experience of awakened awareness enabled her to come to her first teacher with an already profound understanding, and speak from somewhere beyond the limitations of her own ego. I regret that space prevents me in this essay from further explicating each of the thrusts and parries in the dialogues and poems presented in her biography so that the reader unfamiliar with Ch'an and Zen discourse can fully understand how each marvelously manifests a deep understanding of the Buddha's Dharma as taught in the Mahayana tradition.[68]

She married as was expected of her, but tired of ordinary household life. In a world where elite women were expected to marry, bear children, and stay chastely in the "women's quarters," never allowing men outside the family to see them, Miao-tsung broke out of this restrictive pattern placed on women regarded as virtuous and went in search of male teachers, even spending a summer three-month rainy season retreat at a large male monastery. If we take the story of the interview between Miao-tsung and Wan-an as true, that is, at face value, then Miao-tsung was willing to sacrifice her reputation as a chaste woman by lodging in the abbot's quarters and by using her body and her apparent shamelessness as a teaching device in a Dharma interview. Chinese readers might find her behavior transgressive of ordinary morality, and thus not in a straightforward way emulable, exemplary. Nonetheless, her dedication to the pursuit of awakening, and her willingness to step outside the bounds of ordinary morality and risk her reputation to do it would be seen as examples of heroic virtue in their own right. (See p. 000 above.)

Various male Ch'an teachers certified her awakening, her extraordinary gnosis, when she showed herself able to meet various kinds of verbal challenges with appropriate, even astonishingly effective words. She demonstrated the fruit of her awakening by being able to live the simple life of a strict ascetic nun teacher. In this way her life displayed other more conventional heroic Buddhist virtues and was exemplary. She became the abbess and Ch'an master at a famous temple for women, and gave novice ordination and advanced instruction to women students.

Other texts not translated here recorded for posterity her sermons, her poetry and Buddhist verses, as well as her own performance of the intense and challenging dialogues with students through which students in Ch'an and Zen test a master and become enlightened. All of these verbal manifestations of her enlightened mind were understood to be spontaneous; as in the case of van der Leeuw's "speaker," she is understood to have uttered the word of Power with no intention of her own, and her words are recorded because as demonstrations of enlightened mind they have the power to enlighten others.

Very unusually for a woman during the Sung period, she was asked by a leading male Ch'an literary figure to write a preface for his book. She thus became one of the extremely few women in the Sung dynasty who wrote for wide circulation and publication. Her hagiographical pagoda epitaph does not survive; but in local gazeteers she is the remarkable teacher mentioned when her temple's history is discussed.

Miao-tsung clearly was a woman whom all around her thought remarkable chiefly for her awakened mind and for the tremendous power of her words. Her words were understood to be not merely the product of a good education or great cleverness, but to come from, and be a sign of, the powerful gnosis of enlightened mind, and to be the words of a Bodhisattva who rescued beings by teaching Dharma.

In the absence of miracle stories about healings or special manifestations it may be hard for non-Buddhist readers to feel that Miao-tsung's biography is that of a saint. But her biography is of one who, as Keyes puts it, has "domesticated chaos." It is the biography of one who has been deemed by those in her culture to have a close relationship with the sacred because she has "assimilated some of her actions"—in this case, her words, her power of speech and imagination—"to models that are recognized as sacred signs."

Notes

1. For a comprehensive and learned summary on this topic, see Richard Kieckhefer, "Imitators of Christ: Sainthood in the Christian Tradition," in Richard Kieckhefer and George Bond, eds., *Sainthood* (University of California Press, 1988), pp. 1–42.

2. This study was cooperatively undertaken by the Graduate Theological Union in Berkeley, California, and the Center for the Study of World Religions at Harvard University under the direction of Mark Juergensmeyer and John B. Carman. It was supported by the National Endowment for the Humanities and the Eli Lilly Foundation. The two books are John Stratton Hawley, ed., *Saints and Virtues* (University of California Press, 1987), and Richard Kieckhefer and George D. Bond, eds., *Sainthood* (University of California Press, 1988). William James discusses "saintliness" in his *Varieties of Religious Experience.*

3. John Stratton Hawley, "Introduction: Saints and Virtues," in J. S. Hawley, ed., *Saints and Virtues,* pp. xi–xxiv.

4. Joachim Wach, *Sociology of Religion.* Chicago: University of Chicago Press, 1944, p. 359.

5. Joachim Wach, *Sociology of Religion,* p. 358.

6. Ibid.

7. G. van der Leeuw, *Religion in Essence and Manifestation,* Glocester, Mass., Peter Smith, 1967, vol. 1, pp. 214–235. (First published in German in 1933.)

8. Van der Leeuw, p. 228.

9. Van der Leeuw, p. 236.

10. Van der Leeuw, p. 236.

11. Van der Leeuw, p. 236.

12. Van der Leeuw, p. 237.

13. Van der Leeuw, p. 238.

14. Donald S. Lopez, Jr., "Sanctification on the Bodhisattva Path," in Kieckhefer and Bond, 178.

15. Bernard Faure, "Relics and Flesh Bodies," in Susan Naquin and Chün-fang Yu, eds., *Pilgrimage and Sacred Sites in China.* University of California Press,

1992; and Faure, *The Rhetoric of Immediacy,* Princeton University Press, 1991. Robert Sharf, "The Idolization of Enlightenment: On the Mummification of Ch'an Masters in Medieval China." *History of Religions* vol. 32, no. 1 (1992), 1–31.

16. T. Griffith Foulk and Robert H. Sharf, "On the Ritual Use of Ch'an Portraiture in Medieval China," *Cahiers d'Extreme Asie* no. 7, 149–219.

17. Faure, *Rhetoric of Immediacy,* 106–107. Faure suggests that this may have been a strategy to deny the appeal of Tantric Buddhism, a major rival in the late T'ang, as well as a manifestation of the logic of Ch'an's suddenism. Faure, *Rhetoric of Immediacy,* p. 109.

18. Charles F. Keyes, "Charisma: From Social Life to Sacred Biography," in Michael A. Williams, ed., *Charisma and Sacred Biography,* JAAR Studies, JAAR vol. xlviii, numbers 3 and 4, 1982, p. 1.

19. Keyes, p. 1.

20. Keyes, p. 1.

21. Keyes, p. 2.

22. Keyes, p. 2.

23. Keyes, pp. 2–5.

24. Keyes, pp. 3–4.

25. Keyes, p. 12.

26. Keyes, p. 12.

27. Keyes, p. 8.

28. George D. Bond, "The Arahant: Sainthood in Theravada Buddhism," in Kieckhefer and Bond, p. 160. Lopez, *op. cit.,* also cites this passage: "In the *Kevaddhasutta* the Buddha says there are three kinds of marvels (*pāṭihāriya*): magical powers (*iddhi*), such as flying in the lotus position, walking through walls, and walking on water; the marvel of mind reading (*ādesanā*); and the marvel of teaching (*anusāsanī*). He says that he is distressed by and abhors the first two types of marvels because the power to perform them can be obtained through the use of charms and thus cannot be judged as infallible signs of spiritual attainment. The marvel of teaching is not open to such suspicion." (p. 178).

29. Lopez, p. 192.

30. Lopez, p. 202.

31. Faure also suggests that as Ch'an in the late T'ang, Five Dynasties and Sung clearly demonstrates that it values words over relics and the working of miracles, it is opting for the Confucian over the Taoist pole of Chinese culture. Faure, *Rhetoric of Immediacy,* p. 125. Confucian culture is the place where words are the most miraculous things.

32. The *Jen-t'ien pao-chien* was compiled by the monk Ssu-ming T'an-hsiu in 1230; this is not precisely a geneological history of the "transmission of the flame" genre highly popular in the Ch'an tradition in the Sung and Yuan dynasty periods, nor is it a *kung-an* (J. *koan*) collection. The Zen tradition numbered it as one

of "Seven Books" or "Seven Writings" (*ch'i-shu*). Professor Ishii Shūdō calls it a "*sui-pi-chi*," a more casual collection of biographical matter and anecdotes than are the lamp histories and the *kung-an* collections. Cf. Ishii Shūdō, "*Jūichi shu sōdai zenmon zuihitsushū jinmei sakuin* (*jo*) (Index to the names in eleven Sung dynasty Ch'an school *sui-pi-chi*)," *Komazawa Daigaku Bukkyō gakubu kenkyū kiyō* no. 42, 1985, p. 175. To my translation of the *Precious Mirror* biography I have added material from what her teacher Ta-hui Tsung-kao tells others in a "general instruction" (*p'u-shuo*) and a Dharma-instruction (*fa-yü*) about her awakening; these texts are probably the earliest source available to us, and are by someone who knew her well. I have also added material from "transmission of the flame" geneological histories called the *Lien-teng hui-yao* compiled in 1183, the *Chia-t'ai p'u-teng lu,* and the *Wu-teng hui-yüan.*

33. Su Sung (1020–1101) was prime minister in the period from 1086 to 1094; cf. Ishii Shūdō, "Daie Fukaku Zenji Nenpu no kenkyū (ge)," *Komazawa Daigaku Bukkyō Gakubu kenkyū kiyō,* vol. 39 (1982), p. 165. That Miao-tsung was a granddaughter of Su Sung is fact is given in all the lamp history biographies of her.

34. Ta-hui mentions that the Hsü family is from Ch'ang-chou. *Hōgo,* p. 174.

35. There is no listing for Chien-yen Yüan in the *Zengaku daijiten* genealogy.

36. Lit., your forehead eye, or the eye on your head. *Zengaku daijiten,* p. 868.

37. Slipped through!" You missed the chance.

38. Ta-hui Tsung-kao in telling her story in a Dharma-instruction for another woman says that she was determined to practice Buddhism when she was thirty, and that she then studied with various teachers, receiving the seal of awakening (yin-k'o, J. inka) from all of them. He does not name the teachers. Ishii Shūdō, *Daie Fukaku Zenji Hōgo,* in Ishii Shūdō, *Daijō Butten: Chūgoku, Nihon hen,* vol. 12: *Zen goroku* (Tokyo: Chūo kōron sha, 1992; hereafter *Daie hōgo*) p. 174. According to the *Ta-hui P'u-chüeh Ch'an-shih Nien-p'u,* this Dharma instruction was written when he was 70, in 1158.

39. The text refers to Ta-hui Tsung-kao as "Miao-hsi," an informal name that he used during one period of his life. I have changed all occurrences of "Miao-hsi" to "Ta-hui," a name given by the emperor to honor him much later, but the name by which he is best known in the West.

40. Feng Chi (?–1153), tzu Chi-ch'uan. His father was named Feng Ch'ang-ch'i. He was from Kuang-han in Szechuan, received his *chin-shih* degree in 1118. He studied under many Ch'an teachers, and was a Dharma-heir of Fo-yen Ch'ing-yüan. In 1137 he became a "Supervising Secretary (*chi-shih*)," a position at court held by men of prestige and influence, and began to spend a lot of time with Ta-hui Tsung-kao. Later he had another official post in Szechuan. Ta-hui refers to him here as "Vice Minister," *shao-ch'ing,* a common title for second tier executive officials. (See Charles O. Hucker, *A Dictionary of Official Titles in Imperial China*

(Stanford, California: Stanford University Press, 1985), p. 414 and p. 133.) He paid for a revised edition of the Buddhist Canon out of his own pocket, and late in life became interested in Pure Land Buddhism. Cf. *Zengaku daijiten,* p. 1054a. Biographies can be found in *Wu-teng hui-yüan* 20; *Wu-teng ch'üan-shu* 44; *Chu-shih-fen teng-lu,* hsia; *Chia-t'ai p'u-teng lu* 23.

41. Literally, a ghost or spirit.

42. With this sentence we end for the moment the narrative taken from the *Precious Mirror of Humans and Gods,* which does not have an account of the *kung-a* study with Ta-hui that preceded her full awakening. The following paragraphs describing this critical moment in her life come principally from the *Lien-teng hui-yao* and from Ta-hui's records. Ta-hui in a Dharma-instruction says that at this time despite her having received the approval of other masters, deep in her heart she still feared the sufferings of samsara, and wanted to attain a true understanding of her original face. (*Daie hōgo,* p. 174) According to Ta-hui there were seventeen hundred monks assembled for the retreat.

43. *Shang-t'ang.*

44. In Ta-hui's dharma-instruction for Yung-ning Chun Fu-jen Ta-hui writes: "When Yao-shan first went to study with Shih-t'ou, he asked Shih-t'ou: 'I have completed studying the three vehicles and the twelve divisions of the teachings. I have heard that in the south there is a Ch'an lineage that preaches directly pointing to a person's mind, [letting him or her] see [his or her true] nature and [thus] become a Buddha. But I do not understand at all. Would you please instruct me.' Shih-t'ou replied: 'This way won't do; not this way won't do either. This way and not this way both won't do.' Yao-shan still did not understand. So Shih-t'ou said to him, 'It would be good if you went to Kiangsi and asked Ma-tsu the same question.'" (*Hōgo,* p. 174.) Ishii believes that Ta-hui got this from a text called the *Tsung-men t'ung-yao-chi* which he has found in a Japanese library but which has not been published. Cf. *Daie hōgo,* p. 374. For a published source, cf. *Ma-tsu yü-lu, Hsü-tsang-ching* 119:408c14–17; for an English translation of the passage in the latter, cf. Urs App, Facets of the Life and Teaching of Ch'an Master Yun-men Wen-yan (864–949), University of Pennsylvania Ph.D. unpublished dissertation, 1989, p. 65.

45. *Daie hōgo,* p. 175. The *Chia-t'ai* and the *Wu-teng* add this to the *Lien-teng* account.

46. *Daie hōgo,* p. 175.

47. *Shih-lang* was the title given in these biographies. Hucker translates this title as "Vice Director." A *shih-lang* held the second executive position in the Chancellery, the Secretariat, and the great departments in the Sung. In the Sung the *shih-lang* were included among the officials serving as Grand Councilors. Cf. Hucker, *A Dictionary of Official Titles,* pp. 426–427. Ta-hui told Yung-ning Chun Fu-jen, the wife of Teng Liang-fu (her own surname was Tsao, and one of her names

was Shan-yin [good cause]) in the Dharma-instruction cited earlier that Feng Chi (Feng Chi-ch'üan) was staying at the time in the "Immovable Pavilion" at Ching-shan monastery. He was also called the Immovable Layman (Layman of the Immovable Pavilion); perhaps he stayed there often for long periods.

48. For "will not do," perhaps the meaning is better conveyed by "is no use, is a waste of time." "*Shabaho*" is a rendering into Chinese sounds of the Sanskrit term *svaha,* which often ends dharani, and is usually translated "accomplished." "*Soro*" perhaps renders the Sanskrit term "*surya*" (the sun), and "*hsi-li*" perhaps renders into Chinese sounds the Sanskrit term "*sri*" (auspicious), but their meaning is not clear. In the *Yün-men kuang-lu* the expression "*soro soro*" appears several times. Cf. *Taishō* 47.548c; 549c; 550ab; 554b; 555c.

49. Ta-hui says this in his dharma-instruction for Yung-ning Chun Fu-jen. *Hōgo,* p. 175.

50. Kuo-hsiang, who lived long after Chuang-tzu the person and after the compilation of the text called the *Chuang-tzu,* wrote a commentary on the latter.

51. On this story about Yen-t'ou and the woman carrying a child in her arms, Ishii cites *Tsung-men t'ung-yao-chi, chüan* 8, the Yen-t'ou chapter, as the source that Ta-hui quotes from. More readily available sources include: *Lien-teng-hui-yao, chüan* 21; *Jen-t'ien yen-mu, chüan* 6; *Ching-te ch'uan-teng lu, chüan* 26. On "*pu-hsiao-te,*" cf. *Ching-te-ch'uan-te lu, chüan* 15, Tung-shan Liang-chieh chapter, Chen-shan-mei ch'u-pan-she reprint edition, p. 103, lines 14–16; and Chang Chung-yuan, *Original Teachings of Ch'an Buddhism* (New York: Vintage Books edition, 1971), p. 66.

52. Chuang Chou's dream in which he was a butterfly, and his reflection that on waking he was not sure that he was not a butterfly now dreaming that he was a man, is found in the *Chuang-tzu,* Chapter 2.

53. Literally, an oil-fried steamed rice ball. This reference may be to Te-shan and his eating refreshments (*tien-hsin*).

54. Ch. *chieh,* Skt. *gatha.*

55. This verse appears in the *Precious Mirror of Humans and Gods,* which we now rejoin in our narrative. In the *Lien-teng hui-yao* and elsewhere this verse is called "*T'ou-chi sung* (verse on becoming one with the Way, on personally experiencing the mystery, on reaching enlightenment)." Neither this verse nor the reply by Ta-hui are in his extant records.

56. Ta-hui held up his stick or whisk (insignia of office) and said to his students: "If you say this is a bamboo stick, that is wrong. If you say this is not a bamboo stick, that is wrong. What is it?"

57. With the end of this sentence we depart once more temporarily from the *Precious Mirror of Humans and Gods* narrative.

58. This story does not appear in any of Miao-tsung's biographies in the Ch'an genealogical histories. The story occurs in a collection of verses about famous

Ch'an masters, the *Wu-chia cheng-tsung tsan,* the "Poems of Appraisal of the Correct Tradition of the Five [Ch'an] Schools," that dates from 1254 C.E. It is found in the preface to a poem of appraisal about the Ch'an master Wan-an Tao-yen, a Dharma-heir of Ta-hui Tsung-kao (1089–1163).

59. The Head Monk was second in command to Ta-hui with respect to the training of the monks.

60. Literally: "It ferries [*tu*] [or transports] horses; it does not ferry asses." Her answer is similar to, but notably different from, Chao-chou's answer when asked what the bridge at the city of Chao-chou was like. Chao-chou replied: "Horses can cross it, asses can cross it." See my discussion of this story about Miao-tsung in Levering, "Stories of Enlightened Women in Ch'an and the Chinese Buddhist Female Bodhisattva/Goddess Tradition," in Karen L. King, ed., *Women and Goddess Traditions,* Minneapolis, MN: Fortress Press, 1997, pp. 137–176; discussion of this particular story occurs on pp. 152–161.

61. *Wu-chia cheng-tsung tsan, chüan* 2, *Zokuzōkyō* 2b,8,475a-b. This story is given as *koan* #51 in a Japanese text of 1545, *the Shōnan kattō-roku,* which Trevor Leggett has translated as *The Warrior Koans.* This story is on pp. 106–107 of his translation. The text says that this story is taken from the *Wu-chia cheng-tsung tsan,* [which was printed in Japan in 1349], became a koan used by the Japanese nun teacher Shōtaku, who became the third teacher at the famous nunnery Tokeiji. I have consulted Leggett's translation in producing my own.

62. Leggett, p. 109.

63. With this we return to the biography in the *Precious Mirror of Humans and Gods.*

64. This episode is narrated by Ta-hui in his Dharma-instruction (*Hōgo* p. 175–176) and in the "general instruction (*p'u-shuo*)" in which he tells Miao-tsung's story. It is not in the *Lien-teng,* but is found in the *Chia-t'ai* and the *Wu-teng.*

65. In Ta-hui's "general instruction (*p'u-shuo*)" he says that Feng specially invited Miao-tsung to come from P'ing-chiang fu to meet him. When he went to her boat, he asked about the *kung-an.* Ishii translates what is said about this in the *fa-yü* in the same way. *Daie hōgo,* p. 175. I translated from the *Jen-t'ien pao-chien* as "when he passed through Wu-yang he invited her to come to his boat."

66. This whole sentence is legalese.

67. Chang An-kuo is another name for Chang Hsiao-hsiang, who became governor in 1163. Chang An-kuo had connections with Ta-hui.

68. For a full attempt at explication, please see my forthcoming book on Ta-hui and his women disciples.

VII

Pien Tung-hsüan: A Taoist Woman Saint of the T'ang Dynasty (618–907)

Suzanne Cahill

Introduction

In the region of the bustling capital city of Ch'ang an, around the year 628, a young woman who was to become one of the most important Taoist saints of her era was born. Her name was Pien Tung-hsüan. Her biography appears in a set of twenty-eight accounts of female Taoist transcendents called "Records of the Assembled Transcendents of the Fortified Walled City" by the foremost Taoist master of the Shang-ch'ing (Supreme Clear Realm) school in the late T'ang, Tu Kuang-t'ing (850–933). The present paper translates Tu's hagiographical account of Pien Tung-hsüan.[1] These preliminary remarks are meant to put her life in historical and religious perspective. The introduction briefly describes Taoism during the T'ang dynasty, Tu Kuang-t'ing's motives in writing biographies of saintly women, and the form of a typical biography in his collection. Next it turns to the religious practices in which Tu's subjects engaged and to the life path of a Taoist woman saint in late medieval China. Finally, I consider what difference it makes that these saints were women and in what sense they can be considered models for women or for the whole community of the faithful.

Taoism is the native higher religion of China. It grew up alongside the foreign religion of Buddhism, which influenced Taoist beliefs and practices, and the native humanistic tradition of Confucianism, which formed the basis of Chinese ethical and political thought. For the educated official class of the T'ang dynasty, Taoism meant the tradition known as the Shang ch'ing or Supreme Clear Realm school. This school traces its origins in the fourth century to revelations from the highest deities to a young visionary named Yang Hsi. The Shang ch'ing textual corpus was organized in the fifth century by a great editor, T'ao Hung-ching. Much of it appears in the present day *Tao tsang* or Taoist canon. The body of works includes instructions, directed to the individual adept, on how to become perfected and eventually immortal through practices designed to nourish the vital essence. This is the school of which Tu Kuang-t'ing was a leading master, and Pien Tung-hsüan a noted female transcendent.[2]

When Tu Kuang-t'ing wrote his "Records of the Assembled Transcendents of the Fortified Walled City," he had several motives, some explicitly stated in his introduction and some implicitly present in the work itself. Among the reasons he gives for recording female biographies is a desire to preserve, in a time of tumult and danger, the precious textual heritage of his sect. Another is his wish to redress the lack of balance between women and men in accounts of holy people in the canon; although the lives of men are plentiful, lives of women are rare or nonexistent. Finally, he intends to provide models for women in the religious life.[3]

Not so clearly stated but just as clearly present in the "Records of the Assembled Transcendents of the Fortified Walled City" are motives we can infer from Tu Kuang-t'ing's many other extant writings. By his choice of subjects, Tu honors and combines the two main Taoist traditions of his day: the Ling pao or Numinous Treasure school which emphasized public liturgy and drew upon a deep popular base of support, and the Shang ch'ing school to which Tu himself belonged, which stressed individual practice and appealed to an elite audience. Taoist master Tu wrote commentaries on works of both schools in which he tried to harmonize their teachings and practices. His biographies include exemplary saints of both schools. Pien Tung-hsüan, whose life we consider here, represents the model Shang ch'ing saint.

In compiling lives of women saints, Tu Kuang-t'ing also meant to glorify the T'ang dynasty, in its last throes as he wrote, as a rule worthy of the divine grace their presence attests. He collected and edited his materials while following the T'ang imperial court into exile in Szechwan and then back to the capital at Ch'ang an. After the T'ang fell in 907, he served the succeeding court of Wang Chien in the kingdom of Shu in Szechwan. During his decade of wandering, Tu first composed works which praised the T'ang, then after its collapse asserted that the heavenly mandate had passed to Shu. Along with supporting the legitimacy of the government he served, Taoist master Tu wanted to recommend his church as an institution worthy of imperial patronage. Financial and political support in high places were as essential for the prestige and survival of the Taoist church in T'ang China as they were for the Catholic church in medieval Europe. Finally, Tu meant his accounts of women saints to testify to the power of his faith in times of trouble such as his own.[4]

The lives of women saints in "Records of the Assembled Transcendents of the Fortified Walled City" vary considerably in length, but all follow a pattern which goes back to official biographies from the Chinese dynastic histories. The same model had already been used by Buddhist hagiographers for accounts of monks and nuns.[5] The dynastic biography provided an appropriate format for proselytizing authors, since it was familiar, credible, and authoritative to the medieval Chinese literati audience.

The outline of a typical biography in Tu Kuang-t'ing's "Records of the Assembled Transcendents of the Fortified Walled City" follows its official model very closely. The generic account includes specific information in a predictable order. First comes the subject's name, historical era, and lineage (including offices of male ancestors). Remarkable here is the fact that over half of Tu's subjects are of low birth. Lineage is followed by place of birth registry and career. Geographical associations are important, since these women were often the foci of important local cults; Tu tends to grant prominence to the regions of the two T'ang capitals (as in the biography of Pien Tung-hsüan), the area around Ch'eng tu in Szechwan, and the homeland of Shang ch'ing Taoism in the south.

After the genealogical data comes information about the saint's childhood—special talents, signs of vocation such as unprompted reverence or natural inclinations towards faith, and evidence of selection by the gods. The question of marriage, treated as a problem to be solved, follows the events of childhood. Only a few of Tu's subjects marry; most, like Pien Tung-hsüan, are childless and celibate.

After her marriage crisis, the subject reaches adulthood and the biographer describes her mature religious practice, including good works, austerities, and meditation. Here the women reveal their individual claims to sanctity. Practice leads to such fruits of the faith as renewed youth, magical powers and skills, communication with animals, visits from deities, travel in time and space: all signs of divine grace and perfection. During this period of her life the saint may teach disciples or transmit texts.

Finally her practice leads the holy woman to the ultimate reward bestowed by the deities: transformation or apparent death, followed by immortality and posthumous office in the celestial bureaucracy.

Posthumous titles, in the common practice of the imperial government as recorded in official biographies, are honors conferred by the emperor upon deceased worthies in recognition of meritorious services. Such titles, intended for use in the ancestral cult, increase the prestige of the recipient's descendants. In contrast, the Taoist saint was literally believed, after departing this world, to join the gods and assume in heaven the duties of the office to which she is named.

Tu Kuang-t'ing gives prominence to religious practice in his biographies. He assumes that different forms of practice are arranged in a hierarchical order that represents spiritual progress and increasing attainment. The lives of the saints trace a pilgrim's progress for female transcendents, whose stages of spiritual development are marked along the way. The path begins with the attitude of faith, continues with good works, and reaches its high point in the disciplined practices favored by Supreme Clear Realm Taoism.

Tu Kuang-t'ing does not describe the inner condition of faith or reverence; he simply notes that many saints show it, unprompted, as children. Already, as little girls, many performed good works: acts of charity such as feeding starving animals and people, housing the homeless, and burying abandoned corpses. Hidden good works, in which the practitioner does her kindness in secret expecting no praise or return, are especially meritorious. A special brand of good works which appears in the "Records of the Transcendents of the Fortified Walled City" is defense of the faith. Two of Tu's heroines defend themselves and sacred shrines from attacks by brutal Buddhist monks. Another special type of virtuous act Tu reports is the restoration and preservation of Taoist holy places.

Good works are prerequisites which set the stage for Taoist religious practice. Such practice begins with sexual abstinence and fasting, austerities typical of Supreme Clear Realm Taoism and carried out by nearly all of Tu Kuang-t'ing's subjects, including Pien Tung-hsüan. The key to sexual abstinence is refusal to reproduce and enter the realm of family duties and obligations; the significance of fasting seems to be discipline, self-denial, and departure from the society of people who share common foods. Rejecting normal foods, called "cutting off the five grains," was often accompanied by eating magical or symbolic foods instead, as in the case of Pien.

Sexual abstinence and fasting are followed by meditation and visualization in most cases, and in a few cases also by study of holy scriptures. As a good Supreme Clear Realm master, Tu emphasizes meditation; unfortunately, he does not describe specific disciplines, contents, or products of contemplation.[6] Meditation and visualization, in turn, lead to spiritual rewards which include renewed youth, communication with deities, divine knowledge, and magical powers. During this period of manifesting the fruits of the faith, the saint may acquire a band of disciples, as does Pien Tung-hsüan.

Near the end of her earthly career, as happens in the case of Pien Tung-hsüan, the saint often receives a divine prediction of her future transformation and celestial post. The prediction contains specific details, the exact fulfillment of which is considered proof of sanctity. Her final visible act is her departure. The highest form of transformation is to ascend to heaven in broad daylight in front of a host of witnesses—a destiny reserved only for a few of the most perfected, including Pien Tung-hsüan. The next best fate, called "liberation by means of the corpse," consists of appearing to die and leave behind a body to be buried. But the corpse left behind is only an empty husk; the real person has gone off to paradise.[7]

The pattern Tu records shows a hierarchy progressing from faith to good works to Taoist religious practices and finally to transcendence. This hierarchy represents steps in an ideal woman's religious life, stages of spiritual development from childhood to maturity and old age with the greatest attainments at the last. It is an orderly series of steps through which one progresses from faith to immortality.

We might wonder what difference it makes that the subjects of Tu Kuang-t'ing's biographies are women. Let us assume for the moment that there are only two replies: it makes all the difference in the world or it makes no difference at all. In his "Records of the Assembled Transcendents of the Fortified Walled City," Tu gives both answers. By compiling a separate book of female biographies, by giving different titles to female and male Taoist adepts, and by stating that there is a separate path to transcendence for women, he suggests that important gender distinctions exist within Taoism.[8]

Yet Taoist master Tu also implies that women and men, although separate, are equal. Traditional Taoist cosmology holds that yang and yin (male and female) are equal and opposite forces, both worthy and both required for creation. Tu states elsewhere in the same work that "the positions of male realized ones and female transcendents are regulated . . . the primal father and mysterious mother go along as equals, completing each other. . . ."[9] He asserts at one point that a person is raised to celestial office "according to virtue and talent, unrestricted by distinctions between male and female."[10] It makes no difference in the end whether the practitioner is male or female: both can attain the Way, immortality, and a position in the heavenly bureaucracy. The paths are separate, but the goals of practice are identical and the Tao is one. As Tu states in his introduction to the biographies: "Although the Way is one, its practice reveals distinctions. Therefore they say the ways of the transcendents number in the hundreds. We are not limited by a single route; there is not a single method to grasp."[11]

Contemporary scholars investigating female sanctity in the west sometimes propose two alternatives for women saints in relation to their womanhood: they may embrace it fully or reject it completely. The Taoist women saints, with their sexual abstinence and fasting, seem to fall securely in the rejecting category. But we may not have a real gender distinction here: Taoist men saints also refuse to eat or have sexual relations. It seems that class and sect are more important categories than gender in predicting practice. This is an issue of cultural constructions of both sanctity and gender, a broad topic which needs further research.[12]

It is certainly the case that the woman who pursued a religious career in medieval China faced special social problems. How was she to justify her choice of a celibate life in the context of a patriarchal society that defined women in terms of their roles within the family and valued them according to their contributions to the family? The two most important values of traditional China, filial piety and loyalty to the state, were normally fulfilled for women within the family system. The women Tu chronicles do not criticize the family system, even when they personally reject family life. Tu Kuang-t'ing himself clearly shares the values of his time and station. He explains his subjects' rejection of marriage and childbearing in terms which attest to the importance of the family. The convent itself is an artificial family, in which people address one another by terms of fictitious kinship. Tu calls his collection of lives the "record of one family."[13] And he claims the lives of the saints embody a higher form of filial piety and loyalty than the norm. The women saints are filial because their religious practice saves their kin; they are loyal to the state because their very existence attests to the virtue of the ruling emperor and the presence of the mandate of heaven. Pien Tung-hsüan provides a good example of just such transcendent filial piety and loyalty.

Finally let us inquire what sort of models these women might be. Since early Chinese writing is so often didactic, and Tu Kuang-t'ing's is no exception, we might ask what lesson he is teaching with these lives. Tu certainly has no intention of advising all women to leave the household life and enter convents. His subjects provide examples of women living a religious life according to the tenets of Taoism, progressing gradually by steps along the way which leads from faith to immortality. The path represents idealized stages of a woman's life beginning with reverence in childhood, moving to good works in adulthood, and to austerities and meditation in old age. A woman on this path might remain within her family throughout most of her religious life, only rejecting its claims after her children were grown and her responsibilities diminished. At that point, her family might welcome her following religious pursuits rather than meddling in their business and domestic affairs. In addition to providing models of the female religious career, Tu Kuang-t'ing presents his subjects as conduits to the divine and as centers of community. He also depicts them as living auspicious omens, attesting to the continued vitality and legitimacy of the ruling house in a period of extreme challenge.[14] Finally, the holy women give hope to individual believers living in a time of danger and dread. Pien Tung-hsüan's story provides one of Tu's finest examples of the Taoist path for women, following her personal vocation from childhood compassion to heavenly rewards in old age. She represents the saint as creator of community, as living auspicious omen and as proof of the efficacy of the faith in troubled times. Let us turn now to her life as recorded by Tu Kuang-t'ing.

Translation

Pien Tung-hsüan

Pien Tung-hsüan (Grotto Mystery) was the daughter of a person of Fan yang county.[15] When young, she was lofty and pure, clever and perceptive, humane and compassionate, and loved virtue. When she saw that the life of the most minute creature was in danger or in extremity, she would always bow down to save it. Until she had succeeded in saving it, she forgot her own hunger and thirst. Whenever frost and snow congealed and froze, and birds and sparrows roosted hungrily, she sought foodstuffs like rice and grains to scatter and feed them. As years and months deepened, the birds and sparrows came to look for her and recognize her from afar; some led in front, calling out as they flew, while other followed behind, dancing as they soared.

When she was fifteen, she revealed to her father and mother that she wanted to enter the Way and refine her body by cutting off grains and nourishing her vital essence. Her father and mother were moved by her benevolence and compassion, as well as her filial piety, but would not allow it.

When she reached marriageable age she vowed not to marry, but to serve and nourish her parents with sweet delicacies. After several years, she mourned her mother and father. Broken down and emaciated, she would not eat; her fasting almost reached the point of extinguishing her life-force. When she laid aside her mourning clothes, she went to the women Taoist officials (nuns) and asked to become a Taoist Master. In the end, her older and younger brothers (or cousins) being scarce, the child had no close relatives (so she was admitted). Her nature was clever and perceptive and she was capable with a loom shuttle. The flock of women officials sympathized with and respected her. Her spinning and weaving were so industrious! She worked from daybreak to night without being idle.

Whenever she had some income, aside from sesame, *fu ling* fungus, ginseng, incense, or paper money, she would frequently purchase and store things like the five grains. People questioned her about it: "Since you have not eaten these past several years, why do you store up rice and wheat? Can it possibly be that during those eternal nights and freezing dawns you think about hunger and thirst?" She smiled but did not respond. Thus, each morning she scattered rice and grains in the courtyard to feed the wild birds, and beneath the eaves to feed the rats. Years accumulated this way. She never once had an idle appearance. The whole household of women officials in this belvedere (convent) wove silk as a service. From the time Tung-hsüan lived with them, there were never any cases of rats harming things there. People all passed on this story, interpreting it as an example of hidden virtue reaching a response among creatures.

It was also her nature to love to ingest special morsels. Whenever someone handed over cinnabar (elixir) drugs or bestowed pills or powders upon her, she would always be sure to burn incense, make offerings, and pray in the Audience Hall of those Revered of Heaven.[16] Only afterwards would she ingest them. Occasionally when she was made to suffer by the drug, she would vomit it up, and her retching and diarrhea would bring her to the point of exhaustion and distress. But she never was resentful or sighed in complaint. After her symptoms were over, she would swallow the drug as usual. Those sharing the same Way worried about her; with indirect illustrations they repeatedly urged her to shake loose (this practice). But her heart with its perfected belief was solid as a rock and could not be moved. Numerous times, when the farmers encountered famine at harvest time, she would divide the rice and wheat she had stored and distribute it to the people.

One day an old gent carrying a cloth sack on his back entered the belvedere to sell herbal medicines. The group accordingly asked him what drugs he was selling. The old gent said: "Morsels of Great Recycled Cinnabar (Elixir)[17]—whoever ingests them will gain prolonged life and become a realized transcendent who ascends to heaven in broad daylight."

All those who heard this took it as a joke. The old gent's regard was hazy and dark, his countenance wizened and shriveled, and his walking posture stooped and hunched. When his voice had just left his mouth, the group laughed and said to him: "If this recycled cinnabar can bring deathlessness, extended life, and ascent to the heavens, then why are you so dried up and burned out? Why don't you take pity on yourself?"

The old gent said: "When I first boil up and concoct this cinnabar, I must establish merit by delivering someone. In this case, the requirement of saving someone is not yet satisfied. Those who seek transcendence are hard to come by. I cannot just ingest this at my own convenience and then fly up and soar to the heavens."

The group asked him: "All people in the world wish for prolonged life without death, extended years, and increased longevity—since all people have such hearts, how can you say people who seek transcendence are hard to come by?"

The old gent said: "People all have hearts that love the Way, but they are unable to refine their practice. To be able to love the Way and in addition to refine your practice so as to keep the essential spirits from retreating, to be diligent for a long time in these matters, and not to be enticed by sounds and colors, moved by fame and profit, thrown into confusion by the profligate and flourishing, or led around by being and nonbeing, but to keep your heart as it was in the beginning, unchanging as metal or stone, *that* is difficult. In a hundred thousand myriads of people, there might not be one single such person. So how can you just talk about 'loving the Way'?"

They asked him: "When we have someone as noble as our Son of Heaven, whose wealth includes all within the four seas, then if you have such gold and cinnabar drugs, why don't you submit them to the throne and cause the emperor to obtain prolonged life and eternal longevity?"

The old gent replied: "The great incomparable realized persons from above the heavens, the lofty realized supreme transcendents, and the seven primal lords of the Northern Dipper[18] descend in cyclical order among the people, each to become the Son of Heaven. On the day his term is fulfilled each returns and ascends to the Supreme Heaven; why should they simulate taking elixirs to obtain the Way?"

Then the audience also asked: "Since you know everything, which transcendent is the present Son of Heaven?"

He answered: "The Realized Person of the Southern Palace of the Grand Unity of the Vermilion Yang."[19]

In the astuteness of his replies to questions and the matters he discussed, he was different from other people. His words came out fluently. The people could not fathom him and shrank back uncertainly. Suddenly violent wind, thunder, and rain arose. They alternately looked back and stared at him, startled and alarmed at his being so different from ordinary people. The flock of people gradually diminished, scattering as they departed. The old gent inquired of the group: "There is a Taoist female master around here who loves to practice secret virtue and has cut off eating grains for many years. Where is she?"

Accordingly they showed him by pointing to her cloister. The old gent entered the cloister without knocking or asking permission. Going straight across to stand before Tung-hsüan, he said: "I have here the great drug known as recycled cinnabar. I have come from afar to save you. Can you ingest it?"

Tung-hsüan, startled and pleased, extended an invitation to him to sit and asked him how much money she would need to spend for the drug. The old gent said: "It doesn't cost much—only 500,000 in gold."

Tung-hsüan said: "This impoverished and distressed one has been in extreme want for many years now. I really don't have that kind of money. How can I ever achieve such a drug?"

With that he opened his bag and showed her some two or three dippers of drug pellets that were blue-black in color and about the size of paulownia seeds. He ordered her to feel around for them inside the bag herself. Following her own whim, Tung-hsüan grasped three pellets from his drug bag. The old gent said: "If you ingest this cinnabar (elixir), you will transform your intestines and exchange your blood. After exactly fifteen days you will ascend to heaven. This is a drug of the middle grade."[20]

Then again he took a box as big as a coin from inside the overlap of his robe and brought out a little bit of a drug that had the appearance of peach gum. Its fragrance was also like peaches.[21] The old gent himself drew water from the well to blend with this peach gum, then ordered her to swallow the pill. The old gent became happy and said: "Your perfected sincerity has moved me to great gratitude. The Grand Supreme One has given a command ordering me to summon you.[22] After you take these two drugs, you will no longer need to transform your intestines and exchange your blood. Then, dwelling suitably in a pavilion on top of a platform, you will join with realized ones and meet with transcendents, never again to live in stinking and turbid rooms. After seven days you will be able to ascend to heaven; of course, heavenly clothes and heavenly music will come of their own accord to welcome you."

In an instant, the rain cleared and the old gent disappeared. The flock of women officials rushed to visit Tung-hsüan's room to ask her whether or not she had obtained the drug. She reported to them in full. Some scoffed at her strange exaggerations; others sighed over her encounter. Startled and alarmed, they stared at her.

After this, some among the flock of provincials who knew about the incident raced to be the first to see her. Thereupon Tung-hsüan notified the people: "I don't want to live here. I would like to climb to the top of the storied building over the gates of the compound."

When they turned back to look at it, the storied building in the corner (of the convent) was still barred and locked. Tung-hsüan notified the people: "I won't talk from here. I'm still not finished." Then she soared up bodily to the top of the storied building. A strange fragrance overflowed, while extraordinary clouds scattered, filling the whole prefecture.

Those who viewed her were so numerous as to block the roads. The Grand Protector, staff officers, and people from far and near all performed ritual obeisance and formal visiting ceremonies to her. Tung-hsüan notified the masses: "On the morning of the Central Prime Day (the fifteenth day of the seventh lunar month), I will definitely ascend to heaven. You may come and take leave of me."[23]

The masses then brought about a great fast meeting. On the fifteenth day of the seventh month from the hours of 7 to 9 A.M., heavenly music filled the void. Dense and impenetrable purple clouds wound around the storied buildings of the belvedere. The masses of the people saw Tung-hsüan ascend, with heavenly music preceding and following her, with standards and pennants spread out and arrayed. She departed straight to the south. At noontime, the clouds had just scattered. The Grand Protector and the flock of officials all memorialized the throne about what they had perceived that day between the hours of 7 and 11 A.M.

(At the same time), the Brilliant Illustrious One of the Great T'ang dynasty, dwelling at ease in his basilica, suddenly sensed a strange fragrance as variegated purple vapors filled the courtyard.[24] There were four blue lads leading a woman Taoist scholar whose age might have been about sixteen or seventeen. She approached and said: "Your handmaiden is the woman Taoist scholar Pien Tung-hsüan from Yu chou.

Today I have attained the Way and am ascending to heaven. I have come to say farewell to your majesty (literally: you below the stairs)." Her words finished, she slowly departed.

Thereupon the emperor summoned and questioned all those who had submitted memorials and letters. He also dispatched mounted couriers to rush here with matching tallies. He ordered that her belvedere be called the Belvedere of Climbing to Transcendence and that her storied building be called the Purple Cloud Storied Building, in order to publicize this matter. That year the Illustrious One's younger sister, Princess Jade Verity, requested to enter the Way, approached her own entitled town (convent), and realized her investiture.[25] From this time on, his highness loved the affairs of divinities and transcendents and was even more diligent and faithful towards the Way. Thus he ordered the Esquire of the Office of Comparative Texts, Wang Tuan, respectfully to make a stele to record this splendid affair of the divine transcendents.[26]

Conclusions

The strange and entertaining story of Pien Tung-hsüan presents an instructive case of female spirituality in medieval China. Details such as the form of her biography takes and the specific Taoist practices Pien follows are characteristic for her time and place. Other themes, such as the relation between saints and the state, male authors and female biographies, cultural constructions of female gender and religious paths for women, might be compared across different societies and historical periods.

Notes

1. The biography of Pien Tung-hsüan by Tu Kuang-t'ing, collected in his *Yung ch'eng chi hsien lu,* "Records of the Assembled Transcendents of the Fortified Walled City," is found in the *Cheng t'ung Tao tsang,* "Treasurehouse of the Tao of the Era of Rectified Unity" (the Taoist canon), Taipei, Arts and Literature Press, 1976, volume 38, 30340–30342 (hereafter *Records*). For the life and career of Tu Kuang-t'ing, see Franciscus Verellen, *Du Guangting (850–933): Taoiste de cour à la fin de la Chine médiévale,* Paris, Institut des hautes études chinoises, 1989 (hereafter *Verellen*). Other biographies of Pien Tung-hsüan, translated below, appear in the *T'ai p'ing kuang chi,* "A Broad Record from the Era of Grand Peace" of the Sung dynasty (edited by Li Fang and others. Peoples' Literature Press, Peking,

1959, *chuan* 63, 2a–b), and the *Li shih chen hsien t'i tao t'ung chien,* "A Comprehensive Mirror of Successive Generations of Realized Transcendents Who Embodied the Way," by Chao Tao-yi of the Yüan. (*Cheng t'ung Tao tsang,* Arts and Literature Press, Taipei, 1976, volume 8, 6534).

T'ai p'ing kuang chi entry:

By the end of the "Opened Prime" reign period of the T'ang dynasty (712–742), the female Taoist Master Pien Tung-hsüan of Tsao ching county in Chi province had studied the Way and ingested (elixir) morsels for forty years. When she was eighty-four years old, suddenly there was an old man carrying a vessel of dumplings in soup who came to visit Tung-hsüan and said:

"I am the transcendent of the three mountains. In order that you may attain the Way, I have come to take these dumplings in soup together with you. They are made of the powder of jade blossoms: something the divine transcendents honor. Those who have recently attained the Way in most cases have ingested it. If you just ingest some, in seven days you will undoubtedly undergo a feathered transformation." When Tung-hsüan finished eating them, the old man said: "I will go first, you may come afterwards." When his words were done, he disappeared.

On a later day Tung-hsüan suddenly felt her body getting light and her teeth and hair completely returning to their youthful condition. She called her disciples and said: "I have been summoned by the Supreme Clear Realm. Before long, I will certainly leave. I will look back and think of you all. If you can without hatred become skilled at refining my Way, you won't make yourselves coffins of earth and scatter your cloud-souls by delighting in human affairs."

When seven days were fulfilled, she said to her disciples: "Wait until dawn before you go investigate and inquire about my activities." When she stopped, they could already see purple clouds. As dawn set, they filled every part of the doorways to the courtyard. In addition they heard the sounds of numerous people talking in the void. They did not dare enter but all stopped outside the gate. In an instant, the gate opened. Tung-hsüan, riding on a purple cloud, raised her body and stood in the void, more than a hundred feet above the earth. When she spoke parting words to various disciples and priests, many myriads of people including the goading notary (provincial governor), provincial clerks, lower office holders, and hundred surnames (common people) all paid ceremonial respects from afar. In an instant, the sun came out, the purple vapors changed to five-colored clouds, and Tung-hsüan gradually ascended. After a long time, (the whole sight) was just extinguished. (from the *Kuang yi chi,* "A Record of a Wide Range of Strange Phenomena")

Li shih chen hsien t'i tao t'ung chien entry:

Pien Tung-yüan (yüan substituted for hsüan) was a person of Loyang. When young she was fond of the study of Lao-tzu and Chuang-tzu. Accordingly, she was enrolled and registered to become a Taoist master. Traveling in all four quadrants, she purchased drugs to provision herself. One day when she was climbing O Peak at Mount Sung, she encountered a clerk carrying several fascicles of wooden slips on his back. He also had a great pot. They rested together under an old pine tree. Tung-yüan said: "Where are you going?" He said: "I am going to the Eastern side of Mount Sung to become an apprentice. If you are the one I am to recognize, I wish to revere you as a teacher and show you one text as an introduction." Tung-yüan assented.

Again he said: "It has been decreed that you, my master, drink the wine in this pot; is that all right?" She replied: "It is my lowly nature to love to drink habitually. I would like to regard this as a summons to good fortune." Thereupon, drinking some tens of cups in succession, Tung-yüan became drunk. The clerk said: "Your small disciple possesses an art—I can sober up together with you, master. With wine, great caution is necessary, but don't be afraid of it." Then, taking a wooden slip, he rubbed and wiped it. In a little while he had changed it into a sword. After that he said: "Would it be all right if I borrowed my master's liver and minced it up?" Tung-yüan was startled and sobered up.

Then she bowed down and requested a prediction of her destiny from the clerk, saying: "I see you have an air of transcendence and bones of the Way, the like of which I have never before encountered." Thereupon he brandished his sword and cast it up and away into the void, from whence was thrown down a single scroll of texts. He said to Tung-yüan: "After you receive this, please visit me at Five Clouds Stream." When she unrolled it and looked, it was a scroll of paper with twenty-five colored paintings illustrating tea being ground. She really could not grasp their significance. On the tail of the paper was a short poem which read:

> We met each other unexpectedly on the side of O Peak;
> Facing one another, we overturned wine flotsam and together discussed mysteries.
> You proposed to take up my sword technique; I myself transmitted it to you—
> In the end there has never been a reason to deceive people.

Moved, Tung-yüan sighed over meeting him no more. With a burst of radiance, he disappeared. Seeing some people remaining where he had arrived, she asked them: "Do you know of this place of the five-colored clouds?" They took her for mad and for the most part did not reply. After a long time she returned home to Loyang, where she used drunkenness as a vehicle to enter the water and did not come out again. Later there was a stranger who came from the region of the Hsiang River and Mount Heng (in the south); through him the emended texts which Tung-yüan had preserved and entrusted at the Southern Marchmount

Belvedere reached Loyang. Her teachings belonged to and were exchanged among her friends and close relations. Old acquaintances debated the ink traces (handwriting), in the end deciding the texts were indeed of her own stain. At the time, all those who liked such matters called her story a case of liberation by water.

2. For the history of Shang ch'ing (or Mao shan) Taoism during the Six Dynasties, see Michel Strickman, "The Maoshan Revelations: Taoism and the Aristocracy," "*T'oung pao*, 63, 1977; 1–64. On practices devoted to immortality, see Henri Maspero, translated by Frank A. Kierman, Jr. *Taoism and Chinese Religion*, University of Massachusetts, Amherst, 1981. On the Taoist religion, see Isabelle Robinet, *Taoism: Growth of a Religion*, Stanford, Stanford, 1997, and Eva Wong, *The Shambala Guide to Taoism*, Shambala, Boston, 1997.

3. See *Records*, 30323–30324.

4. For discussion of Tu Kuang-t'ing's works and their motivations during this era, see *Verellen*, Chapters 3 and 4.

5. On biographies of Chinese Buddhist monks, Arthur Wright, "Biography and Hagiography: Hui-chiao's *Lives of Eminent Monks*," in Arthur F. Wright, *Studies in Chinese Buddhism*, Yale, New Haven 1990, 73–111. On biographies of Buddhist nuns, see Kathryn Ann Tsai, *Lives of the Nuns*, University of Hawaii, Honolulu, 1994.

6. For a discussion of Taoist meditation of the Supreme Clear Realm School during the T'ang, see Livia Kohn, *Seven Steps to the Tao: Sima Chengzhen's Zuowanglun*, Steyler, Nettetal, 1987, and Isabelle Robinet, *Taoist Meditation*, Suny, Albany, 1993.

7. On "liberation by means of the corpse," see Isabelle Robinet, "Metamorphosis and Deliverance from the Corpse in Taoism," *History of Religions*, 19,1, 1979.

8. Regarding separate titles, Tu states "The ultimate position for men who attain the Way is Realized Lord, and the ultimate position for women who attain the Way is Primal Ruler (*Records*, 30324)." Regarding separate paths for women, Tu says one of his subjects reached immortality by the path of "female transcendence" (*Records*, 30333).

9. *Records*, 30324.

10. *Records*, 30333.

11. *Records*, 30324.

12. See Donald Weinstein and Rudolph M. Bell, *Saints and Society*, University of Chicago, 1982; Rudolph M. Bell, *Holy Anorexia*, University of Chicago, 1985; Carolyn Walker Bynum, *Holy Feast and Holy Fast*, University of California, 1987.

13. *Records*, 30323.

14. For example, Tu Kuang-t'ing's biography of Hsüeh Hsüan-t'ung (*Record*, 30347), copies a memorial concerning that saint addressed to the emperor from

the governor stationed in Ch'eng-tu. Dated in 882, the document states: "Although she belongs among the auspicious omens of this commandery, her story is also a bountiful event for the nation and the dynasty."

15. Fan yang county in the Ching t'ao commandary was located in the region of the T'ang dynasty capital city of Ch'ang an.

16. "Reverend of heaven" is an honorific usually reserved for the three high deities (one for each heaven) who ruled the celestial bureaucracy of the Supreme Clear Realm Taoists. The audience hall, consciously styled like those of the Chinese emperors, was the main public hall of prayer for the community of nuns and was usually located front and center in the convent compound.

17. On "recycled cinnabar," see Nathan Sivin, *Chinese Alchemy: Preliminary Studies,* Harvard, Cambridge, 1968, 156n.

18. The old man names ideal beings of Supreme Clear Realm Taoism: realized persons and transcendents are the immortals the adepts emulate in the hopes of joining; the Seven Primal Lords are the powerful gods of the stars of the Big Dipper.

19. This realized person is the presiding deity of a grotto heaven (a very auspicious place connected underground to other holy spots) in the south near the place where Supreme Clear Realm Taoism began.

20. There are many lists in the Taoist canon classifying various types of elixir drugs according to virtue and efficacy. One appears in the biography of the Queen Mother of the West in *Records,* 30328.

21. On the medicinal properties of peaches, see Derk Bodde, *Festivals in Ancient China,* Princeton. 1975. See also Li Shih-chen, *Pen ts'ao kang mu,* portions translated in *Chinese Medicinal Herbs,* Georgetown, San Francisco, 1973, 356–358.

22. The Grand Supreme One, one of three celestial emperors who were the highest gods of Supreme Clear Realm Taoism, was worshipped already in Han dynasty.

23. The Central Prime Day was one of the three major religious holidays of the medieval Taoists spread throughout the year which were observed with public liturgy.

24. The Brilliant Illustrious One is the T'ang emperor Hsüan tsung, a great patron of Taoism. On his government see Dennis Twitchett, "Hsüan-tsung (reign 712–756)," *The Cambridge History of China,* Volume 3, *Sui and T'ang China,* Part One, Cambridge University, Cambridge, 1979, Chapter 7, 333–363.

25. On Jade Verity see Edward Shafer, "The Princess Realized in Jade." *T'ang Studies,* 3, 1985, 1–24.

26. On Wang Tuan, a literatus who held office under T'ang, see Ou-yang Hsiu et al., *Hsin T'ang shu,* "The New Book of the T'ang Dynasty," Chung hua shu chü. Shanghai, 1975, *Chuan* 149, 4808.

Index of Names

Index of Terms

Subject Index